TODAY'S GIFT
Daily Meditations for Families

EACH DAY
A NEW BEGINNING
Daily Meditations for Women

HAZELDEN

MJF BOOKS
NEW YORK

Published by MJF Books
Fine Communications
Two Lincoln Square
60 West 66th Street
New York, NY 10023

Today's Gift/Each Day a New Beginning
Library of Congress Catalog Card Number 97-75445
ISBN 1-56731-260-8

10   9   8   7   6   5   4   3   2   1

EACH DAY
A
NEW BEGINNING

Editor's note:

Hazelden Educational Materials offers a variety of information on chemical dependency and related areas. Our publications do not necessarily represent Hazelden or its programs, nor do they officially speak for any Twelve Step organization.

The Twelve Steps of Alcoholics Anonymous and The Twelve Steps of Al-Anon are reprinted with permission of Alcoholics Anonymous World Services, Inc. Permission to reprint the Twelve Steps of AA and Al-Anon does not mean that AA has reviewed or approved the contents of this publication, nor that AA agrees with the views expressed herein. AA is a program of recovery from alcoholism. Use of the Twelve Steps in connection with programs which are patterned after AA but which address other problems does not imply otherwise.

INTRODUCTION

For years I struggled to believe in my worth, my capabilities, my strength. And on many occasions I failed to meet the test. Because I didn't understand the source of all strength and goodness, I turned to men first and then to alcohol and drugs. I expected to find my security but found instead an even deeper level of despair. And then, seven years ago, I found Al-Anon which nudged open the door to a new way of life. A year later I found A.A. and the door swung wide.

The program has given me roots where none existed before. It has given me courage to dare to do that which I shuddered before in years gone by. It has given me a sense of belonging to the human race. I no longer feel that I'm outside of the fish bowl looking in.

And the additional and very fortunate gift which has accompanied my program involvement is friendship with women. For years I had been leery of women, assuming they were after my boyfriends, husband and lovers. I was always quite certain that women were not to be trusted. Coming together with women in meetings, hearing how much alike we all are, eased my anxieties. But more importantly, it offered me the opportunity to love women as sisters, as equal travelers on our parallel spiritual journeys.

From so many women these last few years I've received "just the message I needed at the time." The more I've learned to turn in a woman's direction as she speaks, the greater my desire has grown to "hear" what women in all walks of life, all experiences, all times in history have said. Thus, it seemed only fitting when I wrote this book to let the wise words of many women, close at hand and far *away, some recovering, some still suffering, some free from any particular struggles but who struggled nonetheless, set the tone for a book that speaks to us all. I've taken the liberty to quote from women who represent the full spectrum of womanhood, believing that much spoken by any one of us is sacred, meaningful and necessary to the fuller development of at least one person someplace in time.*

I wrote the meditations to complement the quote chosen for each day. So often I've needed to hear "the right message" in order to move forward when inside I was all a jitter—something to center on which could invite the Spirit within to take charge for me. I hope these meditations may bridge whatever gap exists, on any one day in your life, between you and your Spirit. Their sole intent is to make life easier for you; to give you hope when all seems lost. Please accept each day's meditation as an offering of my hand to you. I've learned that when we travel together, nothing is too great for us to bear. And each day can be a new beginning.

I want to offer my thanks to all women for making this book possible. The efforts of the women all around me to live, to survive, to succeed, gave me strength to push ahead one day at a time.

I offer a special thanks to a woman friend and excellent editor who smoothed the rough spots so these words could touch your life in a more certain way. To my family, friends and spouse I say thanks for being patient when my writing took precedence over all else. My need was great to write a book that I believed was needed by my sister travelers on this journey we share.

—the author

We don't always understand the ways of Almighty God—the crosses sent us, the sacrifices demanded . . . But we accept with faith and resignation the holy will with no looking back, and we are at peace.

—*Anonymous*

Acceptance of our past, acceptance of the conditions presently in our lives that we cannot change, brings relief. It brings the peacefulness we so often, so frantically, seek.

We can put the past behind us. Each day is a new beginning. And each day of abstinence offers us the chance to look ahead with hope. A power greater than ourselves helped us to find this program. That power is ever with us. When we fear facing new situations, or when familiar situations turn sour, we can look to that power for help in saying what needs to be said and for doing what needs to be done. Our higher power is as close as our breath. Conscious awareness of its presence strengthens us, moment by moment.

The past is gone. Today is full of possibilities. With each breath I will be aware of the strength at hand.

I believe that true identity is found . . . in creative activity springing from within. It is found, paradoxically, when one loses oneself. Woman can best refind herself by losing herself in some kind of creative activity of her own.

—Anne Morrow Lindbergh

Creative activity might mean bird watching, tennis, quilting, cooking, painting, writing. Creative activity immerses us fully in the here and now, and at the same time it frees us. We become one with the activity and are nourished by it. We grow as the activity grows. We learn who we are in the very process of *not thinking about* who we are.

Spirituality and creativity are akin. There is an exhilaration rooted deep within us that is a lifeline to God. Creative activity releases the exhilaration, and the energy goes through us and out to others. We find ourselves and our higher power through the loss of our self-conscious selves while creating—a picture, a sentence, a special meal.

Creativity is a given. It is another dimension of the spiritual presence guiding us all. I'll get out of its way today.

Like an old gold-panning prospector, you must resign yourself to digging up a lot of sand from which you will later patiently wash out a few minute particles of gold ore.

—Dorothy Bryant

Sometimes we feel buried in sand, blocked, clogged, unable to move. Then we must remember that we are not alone. Help is at hand, if only we will ask for it. If we invoke our higher power, our source of spiritual strength can help us to believe that there is gold somewhere in all this sand, and that the sand itself is useful.

No one and no thing is good all the time. Let us remember that if we expect nothing but gold, we are distorting life, getting in our own way. We don't want to falsify the texture of our lives; the homespun quality helps us to appreciate the gold when it appears.

I will find some gold among the sand, today.

Once I knew that I wanted to be an artist, I had made myself into one. I did not understand that wanting doesn't always lead to action. Many of the women had been raised without the sense that they could mold and shape their own lives, and so, wanting to be an artist (but without the ability to realize their wants) was, for some of them, only an idle fantasy, like wanting to go to the moon.

—Judy Chicago

There are probably not many of us, in this recovery program, who grappled with life as straight on as Judy Chicago did. It is likely we didn't understand that *we* could mold and shape our lives. How lucky we are to be learning that now with the help of the Twelve Steps and one another. Each day we are confronted with many opportunities to make responsible choices, reasonable decisions. These choices and decisions are the molders, the shapers, of who we are becoming. Our identity as women is strengthened each time we thoughtfully make a choice. The action we take through making each choice gives our identity more substance—our wholeness as women is guaranteed through these choices.

Many opportunities to make choices will arise today. I can be thoughtful and make choices that will lead to my greater wholeness.

*Instead of concentrating on why we can't do a thing,
we would be wise to change our "Yes, but . . ." attitude
to a more positive one. Saying "yes" means I really do
want to change my life for the better.*

—Liane Cordes

We truly can do these things that are our "hearts' pure
desires." However, most of us look at the whole task and
feel overwhelmed. We need, instead, to look at the task's
many parts. One part at a time, one day at a time, we can
accomplish any goal we set for ourselves. I know a recovering woman who wrote a 300-page dissertation, the
final achievement to obtain her Ph.D. When asked at a
meeting how she ever did it, her reply was, "One word at a
time." That's wonderful advice. No matter how many goals
were missed or plans dashed when we were still using, now
that we are recovering, each of us can do whatever is in our
hearts—if we do it little by little, not all at once, today.

*Today, I will do one small task that will contribute toward the
achievement of a life goal.*

There are as many ways to live and grow as there are people. Our own ways are the only ways that should matter to us.

—Evelyn Mandel

Wanting to control other people, to make them live as we'd have them live, makes the attainment of serenity impossible. And serenity is the goal we are seeking in this recovery program, in this life.

We are each powerless over others, which relieves us of a great burden. Controlling our own behavior is a big enough job. Learning to behave responsibly takes practice. Most of us in this recovery program have behaved irresponsibly for much of our lives. Emotional immaturity is slow to depart, but every responsible action we take gives us the courage for another—and then another. Our own fulfillment is the by-product of the accumulation of our own responsible actions. Others' actions need not concern us.

Today, I will weigh my behavior carefully. Responsible behavior builds gladness of heart.

The greatest gift we can give one another is rapt attention to one another's existence.
—Sue Atchley Ebaugh

We all want to matter to others. Very often in the past—and sometimes in the present—our behavior has screamed for the attention we seek from others. Perhaps, instead of trying to get attention, we ought to give it. The program tells us we have to give it away in order to keep it. Wisdom of the ages also dictates that in life there are no accidents. Those people close to us and those just passing through our lives have reason to be there. Giving attention to another's humanity is our calling.

I will fully attend to another person I have occasion to be with today. She will matter to me, and my attention will matter to her.

When people make changes in their lives in a certain area, they may start by changing the way they talk about that subject, how they act about it, their attitude toward it, or an underlying decision concerning it.
—*Jean Illsley Clarke*

Acting "as if" is powerful. It leads the way to a changed attitude, a changed woman. If we are self-conscious in crowds and fearful about meeting new people and yet act poised and extend our hands in friendship, we'll not only behave in a new way, but feel good about it, too. Each act we take in this way brings us closer to the woman we are behaving like. Each positive change we make builds our self-esteem. Realizing that through our own actions we are becoming the kind of women we admire gives us the strength, in fact, encourages the excitement in us that's needed to keep changing. Making positive changes in our lives is the stuff that comprises self-esteem. Each gain makes the next one easier to attempt.

I will accept an opportunity today to act "as if" I can handle a situation I used to run from.

The Chinese say that water is the most powerful element, because it is perfectly nonresistant. It can wear away a rock and sweep all before it.
— *Florence Scovel Shinn*

Nonresistance, ironically, may be a posture we struggle with. Nonresistance means surrendering the ego absolutely. For many of us, the ego, particularly disguised as false pride, spurred us on to struggle after struggle. "Can't they see I'm right?" we moaned, and our resistance only created more of itself. Conversely, flowing with life, "bubbling" with the ripples, giving up our ego, releases from us an energy that heals the situation—that smooths the negative vibrations in our path. Peace comes to us. We will find serenity each time we willingly humble ourselves.

Resistance is more familiar. Nonresistance means growth and peace. I'll try for serenity today.

A complete revaluation takes place in your physical and mental being when you've laughed and had some fun.

—*Catherine Ponder*

Norman Cousins, in his book *Anatomy of an Illness*, describes how he cured his fatal illness with laughter. Laughter recharges our entire being; every cell is activated. We come alive, and full vitality restores us physically and emotionally. Many of us need both emotional and physical healing, but perhaps we've overlooked the times to laugh because we've been caught in a negative posture.

Unfortunately, negativity becomes habitual for many of us. However, it's never too late to turn our lives around, to laugh instead of complain. Choosing to see the bright side of life, to laugh at our mistakes, lessens our pain, emotional and physical. Laughter encourages wellness. It is habit-forming and, better yet, contagious. Bringing laughter to others can heal them as well.

We all want health and happiness in ourselves and others, and we can find it by creating it. The best prescription for whatever ails us may well be a good laugh.

Today I'll seek out those chances to dispense a little medicine.

Fear is only an illusion. It is the illusion that creates the feeling of separateness—the false sense of isolation that exists only in your imagination.
—Jeraldine Saunders

We are one. We are connected, interdependent parts of the whole. We are not separate from each other except in the mind, in our false understanding of reality. As we come to understand our connectedness, our need for one another to complete the whole of creation, our fears will die.

It is often said we learn who we really are by closely observing our behavior toward the people in our lives. We meet ourselves in those others. They are our reflections. They are, perhaps, parts we ourselves have not yet learned to love. The program's message is to trust, to have faith; our higher power is in control. We are faced with no person, no situation too big to handle if we trust the program, if we remember the connections among us all.

I will look around today at others, with knowledge of our oneness. Fearing not, I will smile upon the wholeness of life.

*It isn't sufficient to seek wholeness through men,
it never was and it never will be for any woman,
married or single.*

—Patricia O'Brien

Most of us were encouraged from childhood on to "find a husband." The message, often subtle, was nonetheless there. And many of us did marry. However, no relationship carries a lifetime guarantee. Pinning our hopes on another person keeps us dependent; it keeps us in a "holding pattern." It keeps us from making those choices tailored to who we are and who we want to be.

Our recovery as women is closely aligned with our growth in decision making, our choosing responsible behavior and activities, our personal achievement. We do, each of us, need to discover our own wholeness. We need to celebrate our personhood. We need to cheer one another on as women recovering from an addictive past, as worthwhile women in full measure.

I will respect my wholeness today. I will help another woman nurture hers.

I want, by understanding myself, to understand others. I want to be all that I am capable of becoming . . . This all sounds very strenuous and serious. But now that I have wrestled with it, it's no longer so. I feel happy—deep down. All is well.

—Katherine Mansfield

All is well. In the midst of turmoil, let us remember, all is well; in the midst of the pain of self-awareness, all is well. The struggle of the turmoil, the pain that accompanies the lessons of self-awareness, are preparing us for becoming all we are meant to become. We each have a special gift to offer in this life. We will come to understand those gifts and be able to give them as we grow with the pain of self-understanding. All is well. Deep down happiness ripples; it's rippling to the surface of our lives.

My lesson for today is understanding, of myself and others. Happiness is the grade I earn each day of my "becoming."

In a culture where approval/disapproval has become the predominant regulator of effort and position, and often the substitute for love, our personal freedoms are dissipated.

—Viola Spolin

Wanting others to approve our efforts, our appearance, our aspirations and behavior is perfectly normal, certainly not unhealthy. However, needing the approval in order to proceed with our lives is.

In early childhood we are taught to obey others and to please them. We confuse love with approval, and we begin to march to someone else's drum. Then we get even more approval. But soon we get out of step with ourselves; we neglect our personal needs and become puppets.

Giving away our power to the whims of others weakens our Spirit. Personal freedom means choosing our own behavior; it means acting rather than reacting. It also means allowing ourselves the full adventure of living, of meeting each moment wholly, of responding in a pure, spontaneous, personally honest manner. Only then can we give to life what is ours to give.

Each of us has a unique part to play in the drama of life. And we need to rely on our higher power for our cues, not on those whose approval we think we need. When we turn within for guidance, all the approval we could hope for will be ours.

I will be free today. I will let no one control my actions. I will let God give the only approval that counts. Aligning my will with God's will guarantees it.

Everything is so dangerous that nothing is really very frightening.

—*Gertrude Stein*

Life is full of dangers and risks and challenges. We can choose to meet them fearfully or in a spirit of welcome. To choose fear, to say, "I won't take that risk because I might lose," is to prevent ourselves from ever winning. If we welcome the danger, the risk, or the challenge, we acknowledge that life is made up of losses as well as victories, of gains as well as pain.

Life holds the dangers as well as the rewards. We choose how we will act. Sometimes we may feel trapped in a cycle of fearfulness. If we examine our own part, will we find that we are neglecting to take a balanced view? Perhaps, through a fear of losing, we are missing many chances for satisfaction.

I will remember: I have the power to choose what my attitude will be toward this day's offerings.

I feel we have picked each other from the crowd as fellow-travelers, for neither of us is to the other's personality the end-all and the be-all.

—Joanna Field

We must look around at the people in our lives today, and know that we have something special to offer each of them, and they to us. We do travel separate paths together. We may need to learn tolerance; perhaps a friend's behavior pushes us to be more tolerant. Impatience may be our nemesis, and everywhere we turn are long lines and traffic jams. Our experiences with others aren't chance. Fellow travelers are carefully selected by the inner self, the spiritual guide who understands our needs in this life.

We are both the teachers and the pupils. We need both our friends and those we may label our enemies for what they can help us learn.

I will carefully look about me today with gladness at the travelers I've selected to learn from.

She lacks confidence, she craves admiration insatiably. She lives on the reflections of herself in the eyes of others. She does not dare to be herself.
                                                            —Anaïs Nin

How aptly these words describe the woman so many of us were. Many activities were not attempted, courses weren't taken, conversations weren't initiated because we lacked confidence. The pain, the constant search for acceptance and love in the eyes and behavior of others, still haunts us. But those days are past. We are daring to be ourselves, one day at a time.

Confidence still wavers on occasion, and we may need assurance that we're lovable. Gratefully, we can look to one another for the additional boost we may need to face the day. Being there for one another, knowing that we understand each other's fears as women, offers the strength to go ahead that we may lack today or tomorrow.

Today a woman may need me to dare to be herself. I will be there.

We are born in innocence. Corruption comes later. The first fear is a corruption, the first reaching for a something that defies us. The first nuance of difference, the first need to feel better than the different one, more loved, stronger, richer, more blessed—these are corruptions.

—Laura Z. Hobson

We are corrupted. To be human is to be corrupted. Our corruptions interfere with our happiness at the very time we are seeking happiness. When we think if only we were prettier, smarter, had a better job, then we'd be happy, we are giving in to corruptions. And these corruptions stifle our growth. We are each who we need to be. We have a supporting role in one another's lives. We can teach and learn from one another.

Recovery is choosing to help ourselves and one another to be as we are; to quit making comparisons; to understand our equality as women; to celebrate our differences, knowing they give intensity to life's colors for us all.

I can celebrate our special and different gifts today. My heart will be lightened.

The especial genius of women, I believe to be electrical in movement, intuitive in function, spiritual in tendency.

—Margaret Fuller

We are women, and we are moving, together and alone. We are moving into new images of ourselves. There is a healing power that comes from moving, from sharing one's ideas and changing one's self. And it is by trusting ourselves and trusting others that we bring harmony, thoughtfulness, and courage to all our actions.

Life holds many possibilities, and we are able to realize them when we risk changing ourselves through taking action. Those of us struggling to recover are taking action; we are changing ourselves. And as we listen to and support one another, we encourage the necessary changes in our sisters. As one is healed, we are all healed.

Today holds a special promise for me. I can be in harmony. I can share with others. My courage will strengthen others, and others will strengthen me.

The pain of leaving those you grow to love is only the prelude to understanding yourself and others.
—*Shirley MacLaine*

Life is a process of letting go, letting go of conditions we can't control, letting go of people—watching them move out of our lives, letting go of times, places, experiences. Leaving behind anyone or anyplace we have loved may sadden us, but it also provides us opportunities for growth we hadn't imagined. These experiences push us beyond our former selves to deeper understandings of ourselves and of others.

So often those experiences that sadden us, that trigger pain, are the best lessons life is able to offer. Experiencing the pain, surviving the pain that wrenches us emotionally, stretches us to new heights. Life is enriched by the pain. Our experiences with all other persons thereafter are deeper. Instead of dreading the ending of a time, the departure of a loved one, we must try to appreciate what we have gained already and know that life is fuller for it.

Today will bring both good-byes and hellos. I can meet both with gladness.

Too many activities, and people, and things. Too many worthy activities, valuable things, and interesting people. For it is not merely the trivial which clutters our lives but the important as well.
—Anne Morrow Lindbergh

We need interaction with others, and we need activities. We have many gifts to offer those who cross our paths, and we need the many gifts they have to offer us. But we soon have little to share, to give to others, if we neglect the special times, the empty spaces needed for nurturing the soul.

Some time away from people, activities, and things, some time away to commune with God, to seek guidance, to seek security in the fullest sense, will prepare us to better give our gifts to others. That time alone will also ready us to accept others' gifts to us.

It is true we find God's message in others. But the time alone with God lowers the barriers that too often prevent us from hearing another of God's messages as expressed through the friends and even foes who cross our paths.

My gift to myself is some time alone. I deserve that gift today and every day.

One cannot have wisdom without living life.
—Dorothy McCall

Living life means responding, wholly, to our joys and our pitfalls. It means not avoiding the experiences or activities that we fear we can't handle. Only through our survival of them do we come to know who we really are; we come to understand the strength available to us at every moment. And that is wisdom.

When we approach life tentatively, we reap only a portion of its gifts. It's like watching a movie in black and white that's supposed to be in Technicolor. Our lives are in color, but we must have courage to let the colors emerge, to feel them, absorb them, be changed by them. Within our depths, we find our true selves. The complexities of life teach us wisdom. And becoming wise eases the many pitfalls in our path.

Living life is much more than just being alive. I can choose to jump in with both feet. Wisdom awaits me in the depths.

She had trouble defining herself independently of her husband, tried to talk to him about it, but he said nonsense, he had no trouble defining her at all.
—*Cynthia Propper Seton*

To recover means to learn who we are, independent of friends, children, parents, or intimate partners. It means knowing how we want to spend our time, what books we like to read, what hobbies interest us, what our favorite foods are. It means understanding self-direction. It means charting a daily personal course and staying on it. It means defining our responsibilities and carrying them out.

Having an independent identity does not preclude depending on others for certain needs. Perhaps we revel in massage—both getting and giving. Maybe we share the expenses of a household or the responsibilities of raising children. Depending on others to meet their responsibilities does not negate our independent identity; it strengthens it. We choose where and when to be dependent. Healthy dependency complements healthy independence.

Recovery is giving me options. Each day gives me new opportunities.

I look in the mirror through the eyes of the child that was me.

—Judy Collins

The child within each of us is fragile, but very much alive, and she interprets our experiences before we are even conscious of them. It is our child who may fear new places, unfamiliar people, strange situations. Our child needs nurturing, the kind she may not have received in the past. We can take her hand, coax her along, let her know she won't be abandoned. No new place, unfamiliar person, or strange situation need overwhelm her.

It's quite amazing the strength that comes to us when we nurture ourselves, when we acknowledge the scared child within and hold her, making her secure. We face nothing alone. Together, we can face anything.

I will take care of my child today and won't abandon her to face, alone, any of the experiences the day may bring.

The time of discipline began. Each of us the pupil of whichever one of us could best teach what each of us needed to learn.

—Maria Isabel Barreno

"When the pupil is ready, the teacher appears." Life's lessons often come unexpectedly. They come, nevertheless, and they come according to a time frame that is Divine. As we grow emotionally and spiritually, we are readied for further lessons for which teachers will appear. Perhaps the teacher will be a loving relationship, a difficult loss, or a truant child. The time of learning is seldom free from pain and questioning. But from these experiences and what they can teach us, we are ready to learn. As we are ready, they come.

We all enjoy the easy times when the sailing is smooth, when all is well, when we are feeling no pain. And these periods serve a purpose. They shore us up for the lessons which carry us to a stronger recovery, to a stronger sense of ourselves. To understand that all is well, throughout the learning process, is the basic lesson we need to learn. All is well. The teacher is the guide up the next rung of the ladder.

Let me be grateful for my lessons today and know that all is well.

You've got to get up every morning with a smile on
your face,
And show the world all the love in your heart.
Then people gonna treat you better.
You're gonna find, yes, you will,
That you're beautiful as you feel.

—Carole King

Act "as if." There's magic in behaving the way we want to be, even though we don't yet feel it. The behavior seems to lead the way. The attitude, the mental state, follows.

Many days we may not get up with love in our hearts for our family, our friends, our co-workers. We may, in fact, want them to show their love for us first. But if we reach out, give love unconditionally, focus on another's needs, love will return tenfold. And the act of loving them will lift our own spirits. We will know love; we will feel love for ourselves and the many other persons close to us.

The attitude we cultivate, whether one of love or selfishness, inferiority or superiority, will determine how the events of our lives affect us. The principle is so simple. If we meet life with love, with a smile, we'll find love and something to smile about.

My attitude will make this day what it becomes. Meeting it head-on, with love, will assure me of a lovely day.

Surviving meant being born over and over.
                                        —*Erica Jong*

We have decided to live. And each day we make the decision anew. Each time we call a friend, work a Step, or go to a meeting, we are renewing our contract with life. We are being reborn. Before coming to this program we died, emotionally and spiritually, many times. Some of us nearly died physically. But here we are, starting a new day, looking for guidance from one another. We are the survivors. And survival is there for the taking.

We will have days when we struggle with our decision to live. We will want to throw in the towel. We will want to give in or give up. But we've learned from one another about choices. And the choice to survive, knowing we never have to do it alone, gets easier with time.

I am one of the survivors. Today is my day for celebration.

I think self-awareness is probably the most important thing towards being a champion.

—Billie Jean King

Champions are made. How lucky we are to have the Steps to guide us to become champions. The program promises us self-awareness, but we have to put forth the effort. And the process isn't always easy. We have liabilities, all of us, and it's generally easier to see them than our assets. Self-awareness is recognizing both. To become a champion, whether as an athlete, a homemaker, a teacher, a secretary, or an attorney, is to maximize the assets and minimize the liabilities, but to accept the existence of both. The program that we share offers us daily opportunities to know ourselves, to help other women know themselves, and to strengthen our assets along the way. We can feel our assets growing, and it feels good. We can see our liabilities diminish, and it feels good. The program offers us a championship.

I can strengthen my assets, first by knowing them, and then by emphasizing them repeatedly. I'll focus on one today.

"I can't help it" . . . *that's what we all say when we don't want to exert ourselves.*

—Eva Lathbury

Irresponsible behavior is not unfamiliar to us. Passivity is equally familiar. In the past, excusing ourselves of all responsibility prevented us from being blamed. We have learned that it also prevented us from feeling worthy, from fulfilling our potential, from feeling the excitement that comes with achievement.

Our fear of failure helped us to be irresponsible. We may still fear failure, but the program offers us an antidote. We can't fail if we have turned our lives over to our higher power. We will be shown the way to proceed. Our fellow travelers have messages for us that will smooth our path.

I have chosen recovery. I have already said, "I can help it." I will celebrate that I am taking responsibility for my life today.

Fortunately [psycho]analysis is not the only way to resolve inner conflicts. Life itself still remains a very effective therapist.

—Karen Horney

The passage of time, coupled with an openness to the messages gleaned from our conversations with others, can provide answers we need for the way out of painful situations. Life is ebb and flow, peaks and valleys, struggles and sweet times. What we fail to realize, all too often, is that the struggles make possible the times that are sweet.

Our conflicts are our special lessons in life. We can learn to flow with them, move through them, trust their value to us as growing, changing women. How good it feels to have found security with one another and that power greater than ourselves who can, when we are willing, show us the path to resolution.

Life will never be free of conflict—nor should it be. Our lessons move us to higher planes of awareness. We can experience the joy hidden within the conflict. We can help one another remember that the sweetness of a moment is tied to the pain of a former, forgotten moment.

All events, all experiences, are connected. The path I travel, alone and with others, is bringing me brighter days. I will trust my path. It's right for me.

Woman must not accept; she must challenge. She must not be awed by that which has been built up around her; she must reverence that woman in her which struggles for expression.

—Margaret Sanger

Our desire to grow, to make a place for ourselves in the world of our friends, to know that we have counted in the lives of others, is healthy and necessary to our existence as whole women. The inner urging to move ahead, to try a new approach to an old problem, to go after a new job, to learn a new skill, is evidence of God's eternal Spirit within.

Our meaning in this life is found through following the guidance that beckons us toward these new horizons, perhaps new friends, even new locations. We can trust the urge. We can reverence the urge. It will not lead us astray, provided we do not try to lead it. We each have a special gift to express in this life among those to whom we've been led.

For years, many of us quelled the inner urge out of fear; but, fortunately, it didn't desert us. To be human is to have a constant desire to be more than we are. The fears still come, but as we move through them, with the support of other women, other friends, the program gives us the thrill of achievement. We know there is meaning in our existence.

The need to grow, to change, to affect the world around us is part of God's plan for each of us. I will trust the urge; I will let it guide my steps.

You were there when I needed you. You stood above all of the others with your strength and you guided me. To each of you I offer my being, my love and all that I am.

—Deidra Sarault

Each of us is guided while we act as guides to one another, throughout the day, throughout our lives. We are interdependent. Everywhere we look, someone is learning from us and we from her. We often know not what we give, when we give it. And we seldom realize the value of what we're receiving at the time we accept it.

Resistance to what another person is offering us may be our natural response. But the passage of time highlights the value of the experience. We can look for the comforters in our lives. They are there offering us strength and hope enough to see us through any difficulty.

We need both the rough times and the soft shoulders of a friend. They contribute equally to the designs our lives are weaving. The rough times press us to pray, to reach out to others for solace. And our pain gives others the chance to heal our wounds. We are all healers offering strength. And we all need healing.

One of the greatest gifts of my recovery is giving and receiving strength.

What most of us want is to be heard, to communicate.
                                        —*Dory Previn*

Our personhood is denied; the self we are presenting to the world is negated each time we speak, yet go unheard. "The greatest gift we can give one another is rapt attention." If we want attention, we must also give it. That means letting go of all extraneous thoughts when we're in conversation with someone. We cannot expect to get from others what we are unable or unwilling to give.

Being heard and hearing another person is more than just listening. It's letting ourselves be touched, in an intimate way, by the other's words. We don't want judgment, or shame, or to be discounted when we share who we are with another. We want to know that we have been intimately heard. And when we have a chance to hear another, we listen intently for the words meant for us, words that will stretch our womanhood and bring us closer to our inner selves as well.

The beauty of hearing each other is that it helps us to hear ourselves. We know better who we are when we listen to one another. Every conversation offers us a chance to be real, to help another person be real.

Rapt attention is my greatest gift. If I want to receive it, I must give it.

When we begin to take our failures nonseriously, it means we are ceasing to be afraid of them. It is of immense importance to learn to laugh at ourselves.
—Katherine Mansfield

Perfectionism and its control over our lives stands seriously in the way of our growth and well-being, emotionally, spiritually, and even physically. Life's lessons come through failures probably more than successes. Through our failures we learn humility. We learn to look to others for help and guidance. We learn how to let others fail, too. We fail because we are human.

When we no longer fear failure, we are free to attempt greater feats. We dare to learn more, and life is fuller for it—not just our own lives, but the lives that we touch.

Laughter over our mistakes eases the risk of trying again. Laughter keeps us young, and the lighthearted find more pleasure in each day.

I will fail at something I try today. I can laugh about it, though. My laughter will open the way to another try.

Genius is the talent for seeing things straight. It is seeing things in a straight line without any bend or break or aberration of sight, seeing them as they are, without any warping of vision.

—Maude Adams

We are learning, each day of our abstinence, to see more clearly what lies before us. Less and less are we hampered by our own selfish needs, distorting that which we face. We all have within us the talent for seeing things as they really are. But it is a process that takes practice, a process of turning within to the untapped talent which is one of the gifts of a spiritual life.

We are spiritual entities, one and all. And the genius to see as God sees is ours for the asking. This program is paving our way. Each day it becomes easier to live an honest life. Each day we trust more the people we encounter. And each day we take greater risks being our true selves.

The need to distort that which we see ahead lessens as we begin reaping the benefits of the honest, caring, spirit-filled life. Our unhealthy egos stood in our way in the past. And they can get in the way even now, if we forget to look ahead with the eyes of our inner genius.

My path today is straight, clean, and love-filled, if I choose to follow my genius.

Don't compromise yourself. You are all you've got.
—Janis Joplin

When we don't know who we are, it's easy to compromise ourselves. When we don't know where we stand on an issue, it's easy to be swayed by a forceful voice. Values may be cloudy in our minds, or we may not be aware of them at all. It's then that we are vulnerable to the persuasion of another. In this Twelve Step program, we are offered the way to know ourselves. We are supported in our efforts, and we realize we have friends who don't want us to compromise ourselves—who value our struggle to know and to be true to ourselves.

One of recovery's greatest gifts is discovering we can make decisions that represent us, our inner selves, and those decisions please us. We all are familiar with the tiny tug of shame that locates itself in our solar plexus. When we "go along," when we "give in" on a personally important issue, we pay a consequence. We lose a bit of ourselves. Over the years we've lost many bits. We have a choice, however.

I will have a chance, soon, to act according to my wishes. I will take it.

I believe that a sign of maturity is accepting deferred gratification.

—Peggy Cahn

It's okay to want to feel good all the time. Happiness is something we all deserve. However, there are often preparatory steps we need to take, a number of which will not bring joy, before we arrive at a place of sustained happiness.

The level of our pain at any particular moment has prompted us to seek short-term highs. And with each attempt at a quick "fix," we will be reminded that, just as with our many former attempts, the high is very short-term.

Long-term happiness is not the by-product of short-term gratification. We don't have to *earn* happiness, exactly, but we do have to discover where it's found. How fortunate we are to have the program guiding our search. We will find happiness when we learn to get quiet and listen to our inner selves. We will find happiness when we focus less on our personal problems and more on the needs of others.

Many of us will need to redefine what happiness is. Understanding our value and necessity to our circle of acquaintances will bring us happiness, a happiness that will sustain us. Gratitude for our friends, our growing health, and our abstinence also sustain us. Sincerely touching the soul of someone else can tap the well of happiness within each of us.

I will find happiness. Searching within myself, I will patiently, trustingly share myself with others.

*However confused the scene of our life appears,
however torn we may be who now do face that scene,
it can be faced, and we can go on to be whole.*
—Muriel Rukeyser

We can expect to feel fear, even dread at some points in our lives. We will always have situations that, for a time at least, seem more than we can bear. But the clouds will lift. We are never given more than we can handle, and with each passing day we become more at ease with ourselves and all that life gives us. We are learning that "this too shall pass." Our confidence grows as our spiritual program gains strength.

Our ties to one another and our ties to the program make us whole. When we reflect on who we were and how far we've come, we will see that problems we drank over in days gone by are handled today and often with ease. The joy we share is that no problem is too great to be faced any longer. And no situation will ever have to be faced alone, unless we reject God's help.

I will be grateful for my growth toward wholeness and the opportunities I face today. They are bringing me into harmony with the Divine plan for my life.

Reaction isn't action—that is, it isn't truly creative.
—Elizabeth Janeway

We must learn how to act rather than react. Unfortunately, we've had lots of training at reacting. And we're all such good imitators. We are a society of reactors. We let the good or the bad behavior of another person determine our own behavior as a matter of course. But the opportunities are unlimited for us to responsibly choose our behavior, independent of all others in our life.

Change is ours, if we want it. A scowl from a spouse need not make us feel rejected. Criticism at work doesn't have to ruin our day. An inconsiderate bus driver might still be politely thanked. And when we decide for ourselves just how we want to act and follow through, self-esteem soars.

If we are put down, it may momentarily create self-doubt; but when we quickly reassure ourselves that all is well and respond with respect, we grow. A sense of well-being rushes through our bodies.

Being in command of our own feelings and our own actions prevents that free-floating anxiety from grasping us. We are who we choose to be. And new adventures await us.

The opportunities to react will be many today. But each time I can pause, determine the action I'd feel better about, and take it. My emotional health gets a booster shot each time I make a responsible choice.

We have seen too much defeatism, too much pessimism, too much of a negative approach. The answer is simple: if you want something very badly, you can achieve it. It may take patience, very hard work, a real struggle, and a long time; but it can be done . . . faith is a prerequisite of any undertaking. . . .

—Margo Jones

How many dreams have we let die? How many projects did we start, only to leave them unfinished? How many times have we promised ourselves, "This time will be different," but then didn't work to make it so? Negativity breeds more negativity. Fortunately, its opposite does likewise. Our attitude will carry us a long way. And a positive attitude will make all things possible.

We are meant for good living. But we must seek it out and be open to its invitation, be willing to put forth the necessary effort. Our dreams are our invitations to move forward, to strive for a further goal. And having faith in our ability to achieve our dreams will make easier the necessary steps.

We have been blessed with dreams, all of us. They are gifts meant to stretch our capabilities.

I can trust my dreams and aspirations. They are mine, alone, and special to me. Achievement is possible; faith and a positive attitude will ease my efforts.

God knows no distance.

—*Charleszetta Waddles*

As close as our breath is the strength we need to carry us through any troubled time. But our memory often fails us. We try, alone, to solve our problems, to determine the proper course of action. And we stumble. In time we will turn, automatically, to that power available. And whatever our need, it will be met.

Relying on God, however we understand God's presence, is foreign to many of us. We were encouraged from early childhood to be self-reliant. Even when we desperately needed another's help, we feared asking for it. When confidence wavered, as it so often did, we hid the fear— sometimes with alcohol, sometimes with pills. Sometimes we simply hid at home. Our fears never fully abated.

Finding out, as we all have found, that we have never needed to fear anything, that God was never distant, takes time to sink in. Slowly and with practice it will become natural to turn within, to be God-reliant rather than self-reliant.

Whatever our needs today, God is the answer.

There is nothing to fear. At last, I have come to know God. All roads will be made smooth.

It's odd that you can get so anesthetized by your own pain or your own problem that you don't quite fully share the hell of someone close to you.
—Lady Bird Johnson

Preoccupation with self can be the bane of our existence. It prevents all but the narrowest perspective on any problem. It cuts off any guidance from our higher power that may be offered through a friend. It blocks whatever truths are trying to gain our attention. The paradox is that whatever our pain, it is lessened by turning our attention elsewhere, to another's pain or joy.

When we open our minds to fresh input from others, insights emerge. We need the messages others are trying to give us. Nothing that is said in a loving spirit is empty of meaning for our lives.

We might consider that every conversation we have is a conversation with our Creator. What we need to know, for our own growth, is guaranteed to be revealed in our many conversations with others. But we can't hear another's thoughts until we let go of our own.

Full attention to the persons sent to me will offer me exactly what I need, today. My inner guide has beckoned them. I can be alert, expect solutions, and celebrate the wonder of it all.

There are no new truths, but only truths that have not been recognized by those who have perceived them without noticing.

—Mary McCarthy

We understand today ideas we couldn't grasp yesterday. We are conscious this year of details of our past that we may have glossed over at the time. Our blinders are slowly giving way, readying us for the truths we couldn't absorb before.

"When the student is ready, the teacher appears." And the teacher comes bearing truths that we need to assimilate into our growing bank of knowledge. The truths we may be given today, or any day, won't always make us happy immediately. We may learn that a job is no longer right for us. Or that a relationship has reached an end. And the impending changes create unrest. But in the grand scheme of our lives, the changes wrought by these truths are good and will contribute in time to our happiness.

Let's celebrate the truths as they come and trust the outcome to God. We are traveling a very special road. The way is rocky. The bends limit our vision, but we will be given all the direction we need.

The truths I receive today will guide my steps. I shall move in peace.

I have sacrificed everything in my life that I consider precious in order to advance the political career of my husband.

—Pat Nixon

Putting another person's needs first is what most of us were trained to do when growing up. We were seldom encouraged to embark on an individual course, and years of taking a back seat taught us that our hopes mattered little.

Now, for some of us, the future looks like a blank wall. It is time to carve out a plan for ourselves, yet how do we decide where we want to go? And how do we get there? The program says, "Live one day at a time." Our friends say, "Take one step at a time."

We have chosen to do something about the circumstances we found ourselves in, or we wouldn't be reading these words. We can stop for a moment and reflect on the many changes thus far. We are already on our way. We have taken a number of necessary steps. What an exciting adventure we have embarked upon! And we will be helped all along the way.

We can trust our inner yearnings, the ones we may have stifled in times past. We can realize our hearts' pure desires, if we seek guidance.

My time has come. I can mold my future. I will take each day, each experience, and let it draw me to the next important step.

Friendship of a kind that cannot easily be reversed tomorrow must have its roots in common interests and shared beliefs.

—Barbara W. Tuchman

The gift of friendship has been extended to each of us sharing this program. Our interest is common: we want to stay abstinent. And we share the belief that a power greater than ourselves can restore us to sanity. We trust our commitment to one another here. We are learning to live the program's principles in all our affairs.

In years gone by, friendships were often missing from our lives. We had a friend, here and there, certainly, but could she really be trusted—with our secrets, with our spouse? An overriding fear and one not without reason. It's likely that we, too, failed to be good friends. Friendship, anytime, means risking vulnerability. It means making a decision to be trustworthy. And it means not backing away from either, anytime.

Friendships so enrich our lives; they complete us. The experiences shared among friends give us all an edge on living. It is no accident that we have been drawn here together. What we have will help another.

I must be willing to give away my intimate self to my sisters in trust. My strength as a recovering woman will increase as my ties of friendship increase.

Fortuitous circumstances constitute the moulds that shape the majority of human lives.

—Augusta Evans

Being in the right place at the right time is how we generally explain our good fortune or the good fortune of a friend. But it's to our advantage to understand how we managed to be in the right place at just the right moment.

We have probably heard many times at meetings that God's timetable is not necessarily the same as our timetable. That events will happen as scheduled to fit a picture bigger than the picture encompassed by our egos. And frequently our patience wears thin because we aren't privy to God's timetable. But we can trust, today and always, that doors open on time. Opportunities are offered when we are ready for them. Nary a moment passes that doesn't invite us to both give and receive a special message—a particular lesson. We are always in God's care, and every circumstance of our lives is helping to mold the women we are meant to be.

I will take a long look at where I am today and be grateful for my place. It's right for me, now, and is preparing me for the adventure ahead.

Within our dreams and aspirations we find our opportunities.

—*Sue Atchley Ebaugh*

Our dreams beckon us to new heights. All that we may need is the courage to move toward them, taking the necessary steps to realize those dreams. Trusting that we will be shown the steps, one at a time, patiently waiting for the right step and right time is all we need to do, today.

Our dreams, when they are for the good of ourselves and others, are invitations from God to spread our wings, to attempt new heights. Those dreams are part of the destiny designed for us. They are not happenstance. Our gifts are unique. Our contributions are ours alone. Our dreams reflect the contributions we are called on to make in this life.

Our opportunities for fulfillment are varied and not always recognized as for our good. Again and again we need to turn to God, be patient, and trust that we are being called to offer something very special to those around us. No one of us has escaped a special plan. And everyone of us is inspired in particular ways, with particular talents. Our recovery is clearing the way for us to burst forth with our talents.

I will be grateful for all that I am, for all that I have. And I will remember, what I give today to friends around me is mine only to give.

One can never pay in gratitude; one can only pay "in kind" somewhere else in life.
—Anne Morrow Lindbergh

Life is a series of payments. The common expression, "What goes around, comes around," is a truth that governs each of our lives. As women and as members of the human family, we have received untold "payments" from others. On occasion, the payment may not have been one we'd have chosen for ourselves. It takes the distance of time to realize that our payments are meant for our good. And we can share the goodness; in fact, we need to share the goodness with one another. If we give to another the joy given to us, if we give to another the understanding given to us, if we give to another the friendship given to us, we will be ready to receive more in kind.

You and I meet today to make payments. I will receive yours gladly.

*To keep your character intact you cannot stoop to
filthy acts. It makes it easier to stoop the next time.*
—Katharine Hepburn

Behaving the way we believe God wants us to behave
sounds so easy on the surface. We don't willingly hurt
others, do we? Or do we? . . . When did we last secretly
burn with jealousy over another's good fortune or good
looks? Has there been a time, recently, when we sulked for
lack of attention . . . or perhaps picked a fight?

We can simplify life from this moment forth. There is
only one path to walk, one decision to make, in every
instance, and all our burdens will be lifted, all our anxiety
released. We can decide to act in good faith. We can be
silent a moment with ourselves and let our inner guide
direct our behavior, our words, our thoughts.

Each of us knows, when we dare to let our spiritual nature
reign, the right act in every case. Letting God choose our acts
will ease our lives. No more obsessive confusion. No more
regrets. No more immobility due to fear of wrong moves.

---

*Freedom is guaranteed when I depend on God to direct my
behavior. Life's burdens are lifted. I will go forth today, doing
God's will, and my Spirit will be light.*

No trumpets sound when the important decisions of our life are made. Destiny is made known silently.
—Agnes DeMille

The day ahead offers us choices of many kinds—some big ones, many that will affect other persons close to us, a few that will have profound effects on our destiny. But no choice, no decision we make, will be wrong. A particular decision may lead us slightly astray. Down a dead-end path perhaps—but we can always turn back and choose again.

We are seldom aware of the gravity of a particular choice at the time of making it. Only hindsight reveals the wisdom of an important choice. Nevertheless, no choice is without importance in the overall picture of our lives. And at the same time, no choice is all-powerful regarding our destiny. We are offered chances again and again for making the right choices, the ones that will most contribute to the bigger plan for our lives.

I need not worry about today's opportunities for decision making. I will listen to those around me. I will seek guidance in the messages coming to me. I will make the choices I need to, today.

You must do the thing you think you cannot do.
—*Eleanor Roosevelt*

How can we ever do that which seems impossible? Taking a class, quitting a job, leaving a destructive relationship behind, asking for help; none of these can we do alone or with ease. All of these we can handle when we rely on the help offered by the program, the help of one another, the help promised by our higher power. Tackling with God's help that which seems impossible, reduces it to manageable size. It also deflates the power our fears have given it.

That which we fear grows in proportion to our obsession with it. The more we fear a thing, the bigger it becomes, which in turn increases our fear. How lucky we are that God awaits our call for the strength, the companionship that is guaranteed us! We are in partnership, all the way, every day, if we'd only recognize it. We can move toward and through anything. And the added benefit is that we come to trust our partnership. We soon know that all situations can be met. All experiences can be survived. Avoidance is no longer our technique for survival.

A deep breath invites the inner strength to move through me. I will feel the exhilaration of God's power. And I will know the excitement of growth and peace.

We can never go back again, that much is certain.
—*Daphne DuMaurier*

Yesterday is gone, but its experiences will be reflected in those of today. We learned from both the good and the bad situations of yesterday. Where we travel today, likewise, will influence our direction tomorrow. We can't do over what has gone before, but we can positively incorporate all that life is offering us from this moment forth.

We are moving toward greater understanding of life's mysteries with each experience. As today unfolds, we can be moved by the adventures. What we experience is ours alone and will contribute to the unfolding of our special destiny. We move forward, only forward. The doors behind us are closed forever.

Facing what comes to us, with strength, is a gift from this program we share. Letting go of the yesterdays and the last years is another gift offered by this program. And trust that what we face along with what we let go will weave the pattern of our rightful unfolding—that is the ultimate gift given to us by this program.

I need never go back again. I am spared that. My destiny lies in the future. And I can be certain it will bring me all that I desire, and more.

Toleration is the greatest gift of the mind.
—Helen Keller

Facing conditions we would like to change, letting go of people we wish were different, takes growth, patience, tolerance. We're so easily enticed into thinking we'd be happier, "If only he'd change," or "If I had a better job," or "If the kids would settle down." Yet we carry the seed of happiness within us every moment. Learning tolerance for all conditions will nurture that seed.

Intolerance, impatience, depression—in fact, any negative attitude—is habit-forming. Many of us in this recovery program continue to struggle with the habits we've formed. Bad habits must be replaced with new, good habits. We can develop a new behavior, one that pleases us, like smiling at every stranger in a checkout line. We can repeat it in every line. It becomes a habit and a good one.

Toleration of others opens many doors, for them and for us. It nurtures the soul, ours and theirs. It breeds happiness. Those of us sharing these Steps are truly blessed. We're learning about love, how to give it and how to receive it.

There are so many eyes I'll look into today that don't know love. I will give some away with unconditional tolerance. It's a gift—to myself and others.

I want to dance always, to be good and not evil, and when it is all over not to have the feeling that I might have done better.

—Ruth St. Denis

Our wants in life may be simple, or they may be complex. They may yet be confused in our minds, but the clarity will come if we're patient. God has a way of giving us an "inner tug" when a certain direction beckons. Our responsibility is to follow that tug and trust it, fully. Too often we look back on our lives with regret. What is done, is done. We learned lessons from those mistakes. Every day is a new beginning. And we can close every day with no regrets when we have followed our consciences, that "inner tug" that beckons.

The opportunities will come today. Opportunities to be good or evil. Opportunities for making choices over which we will feel good or full of regret at the day's close. Many of our choices will bring us closer to the satisfaction, the contentment with life, that we all search for as women, as human beings. We need not fear coming to life's close, wishing we had done more or better. Living each day in good conscience, waiting for the tug and following it, will ensure a life well lived.

My ego can block out the tug, if I let it. Or I can trust.

*The beauty of the world has two edges, one of
laughter, one of anguish, cutting the heart asunder.*
—Virginia Woolf

Anguish is undoubtedly more familiar to us than is the
beauty of laughter. We feel anguish over our failings; we
feel anguish over our losses; we feel anguish over the attempts to succeed that beckon to us.

Anguish comes of fear. And we so hope to avoid it.
However, it seasons us as women; it enriches us even while
it momentarily diminishes us. It is a major contributor to
the sum and substance of our lives. The anguish we experience prepares us to help others face their own particular
anguish.

Our laughter, too, must be savored and shared. And
laughter builds more laughter. Laughter lends a perspective
to our anguish. Life is made richer, fuller, by the ebb and
flow, the laughter and the anguish in concert.

If only we could remember, when the anguish is present,
that it is making our Spirits whole. That it, along with
laughter, is a healer of the soul. That it lifts our load at the
same time that it burdens us. That it prepares us to better
receive life's other gifts.

*I can help another face anguish. It brings us together. It softens
me. And it makes way for the laughter soon to come.*

You need only claim the events of your life to make yourself yours.

—Florida Scott-Maxwell

The search is on. Everyone, everywhere, asks the question at some time, "Who am I?" Women like ourselves are fortunate to have this program. It shows us the way to self-discovery. It directs our steps to the celebration of self that is a gift of recovery. The events of our past may plague us. But they did contribute to the fullness we feel today. And for them, for their involvement in who we've become, we can be grateful.

Claiming ourselves, the good and the bad, is healing. It's taking responsibility—for where we were and where we're going. Claiming ourselves makes us the active participants in our lives. The choices are many and varied. Not actively participating in life is also a choice. Passivity may have been our dominant choice in years gone by. But now, today, we are choosing recovery. We are choosing action that is healing, and wholeness is the result.

———

Making myself mine will exhilarate me. It will give me hope. It will prepare me for anything to come. I will know a new joy.

Happiness is a byproduct of an effort to make
someone else happy.
—Gretta Brooker Palmer

We have striven for happiness, generally in self-centered ways. We expected others to favor us with their attention, for example. Or we waited for invitations or gifts. We have probably tried to buy happiness with the purchase of a new dress or shoes. Fleeting moments of happiness were gained, that's all. And soon we were discontent once again. And the search was begun anew.

But things have changed for some of us. We are learning, maybe slowly, how to find a more permanent happiness. And we know the happiness that comes from "getting" is elusive. *Giving* to others, giving attention, sharing hope, sharing our own stories, listening to theirs, is the key to finding the happiness for which we've searched so long. We must get outside of ourselves and focus on another's joy or sorrow. Only then do we get a clear perspective on who we are and the necessary role we play in the lives of others who need our attention and who have a message we also need to hear.

The creative power stirring in me needs recognition. Looking deeply into another person, listening intently to the stirring will elicit joy. I will feel in touch with my own creative power, a lasting thrill, not a fleeting moment of happiness.

Being alone and feeling vulnerable. Like two separate themes, these two parts of myself unite in my being and sow the seeds of my longing for unconditional love.

—Mary Casey

How easily we slip into self-doubt, fearing we're incapable or unlovable, perhaps both. How common for us to look into the faces of our friends and lovers in search of affirmation and love.

Our alienation from ourselves, from one another, from God's Spirit which exists everywhere causes our discontent. It is our discontent. When souls touch, love is born, love of self and love of the other. Our aloneness exists when we create barriers that keep us separate from our friends, our family. Only we can reach over or around the barriers to offer love, to receive love.

Recovery offers us the tools for loving, but we must dare to pick them up. Listening to others and sharing ourselves begins the process of loving. Risking to offer love before receiving it will free us from the continual search for love in the faces of others.

I won't wait to be loved today. I will love someone else, fully. I won't doubt that I, too, am loved. I will feel it. I will find unconditional love.

The weariest night, the longest day, sooner or later must perforce come to an end.
—Baroness Orczy

The difficult spells in our lives come to an end. And no matter the depth of our disturbance, we will survive. We forget that the depths teach us how to better appreciate the heights.

Sorrow heightens joy. Depression heightens laughter. We wouldn't know the joys and laughter were it not for the sorrows. In them we learn to be patient, waiting for the wisdom which will light our way. In them we learn to listen for the guidance that beckons us forth.

We must reflect on the troubling experiences we've passed through of late. They made us wiser; they gave us strength. They changed us, moving us ever closer to the women, whole and happy, we desire to be.

Difficulties often precede enlightenment. They pull us inward, perhaps push us to search for our connectedness to God, a connectedness that is at home in our hearts. The paradox is that these painful periods strengthen our oneness with the Spirit.

If the day looks bleak, I will accept it as a hand reaching toward me, to pull me forward, to secure my place in the spiritual family.

. . . I was taught that the way of progress is neither swift nor easy.

—Marie Curie

We are looking for progress, not perfection; however, we sometimes get lost or confused between the two. Expecting ourselves to be perfect at something we are only now learning is a familiar affliction. As we accept our humanness, we'll allow the mistakes that are a normal part of the process of living and learning—a process we call progress.

Our need to be perfect will lessen with time. And we can help ourselves break the old habits. Perfection and self-worth are not symbiotic, except in our minds. And it's a symbiosis that has done us a grave injustice. Breaking the old thought patterns takes a commitment. We must first decide and believe that we are worthwhile, simply because we are. There is only one of us; we have a particular gift to offer this world. And our being is perfect as is. Affirming this, repeatedly, is our beginning. But with this, too, progress will be slow; perfection need only be worked for, not achieved.

The patterns I am weaving with my life are complex, full of intricate detail and knots. I need to go slow, taking only one stitch at a time. With hindsight I will see that whatever the progress, it was the perfect fit to the overall design.

What a strange pattern the shuttle of life can weave.
—Frances Marion

Each experience we have plays its part in the total picture of our lives. The steps we have taken, the path we travel today, and our direction tomorrow are not by chance. There is a pattern. We each have a destiny. We may have veered off the path in the past, and we may veer off it again. But we'll be guided back, and our paths intersect. None of us is traveling alone. We have each other and the creative force that is at the helm.

When we look around us and reflect on how our lives are influenced by the persons close to us, we become aware that our presence affects their lives as well. Most of us could never have predicted the events that have influenced us. Nor can we anticipate what the future may hold. We can be certain, however, that we are safe; a power greater than ourselves is orchestrating our affairs.

There were times we feared we'd never survive an experience. Perhaps we still struggle with fears about new experiences. But every experience adds a necessary thread to the pattern our life is weaving. We have the gift of reflection. We can understand, today, the importance of particular events of the past. Next month, next year, we'll understand today.

I shall enjoy the richness of today. My life is weaving an intricate, necessary pattern that is uniquely mine.

Everyone has talent. What is rare is the courage to follow the talent to the dark place where it leads.
—Erica Jong

There was a time when we didn't believe we had any talents. We couldn't imagine we had any purpose or any gift to give to the world. But it's true: We all have talents, many of them. If we each haven't yet discovered ours, we soon will. With time and the Steps and friends, we will be encouraged to recognize them, to celebrate them, to cultivate them, to dare to give them away.

Utilizing our talents fully, which is part of life's bigger plan, may lead us to new jobs, new friends, to places presently unknown. The prospect of new horizons may excite us. It may also elicit dread. We can trust that, just as we are given no problems too big to handle, we are given no talents too great to develop. The strength to move ahead will always be available if we have faith. And the program offers us faith.

I will look for my talents today. I will also look for talents in my friends. I can celebrate them, and soon the way to use them will become clear.

Most kids hear what you say; some kids do what you say; but all kids do what you do.
—Kathleen Casey Theisen

We are role models for many people: our children, our co-workers, other women in the program. Step Twelve encourages us to set good examples for anyone who might be looking on. Living a principled life takes practice, and progress, not perfection, is hoped for.

Abstinence has offered us a new set of tools for shaping our behavior. No longer must we regret what we did yesterday or last week. We are learning to monitor our actions, but even more importantly, we are defining our values. They, in turn, influence what we say and do.

Thoughtful responses to the situations we encounter require conscious attention to those events. We need reminding, perhaps, that our behavior is continuously telling others who *we* are, what we value, and how we view the people close to us. All of us, consciously or otherwise, imitate behavior patterns of persons we admire. Unfortunately, we sometimes mimic unfavorable behavior, too.

There are those casting their attention our way. The opportunity to model favorable behavior awaits us.

People will follow my lead. I shall walk softly, humbly and lovingly.

It is good to have an end to journey towards; but it is the journey that matters, in the end.
                              —Ursula K. LeGuin

Goals give direction to our lives. We need to know who we are and where we want to go. But the trip itself, the steps we travel, offer us daily satisfaction moment by moment—fulfillment, if we'd but realize it. Too often we keep our sights on the goal's completion, rather than the process—the day-to-day living that makes the completion possible.

How often do we think, "When I finish college, I'll feel stronger." Or, "After the divorce is final, I can get back to work." Or even, "When I land that promotion, my troubles are over." Life will begin "when"—or so it seems in our minds. And when this attitude controls our thinking, we pass up our opportunity to live, altogether.

Looking back on goals already completed in our lives, what so quickly follows the end of a job well done is a letdown. And how sad that the hours, the days, the weeks, maybe even the months we toiled are gone, with little sense of all they could have meant.

I will not forget that every moment of every day I can be God-centered and joyous. The goal I'm striving toward will carry with it a special gift; it will offer the growing person within me an extra thrill, if I've attended to the journey as much as its end.

Loving, like prayer, is a power as well as a process.
It's curative. It is creative.

—*Zona Gale*

The expression of love softens us and the ones we love. It opens a channel between us. It invites an intimate response that closes the distance.

It feels good to express love, whether through a smile, a touch, or a prayer. It heightens our sense of being alive. Acknowledging another's presence means that we, too, are acknowledged. Each of us is familiar with feeling forgotten, unnoticed, or taken for granted, and recognition assures us all that we haven't been overlooked.

Knowing we are loved may be the key to our doing the things we fear. Love supports us to charge ahead, and we can support others to charge ahead. We know that if we fail, we have someone to turn to.

Love heals. It strengthens, making us courageous both when we receive it and when we give it. Knowing we are loved makes our existence special. It affirms that we count in another's life. We need to honor our friends by assuring them of their specialness, too.

I need others. I need to strengthen my supports, my connections to others for the security, even success, of each of us. I can express my love today, and assure my loved ones that they are needed. Then, they and I will surge ahead with new life.

Life is made up of desires that seem big and vital one minute, and little and absurd the next. I guess we get what's best for us in the end.

—Alice Caldwell Rice

It is often said that we will be granted our heart's "pure desires." When we have many unmet desires, maybe we should be grateful. Wants that are ultimately not for our good can open the way to many unneeded and painful experiences.

How often we sit, wishing for a better job, a more loving relationship, a different weather forecast. How seldom we take positive advantage of what is at hand, not realizing that whatever *is*, right now, is the ticket to the next act in the drama of our lives.

We have before us a very limited picture. We cannot possibly know just what we need to travel the distance that's in store for us. Our desires, when they are pure, will carry us to the right destination. They are inspired. But the desires that are motivated by our selfish egos will lead us astray. Many times in the past we did not give up those desires. And the painful memories linger.

Desiring God's will is my most fruitful desire. It's also what is best for me; thus, what I need. All things are working for good when I let my higher power determine my desires.

Parents can only give good advice or put them on the right paths, but the final forming of a person's character lies in their own hands.

—Anne Frank

We must take responsibility for ourselves, for who we become, for how we live each day. The temptation to blame others may be ever present. And much of our past adds up to wasted days or years perhaps, because we did blame someone else for the unhappiness in our lives.

We may have blamed our own parents for not loving us enough. We may have labeled our husbands the villains. Other people did affect us. That's true. However, we chose, you and I, to let them control us, overwhelm us, shame us. We always had other options, but we didn't choose them.

Today is a new day. Recovery has opened up our options. We are learning who we are and how we want to live our lives. How exhilarating to know that you and I can take today and put our own special flavor in it. We can meet our personal needs. We can, with anticipation, chart our course. The days of passivity are over, if we choose to move ahead with this day.

I will look to this day. Every day is a new beginning.

To create is to boggle the mind and alter the mood.
Once the urge has surged, it maintains its own
momentum. We may go along for the ride, but when
we attempt to steer the course, the momentum dies.
—Sue Atchley Ebaugh

A sense of spiritual well-being warms us when we are selfless, when we step away from our obsessing egos, when we let our pure, unfettered desires direct our thoughts and our steps. Our egos may be keeping us caged in old behavior, old fears. Egos struggle for self-preservation; unfortunately, it's our old, unhealthy self the ego is preserving.

The Steps make it possible for us to unload our baggage from earlier days, baggage that intrudes on our perceptions of today's events. The Steps clear the path so we can move responsibly forward.

Living creatively is living in the thick of the flow, trusting the flow, spontaneously moving with the flow, not controlling the flow. We are Spirit-full when we let ourselves roll forward, resisting not, doubting not. And our greatest contributions will be discovered when our ego takes a rest.

My creativity awaits my discovery. It's there. I will release it from the clutches of my ego.

I want to get you excited about who you are, what you are, what you have, and what can still be for you. I want to inspire you to see that you can go far beyond where you are right now.

—Virginia Satir

Deciding to recover was our first step. That decision meant we did want to go beyond where we were. We did want something better for ourselves. And at times, in fleeting moments, we have been excited about who we are and our prospects for a better life.

The excitement and the inspiration come and go; they are seldom stationary. We can actively create the excitement and the inspiration. We need not wait for them to come to us. That's one of the choices we have as human beings, as women.

Passively waiting for "the good life" is past behavior. Each day, this day, we can set our sights on reaching a goal—we can take a step, or two, toward that goal. Progress is there for the making—achievement is there for the taking.

Whatever our hearts' pure desires, we can move toward that goal. We are what we need to be. We have what we need to move ahead.

Today, I will let my excitement for life's possibilities spur me on.

*It is healthier to see the good points of others than to
analyze our own bad ones.*
—Francoise Sagan

Looking for the good in others is good for one's soul.
Self-respect, self-love grows each time we openly acknowledge another's admirable qualities. Comparisons we
make of ourselves with others, focusing on how we fail to
measure up (another woman is prettier, thinner, more
intelligent, has a better sense of humor, attracts people, and
on and on) is a common experience. And we come away
from the comparison feeling generally inadequate and unloving toward the other woman.

It is a spiritual truth that our love for and praise of others
will improve our own self-image. It will rub off on us, so to
speak. An improved self-image diminishes whatever bad
qualities one has imagined.

Praise softens. Criticism hardens. We can become all that
we want to become. We can draw the love of others to us as
we more willingly offer love and praise. We have an
opportunity to help one another as we help ourselves grow
in the self-love that is so necessary to the successful living of
each day.

I will see the good points in others today. And I will give praise.

*The influence of a beautiful, helpful, hopeful character
is contagious, and may revolutionize a whole town.*
—Eleanor H. Porter

We have met certain people who inspired laughter, hope,
or changes in us, or those close to us. We look forward to
seeing them. We leave their presence believing in ourselves,
aware that we can tackle whatever problems had us
immobilized. That special gift to inspire is ours for the
taking, too. The inspiration comes from God.

We can look to God for the strength we need. It will
come. We can look also to God for direction, for the steps
we need to take today. And then wait. Those persons who
inspire us have developed a secure connection to their God.
And it's their connection that comes through them to
inspire us.

We can take some time today, before the demands
overwhelm us, to weave our connection to our higher power.
When that contact is secure, we won't have to await
inspiration from another person to forge ahead with our
plans. The inspiration will live within us, and it will beckon
us onward. Our way will be illuminated.

*I shall meditate upon this. Conscious contact with God is only a
prayer away. My life will be brightened. My burdens will be
lifted. My hopes will become realities, whenever I look to God for
the gift of inspiration.*

Love is not getting, but giving. It is sacrifice. And sacrifice is glorious!

—Joanna Field

How easily we mistake attention for love. Even more easily, we trick ourselves into thinking our ability to control someone signifies love—especially theirs for us. But love is something far different from either attention or control. Far different.

Love frees others from our grasp—and lets them return on their own. Love is placing another's personal needs above our own, without regret. Love is selfless, yet it exhilarates the self. Giving love softens our edges, completes us, and connects us to the people with whom we are fulfilling our destinies.

Wanting love is a normal human desire, not one we should deny. And we shall receive love, the less our emphasis is on getting it, the more on giving it. We invite love when we freely and honestly give it. Another invitation for love comes from loving ourselves; self-hatred, which trapped many of us for years, hampers us no longer.

Love inspires—ourselves and those we give it to. It brightens our way, lessens our burdens, makes possible our rightful unfolding.

I won't look for love today. I will just give it. It will bless me tenfold.

People need joy. Quite as much as clothing. Some of them need it far more.
—Margaret Collier Graham

Life is not without pain and travail. They are necessary to new awareness which prompts growth. And the gift of growth is joy. Pain and joy are thus intertwined. It is possible to feel only the burden of pain and not the exhilaration of joy, however.

Before seeking help to change our lives, many of us were heavily burdened by pain. But we were unable to open ourselves to the knowledge made possible by that pain. We were on a treadmill, accumulating painful experiences at every step, unable to capture the joy that was ever present.

We can have hope. Joy does await each of us today. We must open our eyes to it, just as we must open our hearts to one another. We must be willing to peel away the layers of pain to expose the core, the seedling of joy. And we need joy in our lives, just as surely as we need rest and a good diet. We need the light heart that joy fosters for a better perspective on the many experiences we'll face today, and every day.

Recovery has given me this new option. It guarantees me that every burden will be lightened. The knowledge that joy is inherent, within every experience, is mine, now and forever.

The child is an almost universal symbol for the soul's transformation. The child is whole, not yet divided . . . when we would heal the mind . . . we ask this child to speak to us.

—Susan Griffin

Was there ever a time when we did not feel divided from ourselves? Occasionally we get a glimpse of what such spiritual wholeness would be like, but most of the time we struggle with feelings of conflict, unevenness, a divided heart. Perhaps "the child" is a metaphor for a spiritual guide, like our own higher power, that can help us in our journey toward self-acceptance.

"I may not be perfect, but parts of me are excellent," writes author Ashleigh Brilliant. If we can be happy with this proud, funny boast then perhaps we can stop berating ourselves for our imperfections. If we dwell on our own contradictory impulses, we give them too much importance, too much power.

Let me trust to my glimpses of harmony and wholeness and be grateful for the richness of my spirit.

Flattery is so necessary to all of us that we flatter one another just to be flattered in return.
—Marjorie Bowen

We are all deserving of unconditional love and acceptance. And all the people in our lives, past and present, deserve our unconditional love and acceptance, too. However, it's doubtful that we either feel it all of the time from others or give it away.

It's human of us to find fault—to have expectations that are too high. But for this we pay a price. Instead of experiencing our lives serenely, contentedly, flowing with what is, we often criticize, judge, and feel generally disgruntled throughout the day. What a waste! We do have another choice, fortunately. We can let go and let God, and live and let live. Also we can recall, today and every day, that we are all special individuals in this world who are loved, fully, by our Creator.

The greatest contribution we can make to the lives of others is to be affirming. We can let our spouse, children, and friends know we care about them. That we love and accept them. The love that we also long for will come back to us. We thrill at being affirmed. And we will thrill at affirming.

It feels good to help another feel appreciated. Love and acceptance are my lifeline, from God around us all.

True intimacy with another human being can only be experienced when you have found true peace within yourself.

—*Angela L. Wozniak*

Intimacy means disclosure—full expression of ourselves to another person. Nothing held back. All bared. There are risks, of course: rejection, criticism, perhaps ridicule. But the comfort we feel within is directly proportional to the peace we've come to know.

Each day we commit ourselves to recovery, we find a little more peace. Each conversation we have with our higher power brings us a little more security. Each time we turn our full attention to another person's needs, we feel our own burdens lightened.

Peace comes in stages. As we continue to accept our powerlessness, the depth of our peace increases. Turning more often to a power greater than ourselves eases our resistance to whatever condition prevails. Forgiving ourselves and others, daily, heightens our appreciation of all life and enhances our humility. Therein lies peace.

We each are a necessary part of the creative spirit prevailing in this world. The details of our lives are well in hand. We can be at peace. Who we are is who we need to be.

Intimacy lets me help someone else also live a full and peace-filled life. I will reach out to someone today.

A woman who is loved always has success.
                                                —Vicki Baum

Being loved, and knowing that we are loved, assure us of our connection to the world outside of ourselves, affirming us as participants in the bigger picture. And all of us need to know that we count—that what we say and do matter to others—that we are contributing in an important way.

Often we feel unloved, however. And we search for love. We may have begged for love and still didn't feel it. We have probably become very self-centered in our search. Fortunately, the program helps us to give love to others; the paradox is that love is returned, tenfold.

The wonders of love are many. Love is a healing balm for wounds. And it nurtures, both the one loving and the one loved. Love is an energizer. It spurs us on to successes in work and in play. Love multiplies. If we aren't feeling loved, we can love someone else—and love will visit us, too.

We can help the women in our lives find the successes they deserve. The confidence to tackle new situations is packaged in the gift of love. We need to help one another count.

My love of another is a contributing factor in her success. Her loving gratitude will enhance my own endeavors. I will take a moment, today, with a friend who needs my love.

Noble deeds and hot baths are the best cures for depression.

—Dodie Smith

Depression feeds on itself. With attention it worsens, but there are places for our attention. We can move our focus to a woman who is close by, a woman who is struggling to determine her direction in life. We can offer our ears. Or we can observe attentively, today, all the women, children, and men we see on the streets. When we notice their expressions, we realize they, too, may be suffering.

Doing something for someone else will lessen our own problems, no matter what the cause. In fact, just doing something will lift our spirits. Depression becomes habitual, and habits, even those that are detrimental, are easy to hang on to. When we take an action, even a small one, we can note the change: Action that benefits another is guaranteed to benefit us as well.

Depression does get worse with self-pitying attention; however, attention to ourselves that is nurturing has its place. We can pamper ourselves, but not pity ourselves. Pampering reflects approval, caring, self-respect; three attitudes inconsistent with depression. Even more than inconsistent, pampering and depression are incongruent.

Depression must be coddled to maintain it. It's my choice to move beyond it at any moment. I can put something besides my problem at my center today and enjoy the results.

I realized a long time ago that a belief which does not spring from a conviction in the emotions is no belief at all.

—Evelyn Scott

From pillar to post we bounced, most of us not knowing what we actually believed about nearly any situation before getting to this program. Perhaps we believed what was most convenient at the time because of the people we were with. And maybe we jumped the fence quickly when in a new setting. Values were sometimes talked about but not defined, and certainly not adhered to.

It's difficult to develop a strong sense of self, to have a very secure self-image when the parameters offered by a value system are lacking. Our values define who we are. They offer us direction when making choices. They quietly demand that we behave responsibly. Living in concert with our values brings peace to our souls.

Gone are the days when we rode first one fence and then another, never knowing what side of any issue we honestly believed in. The program has offered us a plan for living, a plan that erases the many uncertainties, the inner turmoil of past years.

Today will have a clarity about it that I can appreciate. I know who I am. I know what I believe. All I need do is act accordingly.

*There's a period of life where we swallow a knowledge
of ourselves and it becomes either good or sour inside.*
—Pearl Bailey

For too many of us, feelings of shame, even self-hatred,
are paramount. No one of us has a fully untarnished past.
Every man, every woman, even every child experiences
regret over some action. We are not perfect. Perfection is
not expected in the Divine plan. But we are expected to take
our experiences and grow from them, to move beyond the
shame of them, to celebrate what they have taught us.

Each day offers us a fresh start at assimilating all that we
have been. What has gone before enriches who we are now,
and through the many experiences we've survived, we have
been prepared to help others, to smooth the way for another
woman, perhaps, who is searching for a new direction.

We can let go of our shame and know instead that it
sweetens the nuggets of the wisdom we can offer to others.
We are alike. We are not without faults. Our trials help
another to smoother sailing.

*I will relish the joy at hand. I can share my wisdom. All painful
pasts brighten someone's future, when openly shared.*

Children are surely one of God's greatest gifts and truest challenges. To share your life with a child is to humble yourself so that you may learn from them and discover with them the beautiful secrets that are only uncovered in searching.

—Kathleen Tierney Crilly

Humility accompanies every experience wherein we let ourselves fully listen to others, to learn from them, to be changed by their words, their presence. Each opportunity we take to be fully present to other people, totally with them in mind and spirit, will bless us while it blesses them. Offering and receiving the gift of genuine attention is basic to the emotional growth of every human being.

Before recovering, many of us so suffered from obsessive self-centered pity that we seldom noted the real needs or pain of the people close to us. We closed ourselves off, wallowing in our own selfish worries, and our growth was stunted.

Some days we still wallow. But a new day has dawned. The Steps offer us new understanding. They are helping us look beyond ourselves to all the children of God in our daily lives. From each of them we have many secrets to learn.

I will be joyous today. Many secrets about life are mine to learn if I will stay close to all the people who cross my path. I will be mindful they are there because they have something to give me. I will be ready to receive it.

Reared as we were in a youth and beauty oriented society, we measured ourselves by our ornamental value.

—Janet Harris

Rare is the woman who doesn't long for a svelte body, firm breasts, pretty teeth, a smooth complexion. Rare is the woman who feels content, truly satisfied with her total person. We are often torn between wanting to be noticed and yet not wanting eyes to gaze upon us.

We are all that we need to be today, at this moment. And we have an inner beauty, each of us, that is our real blessing in the lives of others. Our inner beauty will shine forth if we invite it to do so. Whatever our outer appearance, it doesn't gently touch or bring relief where suffering is—like our words which come from the heart, the home of our inner beauty.

Perhaps a better mirror for reflecting our true beauty is the presence or absence of friends in our lives. We each have known stunning women who seemed to cast only cold glances our way and handsome men who arrogantly belittled others. It's our inner beauty that is valued by others. The surprise in store for each of us is discovering that the glow of our inner beauty transforms our outer appearance too.

My beauty today will be enhanced by my gentle attention to the other people sharing my experiences.

On occasion I realize it's easier to say the serenity prayer and take that leap of faith than it is to continue doing what I'm doing.

—S.H.

The pain of change is a reality. But so is the pain of no change—when change is called for. In spite of our desires, changing others will never be an option, whereas changing ourselves takes only a decision and is a choice always available.

We can take an inventory for a moment. What are we presently doing that makes us ashamed or angry or fearful? We can let go of that behavior and responsibly choose a new tack. If strength is needed, or confidence to try a new behavior, we can simply ask that it be ours. The Third Step promises that our lives are in God's care and our needs are always being attended to—not always our wants, but in every instance our needs.

Most of our struggles, today as in the past, are attached to persons and situations we are trying to forcibly control. How righteous our attitudes generally are! And so imposing is our behavior that we are met with resistance, painful resistance. Our recourse is now and always to accept those things we cannot change, and willingly change that which we can. Our personal struggles will end when we are fully committed to the Serenity Prayer.

The wisdom "to know the difference" is mine today.

Love has a hundred gentle ends.

—Leonora Speyer

Letting go is a process that is seldom easy. For many, its meaning is elusive. How do we "let go"? Letting go means removing our attention from a particular experience or person and putting our focus on the here and now. We hang on to the past, to past hurts, but also to past joys. We have to let the past pass. The struggle to hang on to it, any part of it, clouds the present. You can't see the possibilities today is offering if your mind is still drawn to what was.

Letting go can be a gentle process. Our trust in our higher power and our faith that good will prevail, in spite of appearances, eases the process. And we must let each experience end, as its moment passes, whether it is good or bad, love or sorrow. It helps to remember that all experiences contribute to our growth and wholeness. No experience will be ignored by the inner self who is charting our course. All are parts of the journey. And every moment has a gentle end, but no moment is forgotten.

My journey today is akin to yesterday's journey and tomorrow's too. I will savor each moment and be ready for the next.

When I slow down long enough to smell the roses,
I usually see the beauty and all else that is ours
to share.

—*Morgan Jennings*

We overlook so many joys, so many hidden treasures, when we hurry from place to place, person to person, experience to experience, with little attention anywhere. All that matters passes before us now, at this moment. And assuredly, we will not pass this way again.

It has been said the greatest gift we can give one another is rapt attention; additionally, living life fully attentive to the breezes, the colors, the sorrows and the thrills as well, is the most prayerful response any of us can make in this life. Nothing more is asked of us. Nothing less is expected.

We have just this one life to live, and each day is a blessing. Even the trials we shall understand as blessings in the months, the years ahead, as we can see now how the painful moments of the past played their part. Our attitude toward the lessons life has offered makes all the difference in the world.

I will look closely at everything in my path today. The women and children, the trees and squirrels, the silent neighbors. I will never see them again as I see them today. I will be at attention.

To believe in something not yet proved and to underwrite it with our lives; it is the only way we can leave the future open.

—Lillian Smith

Today stands before us, ready for our involvement. And it will offer us opportunities for personal growth and occasions to help another make progress on her path to the future. Challenges are to be expected. They further our purpose. They foster our maturity.

How different it is, for many of us, to look forward today with secure anticipation, to trust in what the future holds! We can still remember, all too vividly perhaps, the darker periods in our lives, periods that seemed to hold no promise; a time when we dreaded the future, fearing it would only compound those awful times.

The fear and the dread are not gone completely. They hover about us, on occasion. They no longer need to darken all of a day, however. We can recognize their presence as parts of our whole, not all of it. How free we are, today! Our choices are many.

I can step toward today with assurance, reaching out to others along the way, trusting that my accumulated steps add stability to my future.

*It takes time, love, and support to find peace with the
restless one.*

—Deidra Sarault

Restlessness is born of frustration. Perhaps we want to
move ahead with our lives more quickly. Does a job have us
trapped? Do past troubles haunt us still? Maybe perfectionism tarnishes every attempt to achieve. We can learn
from our restlessness, if we let it guide us to our inner
reservoir of peace and spiritual support.

The search for serenity often takes us farther from it. We
mistakenly think a different job or home or relationship will
answer all our needs. But we find that our restlessness has
accompanied us to our new surroundings. Peace has its
home within. And prayer opens the door to it. In the stillness of our patience, we are privy to its blessing.

Restlessness indicates our distance from our higher
power. It may be time for a change in our lives. Change is
good; however, our relationship with God will vouchsafe
any needed changes. Restlessness is self-centered and will
only hamper the steps we may need to take.

---

*Restlessness is a barometer that reveals my spiritual health.
Perhaps prayer is called for today.*

Is there ever any particular spot where one can put one's finger and say, "It all began that day, at such a time and such a place, with such an incident"?
—Agatha Christie

No experience of our lives is pure, unadulterated, set apart from all other experiences. There is an eternal flow in our lives. It carries us from one moment, one experience, into the next. Where we are today, the growth we have attained as recovering women and the plans we have for further changes are prompted by the same driving desires that contributed to our many actions in years gone by.

We can reflect on a particular experience and tag it a turning point. However, neither a lone prescription nor a single martini opened the door we passed through when we chose recovery. But they each may have played a part, and it's the many parts of our lives, past and present, that guarantee us the turning points that nudge us further up the mountain. We will see the summit. And we will understand how, each time we stumbled, new strength was gained.

Every day is a training ground. And every experience trains me to recognize the value of succeeding experiences. With richness, I am developing, one moment at a time.

Love is an expression and assertion of self-esteem, a response to one's own values in the person of another.
—Ayn Rand

The struggle to love one another may be a daily one for us, and it is made more difficult because we are still stumbling in our attempts at self-love. Many of us have lived our whole adult lives feeling inadequate, dull, unattractive, fearing the worst regarding our relationships with others.

But this phase, this struggle, is passing. We see a woman we like in the mirror each morning. We did a task or a favor yesterday that we felt good about. And when we feel good about our accomplishments, we look with a loving eye on the persons around us. Self-love does encourage other love.

Self-love takes practice. It's new behavior. We can begin to measure what we are doing, rather than what we haven't yet managed to do, and praise ourselves. Nurturing our inner selves invites further expression of the values that are developing, values that will carry us to new situations and new opportunities for accomplishments, and finally to loving the woman who looks back at us every morning.

Self-love makes me vulnerable and compassionate towards others. It's the balm for all wounds; it multiplies as it's expressed. It can begin with my smile.

The pure relationship, how beautiful it is! How easily it is damaged, or weighted down with irrelevancies— not even irrelevancies, just life itself, the accumulations of life and of time.

—Anne Morrow Lindbergh

Many of us are presently rebuilding old relationships and searching for new ones, ones that we hope we can protect. We can't survive without relationships, some intimate, some close, some casual. And we discover ourselves through our relationships with others.

The purity of a relationship is directly proportional to the undivided attention we both give to those shared moments, hours, experiences, to being *there* with one another. This communion with another is the celebration of life and God that quickens hearts and ushers in serenity.

Each day I can look for those chances to give myself wholly. And gifts will abound.

Anger repressed can poison a relationship as surely as the cruelest words.

—Joyce Brothers

Anger is familiar to us all. We feel it toward others and from others. The expression and acceptance of anger are where we often falter. Most of us were told when we were small girls that we shouldn't be angry, but we were. And we are, even yet. However, we often still feel like a little girl when it comes to angry feelings.

We need to accept our anger and learn to express it, honestly, openly and assertively, not aggressively. We can't afford to hang on to anger. It grows and then festers and then boils. Soon it is interfering in all our relationships, and it provides a ready excuse for an old, self-destructive pattern we don't want to entertain for even a moment.

Nothing we set out to do today will have the right outcome if we carry anger within us. How we interpret life, how we treat our friends, what we do with our opportunities and our challenges—all these are determined by our attitudes. Repressed anger always blocks the way to a positive attitude.

Every experience can uplift me if anger doesn't weigh me down.

To be wildly enthusiastic, or deadly serious—both are wrong. Both pass. One must keep ever present a sense of humor.

—Katherine Mansfield

How familiar wild enthusiasm and deadly seriousness are to most of us. We experience life within the extremes. The thrill of wild enthusiasm we try to trap, to control. We are exhilarated and feel good. Our serious side traps us, controls us, lowers a pall on all our activities. Both expressions keep us stuck. Neither expression allows the freedom of spontaneity so necessary to a full, healthy life.

Through our addiction—the liquor, the upper, the person, the food—we were searching for a feeling we didn't feel. We were searching for an unnatural state of happiness, even perhaps wild enthusiasm, because we had so little of any enthusiasm for life. Our search failed. Again and again we'd "catch it," only to have it elude us.

We may not have given up the search. But we will come to accept both states of mind as temporary and search instead for the middle ground. A sense of humor will make all of life's loads easier to bear. A sense of humor will offer us the balance that has been missing for so many years.

Today will offer me a chance to be wildly enthusiastic and a chance to be deadly serious. I'll try to focus on the middle ground and cultivate my sense of humor.

Courage is the price that life exacts for granting peace.

—Amelia Earhart

We have learned from experience that a wave of peacefulness washes over us after we have successfully finished a task that was difficult to face. Courage has its reward. However, from time to time, and from task to task, we find we need the reminder that peace will come once the loose ends have been tied by us.

Our search for peace was desperate and unending in past years. Our fears overwhelmed us more often than not. Courage was seldom displayed. Tasks were often left half done or not done at all. Challenges went unmet. And peace eluded us.

We are so lucky that the program found us, and that we found the program! We are looking forward, at last, with the courage that trusting a higher power has given us. Peace is ours, now and always, as we go forth with the strength of the program to bolster us. New jobs, new friends, new situations may still elicit our old fears. But their hold on us is gone. We have learned that we face nothing alone. What relief that simple truth brings.

Courage is one of the program's gifts. I will have courage to go forward: to meet the new day, to handle whatever confronts me. Peace is coupled with courage, now and forever.

Those who do not know how to weep with their whole heart don't know how to laugh either.

—Golda Meir

We all know people who live on the fringes of life. They seem uninvolved with the activity in their midst, as though a pane of glass separated them from us. And there are times when we join the persons standing alone away from the vibrancy of life. Fears keep people apart, particularly the fear of letting go of the vulnerable self and joining in the feelings of the moment.

To fully reap the benefits of life, we have to risk full exposure to one another and to the experience of the moment. Full involvement in the ebb and flow of life will bring the weeping that accompanies both the pain and the joy of life. It will also bring the fruits of laughter.

Both laughter and weeping cleanse us. They bring closure to an experience. They make possible our letting go. And we must let go of pain, as well as joy, to ready ourselves for the next blessing life offers us.

When we keep ourselves apart, when we hold off the tears or the laughter, we cheat ourselves of the richness of life. We have to go through an experience fully in order to learn all it can teach us and then be free of it.

Past experiences never let me go until I fully grieve those that need to be grieved or laugh over those that deserve the light touch. The present is distorted when the past shadows it.

All we are asked to bear we can bear. That is a law of the spiritual life. The only hindrance to the working of this law, as of all benign laws, is fear.
—Elizabeth Goudge

There is no problem too difficult to handle with all the help available to us. Let's not be overwhelmed. The program tells us to "Let go and let God," to turn it over. And that's where the solution lies.

Our challenges, the stumbling blocks in our way, beckon us toward the spiritual working-out of the problem, which moves us closer toward being the women we are meant to be. Our fear comes from not trusting in the power greater than ourselves to provide the direction we need, to make known the solution.

Every day we will have challenges. We have lessons to learn, which means growing pains. If we could but remember that our challenges are gifts to grow on and that within every problem lies the solution.

I will not be given more than I and my higher power can handle today, or any day.

I came to the conclusion then that "continual mind-fulness". . . must mean, not a sergeant-major-like drilling of thoughts, but a continual readiness to look and readiness to accept whatever came.
—Joanna Field

Resistance to the events, the situations, the many people who come into our lives blocks the growth we are offered every day. Every moment of every day is offering us a gift: the gift of awareness of other persons, awareness of our natural surroundings, awareness of our own personal impact on creation. And in awareness comes our growth as women.

Living in the now, being present in the moment, guarantees us the protection of God. And in the stretches of time when we anxiously anticipate the events of the future, we cheat ourselves of the security God offers us right now.

We are always being taken care of, right here, right now. Being mindful, this minute, of what's happening, and only this, eases all anxieties, erases all fears. We only struggle when we have moved our sights from the present moment. Within the now lies all peace.

The most important lesson I have to learn, the lesson that will eliminate all of my pain and struggle, is to receive fully that which is offered in each moment of my life.

Treat your friends as you do your pictures, and place them in their best light.

—*Jennie Jerome Churchill*

Taking our friends and loved ones for granted, expecting perfection from them in every instance, greatly lessens the value we have in one another's lives. Being hard on those closest to us may relieve some of the tension we feel about our own imperfections, but it creates another tension, one that may result in our friends leaving us behind.

We need the reminder, perhaps, that our friends are special to our growth. Our paths have crossed with reason. We complete a portion of the plan for one another's lives. And for such gifts we need to offer gratitude.

Each of us is endowed with many qualities, some more enhancing than others; it is our hope, surely, that our lesser qualities will be ignored. We must do likewise for our friends. We can focus on the good, and it will flourish—in them, in ourselves, in all situations. A positive attitude nurtures everyone. Let us look for the good, and in time, it is all that will catch our attention.

I can make this day one to remember with fondness. I will appreciate a friend. I will let her know she matters in my life. Her life will be enhanced by my attention.

It is only when people begin to shake loose from their preconceptions, from the ideas that have dominated them, that we begin to receive a sense of opening, a sense of vision.

—*Barbara Ward*

A sense of vision, seeing who we can dare to be and what we can dare to accomplish, is possible if we focus intently on the present and always the present. We are all we need to be, right now. We can trust that. And we will be shown the way to become who we need to become, step by step, from one present moment to the next present moment. We can trust that, too.

The past that we hang onto stands in our way. Many of us needlessly spend much of our lives fighting a poor self-image. But we can overcome that. We can choose to believe we are capable and competent. We can be spontaneous, and our vision of all that life can offer will change—will excite us, will cultivate our confidence.

We can respond to life wholly. We can trust our instincts. And we will become all that we dare to become.

Each day is a new beginning. Each moment is a new opportunity to let go of all that has trapped me in the past. I am free. In the present, I am free.

*Life is patchwork—here and there, scraps of pleasure
and despair. Joined together, hit or miss.*
                                        —Anne Bronaugh

As you look ahead, to this day, you can count on unexpected experiences. You can count on moments of
laughter. And you can count on twinges of fear. Life is
seldom what we expect, but we can trust that we will survive
the rough times. They will, in fact, soften our edges. Pleasure
and pain share equally in the context of our lives.

We so easily forget that our growth comes through the
challenges we label "problems." We do have the tools at
hand to reap the benefits inherent in the problems that may
face us today. Let us move gently forward, take the program
with us, and watch the barriers disappear.

There is no situation that a Step won't help us with.
Maybe we'll need to "turn over" a dilemma today. Accepting
powerlessness over our children, or spouse, or co-worker
may free us of a burden today. Or perhaps amends will
open the communication we seek with someone in our
lives. The program will weave the events of our day together. It will give them meaning.

---

*Today, well lived, will prepare me for both the pleasure and the
pain of tomorrow.*

For is it not true that human progress is but a mighty growing pattern woven together by the tenuous single threads united in a common effort?
—*Soong Mei-ling (Madame Chiang Kai-shek)*

We each are spinning our individual threads, lending texture, color, pattern, to the "big design" that is serving us all. Person by person our actions, our thoughts, our values complement those of our sisters, those of the entire human race. We are heading toward the same destination, all of us, and our paths run parallel on occasion, intersect periodically, and veer off in singleness of purpose when inspiration calls us.

It's comforting to be reminded that our lives are purposeful. What we are doing presently, our interactions with other people, our goals, have an impact that is felt by many others. We are interdependent. Our behavior is triggering important thoughts and responses in someone else, consistently and methodically. No one of us is without a contribution to make. Each one of us is giving what we are called upon to give when we are in a right relationship with God, who is the master artist in this design we are creating.

Prayer and meditation will direct my efforts today. My purpose can then be fulfilled.

*Even though I can't solve your problems, I will be
there as your sounding board whenever you need me.*
—Sandra K. Lamberson

The prize we each have been given is our ability to offer
full and interested attention to people seeking our counsel.
And seldom does a day pass that we aren't given the
opportunity to listen, to nurture, to offer hope where it's
been dashed.

We are not separate, one from another. Interdependence
is our blessing; however, we fail to recognize it at our
crucial crossroads. Alone we ponder. Around us, others,
too, are often suffering in silence. These Steps that guide
our lives push us to break the silence. The secrets we keep,
keep us from the health we deserve.

Our emotional well-being is enhanced each time we share
ourselves—our stories or our attentive ears. We need to be a
part of someone else's pain and growth in order to make use
of the pain that we have grown beyond. Pain has its purpose
in our lives. And in the lives of our friends, too. It's our
connection to one another, the bridge that closes the gap.

We dread our pain. We hate the suffering our friends must
withstand. But each of us gains when we accept these challenges as our invitations for growth and closeness to others.

Secrets keep us sick. I will listen and share and be well.

An element of recovery is learning that we deserve success, the good things that come to us, and also that pain is a reality. We have the strength to deal with that pain without medicating, and it will pass.
—Dudley Martineau

Many of us didn't understand the changing variables in being human. Our coping skills were at a minimum until we discovered what alcohol or pills, even food, could do for us. And then, a drink or two—or six, maybe—got us through many a lonely evening.

The desire for an easy solution might still haunt us, but time, new experiences, and program friends have taught us that our past habits weren't really easy solutions. In reality, they increased our problems and led us nowhere.

The Steps and the principles of the program, if applied, guarantee success, living success. We come to believe that strength enough to handle any situation is ours for the asking. And experience with these principles shows us that when we live the way our conscience dictates, the rewards are many.

Every day, especially this one facing us, our choices and decisions will be many. But there is only one solution to any problem, and that's the one our higher power guides us to. The answer, the choice, always lies within, and the good life will accompany our thoughtful, reverent choices.

The power of the program is mine for the taking. All of today's problems can be eased, if I choose to do so.

Make yourself a blessing to someone. Your kind smile or pat on the back just might pull someone back from the edge.

—Carmelia Elliott

Someone will be helped today by our kindness. Compassionate attention assures others that they do matter, and every one of us needs that reassurance occasionally. The program has given us the vehicle for giving and seeking the help we need—it's sponsorship.

Not all of the people we encounter share our program, however. Sponsorship as we know it isn't a reality in their lives. Offering words of encouragement to them, or a willing ear, can be unexpected gifts. They will be deeply appreciated.

The real gift, though, is to ourselves. Helping someone in need benefits the helper even more. Our own closeness to God and thus assurance about our own being is strengthened each time we do God's work—each time we do what our hearts direct.

We are healed in our healing of others. God speaks to us through our words to others. Our own well-being is enhanced each time we put someone else's well-being first.

We're all on a trip, following different road maps, but to the same destination. I will be ready to lend a helping hand to a troubled traveler today. It will breathe new life into my own trip.

The world is a wheel always turning. Those who are high go down low, and those who've been low go up higher.

—Anzia Yezierska

Everything changes. Nothing stays the same. And letting go of the way things are, anticipating instead what they might become, frees us to live each moment more fully.

Time marches on, and our destiny marches with it. There is purpose in how our lives unfold; the ups and downs serve our growth. We must neither resent the doldrums nor savor too long the elation. Giving too much attention to either state interferes with our awareness of the present. And the present has come to teach us.

We must move with time. We must focus our attention on the moment and accept whatever feelings each experience elicits. Emotional maturity is accepting our feelings and letting them go and facing the next moment with fresh receptivity. Our lessons are many, and they accompany the lows as well as the highs. We can be grateful for both.

The program has taught us freedom from lingering lows. It has given us the tools to move confidently forward, trusting that all is well. Nothing lasts forever, and within each struggle is the opportunity for real growth.

The highs will pass away, just as will the lows. They visit us purposefully. I will give them their freedom and find mine as well.

Only those who dare, truly live.
—Ruth P. Freedman

We receive from life, from every experience, from each interaction, according to what we have given. When we commit ourselves fully to an experience, it will bless us. When we give ourselves wholly to any moment, our awareness of reality will be heightened. When we risk knowing others, truly knowing them, we will find ourselves.

How common, and how unfortunate, that so many of us "escape" life! We escape through hiding, hiding from ourselves and others. We fear self-disclosure, our own and someone else's. Before choosing abstinence, our escape was easier. Now, the Steps make escape hard, fortunately.

Having a sponsor—and being one—helps. Taking the Fifth Step and working the Twelfth help. Going to meetings and sharing help. Our experiences today won't come around again—in just the same way. The people in our lives won't say again just what they'll say today. We must not miss out on what life offers. We can risk feeling it all, hearing it all, seeing it all.

The riches of a full life are so easily mine, and so deservedly mine.

It seems to me that I have always been waiting for something better—sometimes to see the best I had snatched from me.
                              —*Dorothy Reed Mendenhall*

Gratitude for what is prepares us for the blessings just around the corner. What is so necessary to understand is that our wait for what's around the corner closes our eyes to the joys of the present moment.

We have only the 24 hours ahead of us. In fact, all we can be certain of having is the moment we are presently experiencing. And it is a gift to be enjoyed. There is no better gift just right for us than this moment, at this time.

We can, each of us, look back on former days, realizing that we learned too late the value of a friend or an experience. Both are now gone. With practice and a commitment to ourselves, we can learn to reap the benefits of today, hour by hour. When we detach from the present and wait for tomorrow, or next week, or look to next year, we are stunting our spiritual growth. Life can only bless us now, one breath at a time.

I can live in the present if I choose to. Gentle reminders are often necessary, however. I will step into my life, today. It can become a habit, one I will never want to break.

In the face of an obstacle which is impossible to overcome, stubbornness is stupid.
—Simone de Beauvoir

Sudden obstacles, barriers in the way of our progress, doors that unexpectedly close, may confuse, frustrate, even depress us. The knowledge that we seldom understand just what is best for us comes slowly. And we generally fight it, even after we've begun to understand. Fortunately, the better path will keep drawing us to it.

We may wonder why a door seems to have closed. Our paths are confounded only when our steps have gone astray. Doors do not close unless a new direction is called for. We must learn to trust that no obstacle is without its purpose, however baffling it may seem.

The program can help us understand the unexpected. We perhaps need to focus on the first three Steps when an obstacle has surfaced. We may need to accept our powerlessness, believe there is a higher power in control, and look to it for guidance. We may also need to remind ourselves that fighting an obstacle, pushing against a closed door, will only heighten our frustration. *Acceptance of what is* will open our minds and our hearts to the better road to travel at this time.

The obstacles confronting me invite me to grow, to move beyond my present self. They offer me chances to be the woman I always dreamed of being. I will be courageous. I am not alone.

I can stand what I know. It's what I don't know that frightens me.

—Frances Newton

Fear of the unknown, often referred to as free-floating anxiety, catches up to us on occasion. But it needn't. The program offers us strength whenever we need it, and faith diminishes all fear. It is said that fear cannot exist where there is faith.

We have many days when we feel strong, in touch with our higher power, able to meet all situations. On those days, we are seldom conscious of how our faith is guiding us. But the hours of fear that we experience on other days make us aware of faith's absence. There is a simple solution: We can reach out to a friend. We can be attentive to her needs, and the connection to God will be made.

Shifting our focus from self-centered fears to another person's needs offers us a perspective on our own life. It also offers us a chance to let God work through us. Our own faith is strengthened each time we offer our services to God and to a friend in need. What may frighten us seems less important the closer we are to the people in our lives.

When I touch someone else, God touches me in return.

To oppose something is to maintain it.
                                    —*Ursula K. LeGuin*

Most of our struggles are with other persons or perhaps situations we want to change. We discover that our continual opposition adds fuel to the fires (at least our own internal ones). But can we turn our backs when we feel justified in our opposition? There's perhaps no more difficult action to take than to walk away from those situations we feel so strongly about, but the wisdom of this program says, "Let go and let God." And when we do let go, as if by magic, relief comes. The fires die out. That which we opposed is less troubling, maybe even gone. We no longer feel the need to struggle today. The need may rise again, but again we can turn to our higher power. Trusting that relief awaits us, ensures its arrival.

As women we discover many opportunities for opposition, too many persons and situations that make our changing roles difficult—too many persons who don't easily accept our changing characters. We must share with one another the strength to let go and let God.

I maintain my struggles with righteous behavior. They lose their sting when they lose my opposition. I will step aside and let God.

In the process of defining myself, I have a tendency to set up rules and boundaries and then forget that rules are made to be broken, as are boundaries to be expanded and crossed.
—Kathleen Casey Theisen

Recovery has given us the freedom to address life honestly, with forethought and a certainty about the rightness of our actions. We need be mindful that what is right today may not be right tomorrow or thereafter. As we move through our experiences, we are changed, and then we look with a new perspective on old conditions. Our new perspective hones our value systems, and yesterday's rules and boundaries no longer fit today's situations.

Our growth as women is an unending process. What we confront today with assurance, we prepared for yesterday. And tomorrow will be eased by our definition of today. The program has gifted us with clarity—clarity about ourselves, clarity regarding others, and clarity on how to continue our growth.

My value system awaits finer definition, and every experience today presents me with an opportunity for that definition.

One has to grow up with good talk in order to form the habit of it.

—Helen Hayes

Our habits, whatever they may be, were greatly influenced, if not wholly formed, during childhood. We learned our behavior through imitation—imitation of our parents, our siblings, our peer group. But we need not be stuck in habits that are unhealthy. The choice to create new patterns of behavior is ours to make—every moment, every hour, every day. However, parting with the old pattern in order to make way for the new takes prayer, commitment, determination.

All of us who share these Steps have broken away from old patterns. We have chosen to leave liquor and pills alone. We may have chosen to leave unhealthy relationships. And we are daily choosing to move beyond our shortcomings. But not every day is a successful one. Our shortcomings have become ingrained. Years of pouting, or lying, or feeling fearful, or overeating, or procrastinating beckon to us; the habit invites itself.

We can find strength from the program and one another to let go of the behavior that stands in the way of today's happiness. And we can find in one another a better, healthier behavior to imitate.

The program is helping me to know there is a better way, every day, to move ahead. I am growing up again amidst the good habits of others, and myself.

To look backward for a while is to refresh the eye, to restore it, and to render it the more fit for its prime function of looking forward.
—Margaret Fairless Barber

When we contemplate last month, last year, the period of time just before we came into this Twelve Step program, we can see many changes, good changes, have come our way. But we take the changes for granted sometimes. Or maybe we fail to reflect on them at all. We get caught up in the turmoil of the present, believing it will last forever, forgetting that yesterday's turmoil taught us much that we needed to know.

The past, for most of us, was rife with pain. But now we have hope. We have gained on life. We may be back in the good graces of our family. Perhaps we have patched up some failed relationships. A career has beckoned to us. Good experiences have come to pass. But we aren't free of difficulties. They need not get us down again. Hindsight assures us that this, too, will pass. It also guarantees that we will move forward, just as we have again and again, if only we have faith.

I will take this moment to look back at last year or the last binge. I can rest assured that I am moving forward. I will continue to do so.

*Our own rough edges become smooth as we help a
friend smooth her edges.*

—Sue Atchley Ebaugh

Focusing on a good point in every person we encounter
today will benefit us in untold ways. It will smooth our
relations with that person, inviting her to respond kindly
also. It will increase our awareness of the goodness all
around us. It will help us realize that if everyone around us
has positive traits, then we must also have them. But
perhaps the greatest benefit of focusing on good points is
that it enhances us as women; a healthy, positive attitude
must be cultivated. Many of us had little experience with
feeling positive before the turning point, recovery.

Recovery is offering us a new lease on life every moment.
We are learning new behaviors, and we are learning that
with the help of a higher power and one another, all things
that are right for us are possible. It is energizing to focus on
the good points of others, to know that their good points
don't detract from our own.

In the past, we may have secretly hated other women's
strengths because we felt inferior. We are free from that hate
now, if we choose to be. A strength we can each nurture is
gratitude for being helped by, and privy to, the strengths of
our friends and acquaintances.

---

*Bad points get worse with attention. My good points will gain
strength.*

When you cease to make a contribution, you begin to die.

—*Eleanor Roosevelt*

We need to take note, today, of all the opportunities we have to offer a helping hand to another person. We can notice too the many times a friend, or even a stranger, reaches out to us in a helpful way. The opportunities to contribute to life's flow are unending.

Our own vibrancy comes from involvement with others, from contributing our talents, our hearts, to one another's daily travels. The program helps us to know that God lives in us, among us. When we close ourselves off from our friends, our fellow travelers, we block God's path to us and through us.

To live means sharing one another's space, dreams, sorrows; contributing our ears to hear, our eyes to see, our arms to hold, our hearts to love. When we close ourselves off from each other, we have destroyed the vital contribution we each need to make and to receive in order to nurture life.

We each need only what the other can give. Each person we meet today needs our special contribution.

What a wonderful collection of invitations awaits me today!

She knows omnipotence has heard her prayer and
cries "it shall be done—sometime, somewhere."
                                    —*Ophelia Guyon Browning*

Patience is a quality that frequently eludes us. We want what we want when we want it. Fortunately, we don't get it until the time is right, but the waiting convinces us our prayers aren't heard. We must believe that the answer always comes in its own special time and place. The frustration is that our timetable is seldom like God's.

When we look back over the past few weeks, months, or even years, we can recall past prayers. Had they all been answered at the time of request, how different our lives would be. We are each on a path unique to us, offering special lessons to be learned. Just as a child must crawl before walking, so must we move slowly, taking the steps in our growth in sequence.

Our prayers will be answered, sometime, somewhere. Of that we can be sure. They will be answered for our greater good. And they will be answered at the right time, the right place, in the right way.

I am participating in a much bigger picture than the one in my individual prayers. And the big picture is being carefully orchestrated. I will trust the part I have been chosen to play. And I can be patient.

Everything has its wonders, even darkness and silence, and I learn, whatever state I may be in, therein to be content.

—Helen Keller

There is wonder in the moment, if we but look for it, let it touch us, believe in it. And with the recognition and celebration of the wonder comes the joy we desire and await.

Being wholly in tune with the present moment is how we'll come to know the spiritual essence that connects all of life. We search for peace, happiness, and contentment outside of ourselves. We need instead to discover it within us, now and always, in whatever we are experiencing.

We can let our experiences wash over us. Longing for a different time, a distant place, a new situation breeds discontent. It prevents us from the thrill, the gifts offered in this present moment. But they are there.

We can practice feeling joyful in the present, be thrilled with the realization that right now, all is well. All is always well. Life is full of mystery and wonder and each moment of our awareness adds to the wonder.

I am moving forward; we all are. I am on target. I am participating in a glorious, wonderful drama. Let me jump for joy. I have been specially blessed.

. . . pain is the root of knowledge.

—*Simone Weil*

We don't want pain in our lives. We dread the situations we anticipate will be painful. We probably even pray to be spared all painful experiences. But they come anyway, at times in profusion. And we not only survive the pain, we profit from it.

It seems that pain stretches us to our limits, generally forcing us to look for guidance from others, and it pushes us to consider new choices in our present situation. Pain is our common denominator as women, as members of the human family. It softens us to one another. It fosters empathy. It helps us to reach out and realize our need for one another.

New knowledge, new awarenesses, are additional benefits of accepting, rather than denying, the pain that accompanies life. This journey that we're on is moving us further and further along the path of enlightenment. We can consider that each problem, each crisis, is our necessary preparation for moving another step down the road.

I learn out of necessity. And when the student is ready, the teacher will appear.

So much to say. And so much not to say! Some things are better left unsaid. But so many unsaid things can become a burden.

—*Virginia Mae Axline*

The occasions are many when we'd like to share a feeling, an observation, perhaps even a criticism with someone. The risk is great, however. She might be hurt, or he might walk away, leaving us alone.

Many times, we need not share our words directly. Weighing and measuring the probable outcome and asking for some inner guidance will help us decide when to speak up and when to leave things unsaid. But if our thoughts are seriously interfering with our relationships, we can't ignore them for long.

Clearing the air is necessary sometimes, and it freshens all relationships. Deciding when to take the risk creates consternation. But within our quiet spaces, we always know when we must speak up. And the direction will come. The right moment will present itself. And within those quiet spaces the right words can be found.

If I am uncomfortable with certain people, and the feelings don't leave, I will consider what might need to be said. I will open myself to the way and ask to be shown the steps to take. Then, I will be patient.

> . . . *suffering . . . no matter how multiplied . . . is
> always individual.*
> —Anne Morrow Lindbergh

Knowing that others have survived experiences equally devastating gives us hope, but it doesn't diminish our own personal suffering. Nor should it; out of suffering comes new understanding. Suffering also encourages our appreciation of the lighter, easier times. Pain experienced fully enhances the times of pleasure.

Our sufferings are singular, individual, and lonely. But our experiences with it can be shared, thereby lessening the power they have over us. Sharing our pain with another woman also helps her remember that her pain, too, is survivable.

Suffering softens us, helps us to feel more compassion and love toward another. Our sense of belonging to the human race, our recognition of the interdependence and kinship of us all, are the most cherished results of the gift of pain.

Each of our sufferings, sharing them as we do, strengthens me and heals my wounds of alienation.

Love between two people is such a precious thing. It is not a possession. I no longer need to possess to complete myself. True love becomes my freedom.
—Angela L. Wozniak

Self-doubt fosters possessiveness. When we lack confidence in our own capabilities, when we fear we don't measure up as women, mothers, lovers, employees, we cling to old behavior, maybe to unhealthy habits, perhaps to another person. We can't find our completion in another person because that person changes and moves away from our center. Then we feel lost once again.

Completion of the self accompanies our spiritual progress. As our awareness of the reality of our higher power's caring role is heightened, we find peace. We trust that we are becoming all that we need to be. We need only have faith in our connection to that higher power. We can let that faith possess us, and we'll never need to possess someone else.

God's love is ours, every moment. Recognition is all that's asked of us. Acceptance of this ever-present love will make us whole, and self-doubt will diminish. Clinging to other people traps us as much as them, and all growth is hampered, ours and theirs.

Freedom to live, to grow, to experience my full capabilities is as close as my faith. I will cling only to that and discover the love that's truly in my heart and the hearts of my loved ones

Accustomed as we are to change, or unaccustomed, we think of a change of heart, of clothes, of life, with some uncertainty.

—Josephine Miles

Being used to a situation, even a painful one, carries with it a level of comfort. Moving away from the pain, changing the situation, be it job, home, or marriage, takes courage and support from other persons. But even more it takes faith that the change will benefit us. For most of us, the pain will need to worsen.

In retrospect, we wonder why it took us so long. We forget, from one instance to the next, that a new door cannot open until we've closed one behind us. The more important fact is that a new one will always open without fail. The pain of the old experience is trying to push us to new challenges, new opportunities, new growth. We can handle the change; we can handle the growth. We are never given more than we can handle, and we are always given just what we need.

Experience can't prepare us for the ramifications of a new change. But our trust in friends, and our faith in the spiritual process of life, can and will see us through whatever comes.

If a change of any kind is facing me today, I will know that I am not alone. Whatever I am facing is right for me and necessary to my well-being. Life is growth. The next stage of my life awaits me.

Insight is cheap.

—*Martha Roth*

For years we kept ourselves in a split condition: With one part of our minds we looked at ourselves and said, "I do some self-destructive things because I don't believe I deserve love." When we became involved with unsuitable people or abused our bodies, we said, "I am punishing myself—I am expecting too much—I neglect my own needs."

We may see clearly how and why we get in our own way. But unless we have faith in a power greater than ourselves, we won't step aside. We won't let go. We'll do the same thing and "understand" ourselves in the same ways. We may even use our "insight" to keep ourselves stuck—to protect ourselves from the risk of change.

Now, having had a spiritual awakening, having come to believe that a higher power can restore us, we possess a gift more powerful than the keenest insight—faith in our ability to grow and change. We are children of God. All the creative power of the universe streams through us, if we don't block it.

Today, I will have faith, and all will be well.

One must be leery of words because they turn into cages.

—*Viola Spolin*

We defeat ourselves with labels. We hem ourselves in; we shorten our vision; we cut off opportunities in the making. We influence how others think of us, too. Someone wise said that we teach others how to treat us. Are we teaching people to expect nothing great from us—because we are always afraid? Do we shatter their vision of our potential—by never thinking we can handle what may come?

We become the persons we have programmed ourselves to be. We can revamp the program, anytime. And right now is a good time to begin. We are surrounded by persons who have done just that.

It's time for praise. We are all that we need to be, and more. We will be helped to do all we are asked to do. We have an inner beauty that only needs encouragement to shine forth. If we smile from within today, we will free ourselves from our negative cages. A new life awaits us.

To catch myself each time I insult myself will be a challenge, but one worth taking on. And it's one I can win!

. . . love is a great beautifier.

—Louisa May Alcott

Meeting life head-on, with a smile, attracts people and situations to us. Our attitudes shape our world—which is not to deny that problems do occur. However, problems can be viewed as special opportunities for personal growth—as gifts, more or less, that we are ready to receive. When the student is ready, the teacher appears. The stumbling blocks we encounter push us beyond our present awareness. They teach us that we are stronger and more creative than we'd thought. Problem solving is esteem-building.

Negatively confronting the day is sure to complicate any experiences. A simple misunderstanding can be exaggerated into a grave situation, requiring the energy of many people to handle it. On the other hand, a patient, trusting, loving attitude can turn a grave situation into a positive learning experience for all affected.

We can beautify the day by smiling throughout all the experiences it offers us. The expression of love to everyone we meet guarantees to make us more lovable in return.

How great is my influence today! I can go forth feeling love, if I choose to—guaranteeing an enjoyable day for me and everyone I meet.

The rare and beautiful experiences of divine revelation are moments of special gifts. Each of us, however, lives each day with special gifts which are a part of our very being, and life is a process of discovering and developing these God-given gifts within each one of us.
　　　　　　　　　　　　　　　　　—Jeane Dixon

Have we discovered what our gifts are? We assuredly have them, and now that we are abstinent we have opportunities, daily, to share them with others. Sharing them knowingly will bring joy to us, but more than that, we will grow in appreciation of ourselves. And we do need to realize how very important we are to others.

Many of us came into this program nearly feet first. Most of us were filled with rage, shame, or both. Life had dumped on us. We had survived only minimally. The knowledge that we had something to offer the human race was not ours, then. It may still be knowledge that escapes us, from time to time. But we can learn to acknowledge it.

We have many talents that are ours alone to offer the world. Perhaps we express ourselves adroitly; maybe we write particularly well. Listening when it's most needed by a friend may be our finest talent today. We might have gifts as a musician or a manager. Our inner self knows our strengths. We can listen for that voice.

God is trying to get my attention today, to direct my energies to make the most of my special talents. I will be aware.

. . . it is a peaceful thing to be one succeeding.
—Gertrude Stein

Success is at hand. While we read these words, we are experiencing it. At this very instant, our commitment to recovery is a sign of success, and we feel peace each time we let go of our struggle, turning to another for help, for direction. Because we strive only for perfection, we recognize nothing less; we block our awareness of the ordinary successes that are ours again and again. Thus, the serenity the program promises us eludes us. But we *are* succeeding. Every day that we are abstinent, we succeed.

We can think of the times—perhaps only yesterday—when we listened to a friend in need, or finished a task that was nagging at us. Maybe we made an appointment to begin a project we've been putting off. Success is taking positive action, nothing more.

Many of us, in our youth, were taught that success only came in certain shapes and sizes. And we felt like failures. We need new definitions; it's time to discard the old. Luckily for us, the program offers us new ones.

Every person, every situation, can add to my success today. My attitude can help someone else succeed, too.

I stand before you as a tower of strength, the weight of the world on my shoulders. As you pass through my life, look, but not too close, for I fear I will expose the vulnerable me.

—*Deidra Sarault*

Vulnerability is as much a part of being human as is strength. Our vulnerability prevents our strength from becoming hard, brittle, self-serving. Our soft edges invite others' openness and their expressions of love.

We learned long ago to be "strong." We were encouraged to need no help, to need nobody. Now, we struggle to ask for help. As we grow in understanding of our human needs, and as we become more aware of the spiritual help available, the difficulty of reaching out to others is eased.

No longer need we look to pills, booze, food, or lovers for strength. All the strength we'll ever need is as close as our thoughts. At this moment, we are a tower of strength, not one weighted with burdens. Rather, our strength is a gift of our connection to a spiritual power that can free us from all the troubles we shoulder. Our vulnerable selves will open our souls to the flood of strength just waiting for our prayers.

I will be as strong as I need to be when I tap the spiritual source that awaits my call. I will risk my vulnerable self today.

We tend to think of the rational as a higher order, but it is the emotional that marks our lives. One often learns more from ten days of agony than from ten years of contentment.

—Merle Shain

Pain stretches us. It pushes us toward others. It encourages us to pray. It invites us to rely on many resources, particularly those within.

We develop our character while handling painful times. Pain offers wisdom. It prepares us to help other women whose experiences repeat our own. Our own pain offers us the stories that help another who is lost and needs our guidance.

When we reflect on our past for a moment, we can recall the pain we felt last month or last year; the pain of a lost love, or the pain of no job and many bills; perhaps the pain of children leaving home, or the death of a near and dear friend. It might have seemed to us that we couldn't cope. But we did, somehow, and it felt good. Coping strengthened us.

What we forget, even now, is that we need never experience a painful time alone. The agony that accompanies a wrenching situation is dissipated as quickly and as silently as the entrance of our higher power, when called upon.

I long for contentment. And I deserve those times. But without life's pain I would fail to recognize the value of contentment.

*The battle to keep up appearances unnecessarily,
the mask—whatever name you give creeping
perfectionism—robs us of our energies.*
                                   —Robin Worthington

How familiar we are with trying to be women other
than ourselves; ones more exciting, we think, or sexier, or
smarter. We have probably devoted a great deal of energy
to this over the years. It's likely that we are growing more
content with ourselves now. However, aren't there still
situations in which we squirm, both because we want to
project a different image, and because we resent our desire
to do so?

We each have been blessed with unique qualities. There
is no other woman just like ourselves. We each have special
features that are projected in only one way, the way we
alone project them.

Knowing that we are perfect as we are is knowledge that
accompanies recovery. How much easier life is, how much
more can be gained from each moment, when we meet each
experience in the comfort of our real selves. The added gift
of simply being ourselves is that we'll really hear, see, and
understand others for the first time in our lives.

*I can fully focus on only one thing, one person at a time. I will
free my focus from myself today and be filled up by my experiences with others.*

*To expect too much is to have a sentimental view of
life, and this is a softness that ends in bitterness.*
—*Flannery O'Connor*

Having too-high expectations is a setup for disappointment. Expectations that are high lend themselves to a
fantasy life, and reality can never match our fantasies. When
we get hooked on the fantasies, somehow thinking they are
reality, or should be reality, we are vulnerable to the hurt
that accompanies the emergence of "the real." Then we feel
cheated—bitter: "Why did this have to happen to me?"

Having too-high expectations was a familiar feeling
before recovery. And it remains familiar to us, even now.
Dreams and aspirations aren't wrong. In fact, they beckon
us on to better and greater things. But dreams of what we
can become through responsible choices are quite different
from idle expectations of what will or should be.

*Every moment of every day opens the way to my aspirations
that enhance reality. I will be open and receptive to reality and
its gifts.*

To wait for someone else, or to expect someone else to make my life richer, or fuller, or more satisfying, puts me in a constant state of suspension; and I miss all those moments that pass. They never come back to be experienced again.

—Kathleen Tierney Crilly

The steps we are taking today will never again be taken in exactly the same way. The thoughts we are thinking are fresh, never to be repeated. All that these moments offer will never pass our way again.

We each have to grab our own happiness, create our own richness through experiences. We may share what we capture with loved ones, but like us, they too must search their own avenues for the satisfaction that lasts. We can neither give happiness to another, like a gift, nor expect it in return.

The fullness of life we all long for is the natural by-product of living every moment as fully as possible. Our higher power will never direct us into waters too deep. When we have willingly turned our lives and our wills over, we'll find an abundance of the rich, the full, the satisfying. Faith in God answers all questions, solves all problems.

I will cherish every moment today. Each one is special and will not visit me again.

Bad moments, like good ones, tend to be grouped together.

—Edna O'Brien

Rough times may be pouring in on us at the moment, and they may seem unending. Difficulties appear to attract more difficulties, problems with loved ones, problems at work, problems with our appearance. A negative attitude, something that we all struggle with at times (some of us more than others), is the culprit.

When the good times come, as they always do, they are accompanied by a positive attitude. We do find what we look for.

Our attitude is crucial. It determines our experiences. A trying situation can be tolerated with relative ease when we have a positive, trusting attitude. We forget, generally, that we have an inner source of strength to meet every situation. We forget the simple truth—all is well, at this moment, and at every moment. When the moments feel good, our presence is light, cheery. When the moments are heavy, so are we.

I can turn my day around. I can change the flavor of today's experiences. I can lift my spirits and know all is well.

Every human being has, like Socrates, an attendant spirit; and wise are they who obey its signals. If it does not always tell us what to do, it always cautions us what not to do.

—Lydia M. Child

Our Spirit is our inner guide. And our Spirit never, never, gives us wrong directions. Because we're human, it's all too easy to deny the voice from within. Some call it conscience. And our behavior, maybe frequently, maybe occasionally, belies what our conscience knows is right. We suffer for it.

We are trying to be healthy—emotionally, spiritually, physically. Each day we can make progress. With each action we take, we have a choice. Our Spirit, our conscience, should be consulted. Right choices make for right actions that will emotionally and spiritually benefit us and the other persons close to us.

It's comforting to rely on the inner voice. It assures us we're never alone. No decision has to be made alone. No wrong action need ever be taken. A sense of security accompanies the partnership between each of us and our Spirit.

I will let the partnership work for me today.

Your sense of what will bring happiness is so crude and blundering. Try something else as a compass. Maybe the moralists are right and happiness doesn't come from seeking pleasure and ease.

—Joanna Field

We think we know what will make us happy. Seldom do we readily accept that painful moments are often the price tags for peaceful, happy times. Nor do we appreciate that happiness lives within each of us; never is it intrinsic to the events we experience. Because we look for happiness "out there" and expect it gift-wrapped in a particular way, we miss the joy of being fully alive each passing moment. How distorted our sense of happiness was before finding our way to this program! How futile our search!

The way still isn't easy every Step we take, but we will find happiness in those fleeting moments when we can get outside of ourselves long enough to be fully attentive to the people in our lives. We'll find it because it's been there all the time. It flows between us when we open our hearts to give and to receive compassion. Being truly there for another person is the key which unlocks the gate holding happiness back.

I will let someone in today and feel the rush of happiness.

Miracles are instantaneous, they cannot be summoned, but come of themselves, usually at unlikely moments and to those who least expect them.
—*Katherine Anne Porter*

Each of us has miraculously been summoned to the road to recovery. We no doubt felt hopeless many times. We no doubt pleaded, aimlessly and to no one in particular, for help. And then it came. Many of us probably do not know just how. But we can look around at one another and appreciate the miracle in our lives.

We still have days when the going is rough. Days when we feel twelve years old, unable to handle the responsibility of our lives, in need of a mother to nurture us and assure us that the pain will pass. We can look to a sponsor on those days. We can look for someone else to help. We can also reflect on how far we've come. In the midst of distress, gratitude for all the gifts of recovery eases the pain, the fear, the stress of the moment.

The miracles continue in my life. Every day offers me a miracle. Thankfulness today will help me see the miracles at work in my life and in the lives of other women on the road to recovery.

Difficulties, opposition, criticism—these things are meant to be overcome, and there is a special joy in facing them and in coming out on top. It is only when there is nothing but praise that life loses its charm, and I begin to wonder what I should do about it.
—Vijaya Lakshmi Pandit

To be alive means to experience difficulties, conflicts, challenges from many directions. What we do with adverse conditions both determines and is determined by who we are. Resistance, most of us have learned, heightens the adversity. Acceptance of the condition, trusting all the while the lesson it offers us is for our benefit, ensures that we'll "come out on top."

Difficulties are opportunities for advancement, for increased self-awareness, for self-fulfillment. So often we hear and remind one another that we grow through pain. We can face any situation knowing we have the strength of the program to shore us up. Strangely, we need challenges in order to grow; without growth we wither. Happiness is the bounty for facing the momentarily unhappy conditions.

Any difficulty I meet today offers me a chance for even greater happiness; it guarantees my growth.

It is only the women whose eyes have been washed clear with tears who get the broad vision that makes them little sisters to all the world.

—Dorothy Dix

The storms of our lives benefit us like the storms that hit our towns and homes and wash clean the air we breathe. Our storms bring to the surface the issues that plague us. Perhaps we still fear a job with responsibilities. Perhaps we still struggle with the significant other persons in our lives. Possessiveness is a particular storm that often haunts our progress. Storms force us to acknowledge these liabilities that continue to stand in our way, and acknowledgment is the step necessary to letting go.

Recovery is a whole series of storms, storms that help to sprout new growth, storms that flush clean our own clogged drains. The peace that comes after a storm is worth singing about.

Each storm can be likened to a rung on the ladder to wholeness, the ladder to full membership in the healthy human race. The storms make climbing tough, but we get strength with each step. The next storm will be more easily weathered.

If today is a stormy day, let me remember it will freshen the air I breathe.

Loving allows us to live and through living we grow in loving.

—Evelyn Mandel

Many days it seems too easy to be centered on ourselves, wondering if others love us rather than loving others. On those days, we may have to act "as if" we love the persons who live on our pathways. The unexpected gift is that we do begin to feel both love and loved. Living becomes easier, and so does loving. Acting "as if" is a good way of learning those behaviors that don't feel natural. And in time, acting "as if" is necessary no more.

I can behave in any way I decide to. I can choose to think about others, and love them. I can choose to forget myself today.

. . . in order to feel anything you need strength . . .
—*Anna Maria Ortese*

Strength for any task, to withstand any pressure, to find the solution to any problem, is always as close as our very breath. We expend all our energy, wearing ourselves down, even getting sick from worry when we fail to turn to the source of strength that is ours for the taking.

We are offered, moment by moment, opportunities to experience the rapture of life. We have the chance, with recovery, to trust our senses, to turn ourselves over to the moment, knowing we can survive every experience, knowing we are guaranteed new knowledge, a greater awareness of the meaning of our own lives when we're fully attuned to the experiences that are uniquely our own, right here, right now.

Our strength increases as we flex it, not unlike muscles. The more we turn to that greater power, the more available that source of strength becomes. With practice, it becomes habitual to let God help us withstand all pressures, solve every problem. In time, the pressures and problems seem to exist no more. We learn to let our higher power circumvent the difficulties in our lives. Free at last, we become free at last to feel the real joys of living.

All the strength I need to face anything that's worrying me is at hand. I will let go and let God help me today.

. . . if we are suffering illness, poverty, or misfortune, we think we shall be satisfied on the day it ceases. But there too, we know it is false, so soon as one has got used to not suffering, one wants something else.
—Simone Weil

Perhaps it's the human condition never to be satisfied and yet always to think, "If only . . ." However, the more we look within for wholeness, the greater will be our acceptance of all things, at all times.

So frequently we hear that happiness is within. But what does that mean when we may have just lost the job that supported us and our children? Or when the car won't start and funds are low? Or when we are feeling really scared and don't know whom to talk to or where to go? "Happiness is within" is such a grand platitude at those times.

Nevertheless, our security in any situation is within, if we but know how to tap it. It is within because that is where the strength we are blessed with resides, the strength given us from the power greater than ourselves. "Going within" first takes a decision. Next, it takes stillness, and then, patience. But peace will come.

We will quit wanting when we have learned how to turn to our inner strength. We will find serenity rather than suffering.

I will go within whenever I feel the rumblings of dissatisfaction today. I will look there for my joy and sense of well-being and know that divine order is in charge.

It only takes one person to change your life—you.
                                                —Ruth Casey

Change is not easy, but it's absolutely unavoidable. Doors will close. Barriers will surface. Frustrations will mount. Nothing stays the same forever, and it's such folly to wish otherwise. Growth accompanies positive change; determining to risk the outcome resulting from a changed behavior or attitude will enhance our self-perceptions. We will have moved forward; in every instance our lives will be influenced by making a change that only each of us can make.

We have all dreaded the changes we knew we had to make. Perhaps even now we fear some impending changes. Where might they take us? It's difficult accepting that the outcome is not ours to control. Only the effort is ours. The solace is that positive changes, which we know are right for us and other people in our lives, are never going to take us astray. In fact, they are necessary for the smooth path just beyond this stumbling block.

When we are troubled by circumstances in our lives, a change is called for, a change that we must initiate. When we reflect on our recent as well as distant past, we will remember that the changes we most dreaded again and again have positively influenced our lives in untold ways.

Change ushers in glad, not bad, tidings.

*Our friends were not unearthly beautiful, Nor spoke
with tongues of gold; our lovers blundered now and
again when we most sought perfection . . .*
                                        —Adrienne Rich

So often our expectations exceed reality. We want more
than we have; our homes, our loved ones, perhaps our jobs
seem not to measure up. "If only"—we say to ourselves. The
time has come to quit saying "if only" and be glad, instead,
for what is.

We are recovering. We do have friends and family who care
about us. We do have exactly what we need at this moment.

We each can make a contribution today for the good of
someone else and thus for ourselves. And in the act of looking to this day—to giving something to another human
being—we will sense the inner perfection we mistakenly
long for in our outer selves.

*I can look around me today and be thankful. I will tell someone
close that I'm glad we share one another's world.*

The change of one simple behavior can affect other behaviors and thus change many things.

—Jean Baer

Our behavior tells others and ourselves who we are. Frequently, we find ourselves behaving in ways that keep us stuck or embarrass us. Or we may feel deep shame for our behavior in a certain instance. Our behavior will never totally please us. But deciding we want to change some behavior and using the program to help us is a first step.

Remember, imperfections are human and very acceptable. However, changing a particular behavior, maybe deciding to take a walk every morning rather than sleeping 30 extra minutes, will change how we feel about ourselves. And a minor change such as this can have a remarkable effect on our outlook, our attitudes.

The dilemma for many of us for so long was the fear we couldn't change. But we can. And we can help each other change, too.

One small change today—a smile at the first person I meet— meditation before dinner—a few minutes of exercise—will help me chart a new course. I will encourage another woman to join me in this effort too, and I will be on my way.

Give as much of yourself as you can to as much of your higher power as you can understand.

—S.H.

The more we are in concert with God, the greater will be our pleasures in life. Recognizing our partnership with our higher power makes every decision easier, facilitates the completion of every task, and removes all uncertainty about our value to this world, particularly to those persons around us.

Knowledge that we are never alone, that in every circumstance our best interests are being cared for, softens whatever blow we encounter. The blows teach us; they are the lessons the inner self has requested, and let us never forget we have a ready tutor to see us through every assignment.

The more we rely on God to see us through the mundane activities as well as the troubling experiences, the greater will be our certainty that all is well, our lives are on course, and a plan is unfolding little by little that has our best interests at its center.

My understanding of God and the power of that presence is proportionate to my reliance on that power. Not unlike the power of electricity, I can plug into the source of the "light" of understanding and for the strength to see my way through any experience today.

It's ironic, but until you can free those final monsters within the jungle of yourself, your life, your soul is up for grabs.

—Rona Barrett

We all have monsters. Maybe it's depression over the past or present circumstances, or resentment about another's behavior, or fear of new situations. Maybe it's jealousy of other women. The more attention we give the monsters, the more powerful they get. The harder we try to resist the jealousy or depression or fear, the greater it becomes.

The program offers us the way to let go. And we find the way through one another. When we share ourselves fully with one another, share our monsters with one another, they no longer dominate us. They seek the dark recesses of our minds, and when we shine the light on them, they recoil. The program offers us an eternal light.

I will let the program shine its light in my life today. My monsters will flee for the day.

One is happy as a result of one's own efforts, once one knows the necessary ingredients of happiness— simple tastes, a certain degree of courage, self-denial to a point, love of work, and above all, a clear conscience. Happiness is no vague dream, of that I now feel certain.

—George Sand

We are as happy as we make up our minds to be, so goes the saying. But happiness is the result of right actions. We prepare for it daily. We chart our course. Many of us have to first determine where we want to go before we can decide on the chart. We have perhaps passively floated along for years. But now the time is right to navigate, to move toward a goal.

We may have fears about moving ahead. We can be courageous, however. Strength is at hand, always, if we but ask for it. We can make a small beginning today. And every day, we can do at least one thing we need to do to bring us closer to our goal. Accomplishment, however small, nurtures good feelings. Happiness is the by-product

---

Today is wide open. I will decide on a course of action and move ahead. All around me help is available for the asking.

Out of every crisis comes the chance to be reborn, to reconceive ourselves as individuals, to choose the kind of change that will help us to grow and to fulfill ourselves more completely.

—Nena O'Neill

Before choosing to recover, most of us lived through crisis after crisis. Many days we sought the oblivion of alcohol and drugs rather than face fears that ate away at us. It probably wasn't possible for most of us to realize that a crisis was a tool for growth.

Even today, even in our recovery program, even though the clouds are clearing and we are feeling better about ourselves, a crisis may overwhelm us for a time. We do find help for it, though. We can breathe deeply, look to our higher power, listen for the messages that are coming through from our friends. And we can choose among the many options for the right action to take at this time.

Life is a series of lessons. Crises can be seen as the homework. They aren't there to defeat us but to help us grow—to graduate us into the next stage of life.

Today, I will look for my lessons and feel exhilarated by the growth that is guaranteed.

As the wheel of the decades turns, so do a person's needs, desires, and tasks. Each of us does, in effect, strike a series of "deals" or compromises between the wants and longings of the inner self, and an outer environment that offers certain possibilities and sets certain limitations.

—Maggie Scarf

What life has measured out may not be what we had dreamed of. Life's lessons may not be those we'd have chosen to learn. Wisdom dictates that the joy of life is proportional to the ease with which we accept those possibilities for growth that have grown out of our inner desires.

Our desires are like an outline for a written assignment, a research project. They help us to see where we want to go at any one time, but as we move, the direction may need to change. The natural flow of "the assignment" will help to refine it.

We may not have tried to "realize" many of our desires in the past. But the time has come. One of the joys of recovery is that we understand our desires are closely related to our spiritual program and our recovery. And we know we are not alone. We need to attend to the inner desires that beckon to us. They are calling us to move forward.

Today, I can take the first few steps.

*Spiritual power can be seen in a person's reverence
for life—hers and all others, including animals and
nature, with a recognition of a universal life force
referred to by many as God.*

—*Virginia Satir*

Taking the time, daily, to recognize the spiritual force
in everyone and everything that is all about us encourages
us to feel humble, to feel awe. Reflecting on our inter-
connections, our need for one and all to complete the
universe, lessens whatever adversity we might feel as we
struggle with our humanity.

Our spiritual power is enhanced with each blessing we
give. And as our spiritual power is enhanced, life's trials
are fewer. Our struggle to accept situations, conditions, and
other people, or our struggle to control them, lessens every
day that we recognize and revere one another's personhood,
one another's existence.

*I can teach myself reverence, and I can begin today. I will look
for "the Spirit" everywhere, and I will begin to see it.*

Women sometimes gossip when they want to get close to people.

—*Joan Gilbertson*

Feeling alone and lonely heightens our fears of inadequacy. In our alienation from others, paranoia grips us. We yearn to feel a connection with someone, and gossip about another someone can draw two lonely people close. We are bonded.

We need a sense of belonging, every one of us: belonging to the neighborhood; belonging to the staff where we work; belonging to the group we call friends. Knowing that we do belong fosters the inner warmth that accompanies security, well-being. And our fears are melted.

The program's Fifth, Ninth, and Tenth Steps guarantee that we'll feel the closeness we long for when we work them. Self-revelation strengthens our ties to the people we long to connect with. Gossip loses its appeal when we know we share a closeness already. Mingling our vulnerabilities secures our closeness.

We need to be attentive to our judgments of others, be they verbalized in gossip or only savored in silence. These judgments act as barometers of our own self-image. Our security in knowing we belong, that we are one, relieves us of the need to judge others unfairly.

Loneliness pushes me to behavior that even compounds the loneliness. Real closeness will come when I talk about myself rather than someone else.

*In anxiety-provoking situations, many women feel
unable to act. They find themselves at a loss to come
up with an effective response, or any response at all.*
—Stanlee Phelps and Nancy Austin

Feeling unable to act is a humiliation, perhaps an embarrassment, and it is habit-forming. Perhaps our inertia is due to our need to act "correctly" and the accompanying fear that we'll err. Unfortunately, our fear of action reinforces itself. The only way to end the vicious cycle is to act—right or wrong. The surprise in store for us is that no action we take will be truly wrong. We will learn not only from the action itself, but from its ripples.

The response to life we make through action will gratify us; it will nourish us and will make us dread less the next situation that calls for a response.

Opportunities for action are the stepping stones to emotional maturity. The more we "act," the more able we are to act. And a new habit is formed.

*Taking action, even when I fear it's wrong, is growth-producing.
Without growth there is no life. Today, I will live!*

That reality of life and living—movement from one place to another either in a project or in a state of mind, does not conform with what we imagine or expect or think we deserve so we often leave things hanging unfinished or unstarted.

—Sandra Edwards

Being dissatisfied—discontented with the experiences life gives us—forever hampers our growth. Reality is not our bane but our gift. The particular reality perceived by any one of us is of special significance because in that reality are our lessons—the very lessons that will awaken us to the awareness that what life offers is just what we deserve, and more.

It's our interpretation of life's realities that is at fault. But as we grow spiritually the clouds will disappear. We'll come to understand the interplay between our realities. And we'll willingly move ahead, fulfilling our part in life's bigger picture.

Sometimes all I can do is trust that all is well, even though it's not as I had hoped. On bad days I need only to reflect on the past to know that I am moving in the right direction.

One cannot collect all the beautiful shells on the beach; one can collect only a few, and they are more beautiful if they are few.
—*Anne Morrow Lindbergh*

Being selective in choosing activities, in choosing friends, in choosing material possessions fosters unexpected appreciation. Too much of any one thing negates whatever specialness might have been realized. If we surround ourselves with acquaintances, we never fully share in knowing a few people well. If we surround ourselves with "toys," we never learn how we really want to spend our time.

When we don't take life slowly, piece by piece (one shell at a time), we avoid the greatest discovery of all, the person within. When our attention to persons, places, things is deliberate and steady, the beauty within the object of our focus shines forth, and we, too, are made more beautiful in the process.

Today, I will take time to smell the flowers.

*I have come to realize that all my trouble with living
has come from fear and smallness within me.*
—Angela L. Wozniak

We create problems for ourselves because we think
we need to be more than we are. We fear that we are inadequate to the task before us, fear that another woman is
more attractive, fear that the friends around us are bored by
our presence.

Fear hinders us; it prevents full involvement with the
experiences we are given to grow on. When we withdraw
from a situation in order to save ourselves from failure, we
have chosen instead another kind of failure: failure to take
all we can from life, failure to be all that we can be. Every
experience can move us forward in the understanding of
ourselves. When we withdraw, we stay stuck in a world we
need to leave behind.

---

*I will not fear whatever looks like trouble today. Nothing I can't
handle—in fact, nothing I can't grow from—will come my way
today. My inner strength can see me through.*

Follow your dream . . . take one step at a time and don't settle for less, just continue to climb.
—Amanda Bradley

Dreams are common to us all. Dreams are special as well. We probably keep to ourselves many of our dreams for fear of derision or misunderstanding. Oftentimes we may have selectively shared some dreams, those we figured would get approval. The ones closest and dearest to us, the ones we feel most vulnerable about, we may choose to treasure to our hearts only, sometimes thinking, "If only you knew," sometimes wondering if we are being silly.

We are coming to believe that our dreams are *spirit-filled.* They are gifts to encourage us. Like a ship at sea needing a "heading" to move forward, our dreams lend direction to our lives. Our frustration may be that we can't realize a dream without many steps and much time. But life is a process of steps. Success in anything comes inch by inch, stroke by stroke, step after step.

My dreams today are meant to guide me. I will take a first step toward making the dream a reality.

We all live with the objective of being happy; our lives are all different and yet the same.

—Anne Frank

Happiness feels so close and yet so far away. Perhaps we look to a person for it, or to a job, or to a new winter coat. We deserve happiness, we know. Yet, we learn so slowly that happiness can only be found within. The person leaves; the job goes sour; the new coat is quickly out of style. Elusive, all of them.

But the happiness that comes from knowing who we are and how our lives fit in the grand design of the Creator never eludes us. We are one of a kind. And there is no other who can offer to the world of friends just what each of us can. We are needed, and knowing that, really knowing it, brings happiness.

Before we found this program, we no doubt failed to realize our worth. We can celebrate it now. We can glory in our worth, our specialness, and we can cherish the design. We can cherish our parts and cherish the part each person plays.

Combined, we are as one big orchestra. The conductor reads the music and directs the movements. Being in tune with the conductor feels good. I can call it happiness. All I need do is play my part.

The level of anxiety I feel when an attractive woman enters the room is the cue informing me of my closeness to God at that moment.

—Anonymous

Our security lies now and always in our relationship with God. When we are spiritually connected, we don't lack confidence, self-assurance. We don't doubt our value to those around us. Having an active friendship with our God keeps us ever aware that whatever is right for each of us at this time will be given us, that each other person in our life is also on a divinely ordained path going somewhere special to her growth.

It's unfortunate, but true, that many of us had painful experiences with other women earlier in our lives. Maybe we lost a lover or a husband to someone we knew. And it's difficult to believe that what is right for us will come to us, that we need never fear another woman.

The program offers us daily opportunities to take stock of our assets in order to know that we count. And more importantly, it promises security and serenity if each day we invite our higher power to be our companion. We need never fear someone else's presence. Nor need we fear any new situation. With God at our side, all is well. And we'll know it!

I will make God my friend today and enjoy the ease of living.

From early infancy onward we all incorporate into our lives the message we receive concerning our self-worth, or lack of self-worth, and this sense of value is to be found beneath our actions and feelings as a tangled network of self-perception.
—Christina Baldwin

Lifting our self-esteem is not a particularly easy task for most of us. It's probable that again and again our confidence wavered before we sought help from the program. It's also probable that our confidence still wanes on occasion. The old fears don't disappear without effort.

But each day we can do some one thing that will help us to feel better about ourselves. All it takes is one small act or decision, each day. The program can give us the strength we need each day to move forward one step.

Today, I will do one thing I've been putting off. A whole collection of "one days" will lay the groundwork for the person I'm building within.

Without discipline, there's no life at all.
—*Katharine Hepburn*

Procrastination is habitual. It's perhaps a habit we've struggled with over the years, and not one that can be willed away. It eats at us, no doubt. How many times have we gone to bed at night depressed, discouraged, angry with ourselves for not finishing a job we promised ourselves, or someone else, we'd do! Sometimes it feels hopeless. The tasks awaiting our attention pile up, seem impossible to complete. But there is hope. The program has offered us an easy solution.

We have only this day to concern ourselves with. We can break the spell of procrastination, lethargy, immobility, if we choose. We can pick a task that needs attention, any task, preferably a small one for today. Maybe it's writing a letter, or fixing a hem, or making an appointment to see a doctor. Deciding to do something, and then doing it, breaks through the barriers that have caged us. Immediately we will sense the surge of freedom. In this moment we can always act. And any act will free us.

When procrastination blocks us, our senses are dead to the friends close to us. It's as though we have stepped outside of the circle of life. The real gifts of sobriety are beyond our reach when we choose inaction.

I will get free. I will tackle a small task today. It will bless me in special ways.

The process of living, for each of us, is pretty similar.
For every gain there is a setback. For every success, a
failure. For every moment of joy, a time of sadness.
For every hope realized, one is dashed.
—*Sue Atchley Ebaugh*

The balance of events in our lives is much like the balance of nature. The pendulum swings; every extreme condition is offset by its opposite, and we learn to appreciate the gifts . . . of the bad times as well as the periods of rest.

On occasion we'll discover that our course in life has changed direction. We need not be alarmed. Step Three has promised that we are in caring hands. Our every concern, every detail of our lives, will be taken care of, in the right way, at the right time.

We can develop gratitude for all conditions, good or bad. Each has its necessary place in our development as healthy, happy women. We need the sorrows along with the joys if we are to gain new insights. Our failures keep us humble; they remind us of our need for the care and guidance of others. And for every hope dashed, we can remember, one will be realized.

Life is a process. I will accept the variations with gratitude. Each, in its own way, blesses me.

Many of us achieve only the semblance of communication with others; what we say is often not contingent on what the other has just said, and neither of us is aware that we are not communicating.
—Desy Safán-Gerard

When we don't listen fully to each other, when we don't revere the Spirit within others that's trying to talk to us, we destroy the connection that wants to be made between our Spirits. Our inner selves have messages to give and messages to receive for the good of all. Our ego selves often keep us from hearing the very words that would unravel a problem in our lives.

How hard it is, how often, to be still and to fully listen to the words, rather than the person. How much more familiar it is to filter the message with our own ongoing inner dialogue—our own ongoing continual assessment of another's personhood at the very time our higher power is trying to reach us through them.

There really are no wasted words. Messages are everywhere. We can learn to listen.

I will hear just what I need to hear today. I will open myself fully to the words.

*When we start at the center of ourselves, we discover
something worthwhile extending toward the periphery
of the circle. We find again some of the joy in the now,
some of the peace in the here, some of the love in me
and thee which go to make up the kingdom of heaven
on earth.*

—G. F. Sear

Perhaps we have feared discovering our center; perhaps
we have feared finding nothing there. The struggle to believe in ourselves, to know we have an important part to
play in the circle of life, the circle encompassing all life, is
a hard-fought struggle for many of us. But we are learning. We are finding treasures within ourselves. Others are
helping us to find those treasures. Sharing special moments
in time with loved ones and ones we are learning to love
reveals many treasures.

All we have is here—now—us. We are all we ever need to
be—here and now. We are, at every moment, what we need
to be if only we'd trust revealing our true selves, our centers,
to one another. Our centers each need that of another.

This program needs each of us for what we add to it. The
worthiness of the program, of the whole circle, is enhanced
by the inclusion of our centers.

I will share my center today with you.

My lifetime listens to yours.

—Muriel Rukeyser

Our experiences educate us to help show each other the way. Others' experiences, likewise, will help still others. We need to share our histories. And the program offers us the way. There is no greater honor we can give one another than rapt attention. We each want to be heard, to be special, to be acknowledged. And recognition may well be the balm that will heal someone's hurt today.

A new day faces us, a day filled with opportunities to really listen to someone who needs to be heard. And the surprise is that we will hear a message just right for us, where we are now. A message that may well point us in a new, better direction. Guidance is always at hand, if only we listen for it. But when we are trapped in our own narrow world of problems and confusion, we scramble whatever messages are trying to reach us. And we miss the many opportunities to make another person feel special and necessary to our lives.

My growth is enhanced every time I give my attention fully to another person. And this process is multiplied over and over and over. I will be there for someone today.

If people only knew the healing power of laughter and joy, many of our fine doctors would be out of business. Joy is one of nature's greatest medicines. Joy is always healthy. A pleasant state of mind tends to bring abnormal conditions back to normal.

—Catherine Ponder

Feeling joy may not come naturally to us most of the time. We may, in fact, have to act "as if" with great effort. We may not even recognize genuine joy in the beginning. A technique for finding it is living fully in the present and with gratitude for all we can see, touch, and feel.

The open and honest expression of gratitude for the presence of the ones closest to us now creates a rush within our breasts, a rush that will be shared by our friends, too. Joy is contagious. Joy is freeing. Joy brings into focus our distorted perceptions. Greeting life with joy alters every experience for us and for those we share it with.

I will bring joy wherever I go today. I will give the gift of joy to everyone I meet.

Everyday . . . life confronts us with new problems to be solved which force us to adjust our old programs accordingly.

—Dr. Ann Faraday

Facing the day straight on is occasionally difficult to do. There are those days we feel like crawling under the covers and staying there, certain that we can't handle whatever might be asked of us. Maybe today is one of those days. Perhaps we feel 12 years old, instead of 42. To consciously behave like a responsible 42-year-old is out of the question. Acting "as if" is the next best thing, the program tells us, and it is.

Acting "as if" also comes in handy when only a minor kink interferes with the day's progression. Most problems don't fit an easy solution or a familiar one. However, most problems are dispensed with by seeing them as opportunities for creative response, calmly seeking guidance and then moving ahead slowly, being aware of the effects of our actions.

Today, and every day, I will have an opportunity to think creatively and to rely on my inner guide. Instead of dreading the unfamiliar, I will be glad for it. It's moving me ever closer to understanding life's mysteries.

All of us have unique talents and gifts. No obstacle, be it physical, mental or emotional, has the power to destroy our innate creative energies.
—Liane Cordes

Believing this fully is difficult at times; for some of us, most of the time. But it is true. What each of us can contribute to the world is unlike every other contribution. Each talent is slightly different from every other talent. And they are all needed. We are all needed.

Creativity—any kind—writing, photography, cooking, child care, weaving, managing, woodworking—nourishes the self that feels isolated and worthless. And as the self is nourished, it grows; it recovers.

Recovery means changing our lifestyle. It means reaching out to others and being there for one another. It means rejoining the human race by giving of ourselves. Our talents are the gifts the human race awaits—needs, in fact. Do we know our talents?

I will search out my secret dreams today. In them lie my talents. I will develop them. Help awaits me.

For many years I was so flexible I didn't know who I was, and now that I'm discovering who I am, I think "OK, I know where I stand on that issue. Now on to the next one." But I have to remind myself that all issues are interrelated—no one is separate.
—Kathleen Casey Theisen

Today flows from yesterday, the day before, the day before that. Tomorrow repeats the pattern. What we are given on any one day will have its beginning in the past and its finale in the future. No incident is isolated entirely; no issue is self-contained.

Maturity is being able to let go of outgrown attitudes, stifling opinions, no matter how good and right they were at one time. Our egos often get too attached to some of our opinions, and new ideas can't filter in. Some will try to get our attention today. We are ready for new growth. The choice not to hamper it is ours to make.

The opinions we held certain yesterday may not be adequate to the problems of today. They need not be. They served us well. They are not for naught.

Today's issues need today's fresh responses. I will be unafraid. Today flows from yesterday, the day before, and the day before that. Tomorrow follows suit.

The pain of love is the pain of being alive. It's a perpetual wound.

—*Maureen Duffy*

We live in one another's company. We grow to yearn for one another's company at a deeper level. The yearning reciprocated opens the way to a love relationship, a relationship both blessed and torn by intimacies.

It's human to long for love, to want to shower it and receive it. But the pain of waiting for it doesn't match the pain that accompanies its arrival. Love heightens our sensitivities. Any separations, any discrepancies, physical or emotional, wound the partners in love. The pain that accompanies never having something is less than the pain of projected loss after its arrival.

Love should bring only happiness, we mistakenly think. But love, giving it and receiving it, beckons us to bare our souls, to expose our hidden selves. The fear of rejection, the anxiety that we'll be rejected "when they know the real me," is large and looms over our shoulders.

How lucky we are to have this program, these Steps, which if practiced in all our affairs will prepare us for love and loving. They will help us to live with the pain of love, knowing that it increases our humanity—that it deepens our awarenesses and thus heightens our appreciation of all of life.

The pain of love increases my rapture.

Wisdom never kicks at the iron walls it can't bring down.

—Olive Schreiner

God grant us the serenity to accept the things we cannot change. Many times—yesterday, last week, today, and even tomorrow—we'll come face-to-face with a seemingly intolerable situation. The compulsion to change the situation, to demand that another person change the situation, is great. What a hard lesson it is to learn we can change only ourselves! The hidden gift in this lesson is that as our activities change, often the intolerable situations do, too.

Acceptance, after a time, smooths all the ripples that discourage us. And it softens us. It nurtures wisdom. It attracts joy and love from others. Ironically, we often try to force changes that we think will "loosen" love and lessen struggle. Acceptance can do what our willpower could never accomplish.

As we grow in wisdom, as we grow in understanding, as we realize the promises of this program, we'll stand ready, as women, to weather all our personal storms. Like the willow in the wind, we'll bend rather than break. And we'll be able to help our sisters become wise through our example.

My lessons are not easy. But they will ease my way. Better days begin today.

. . . we could never learn to be brave and patient if there were only joy in the world.

—Helen Keller

We chase after joy, like a child after a firefly, being certain that in joy all problems are solved, all questions are answered. Joy has its rewards, and we deserve them. But life has more to teach us.

We need to learn patience; through patience we come to respect time and its passage, and we are mellowed. We need to learn tolerance; through tolerance our appreciation of another's individuality is nurtured. We need to learn self-respect; self-respect prepares us to contribute more freely to our experiences, and we find wholeness.

Life's travails are our opportunities for lasting, enriching joy. The rough spots deepen our understandings. And these help us to bring joy to the lives of friends near and dear.

I need not turn my back on joy. But I will be glad for all life's experiences. The panorama will sustain me more fully.

One receives only that which is given. The game of life is a game of boomerangs. Our thoughts, deeds and words, return to us sooner or later, with astounding accuracy.

—Florence Scovel Shin

Each of us can attest to the truth of this passage. During the difficult times, however, it is not uppermost in our minds that "what goes around, comes around." It feels all too easy to be justifiably resentful or to gossip or to ignore another's presence. And the repercussions are seldom immediate. They will come, though.

Goodness is likewise repaid. Giving love, attention, and respect to the individuals who share our lives and to the people who cross our paths by chance will smooth our own passage day by day. The effects of our goodness will often be felt quickly. A smile elicits a smile. Kind thoughts bless us as well as the receiver. Life events do come full circle.

With a bit of effort, I can smile at someone today, even though I'm frowning inside. Both will be better for it.

There were deep secrets, hidden in my heart, never said for fear others would scoff or sneer. At last I can reveal my sufferings, for the strength I once felt in silence has lost all its power.

—Deidra Sarault

There is magic in sharing ourselves with someone else. We learn from Steps Four and Five that what we thought were heinous acts are not unusual. Our shameful acts are not unique, and this discovery is our gift when we risk exposure.

Realizing how much we are like others gives us strength, and the program paves the way for us to capture that strength whenever and wherever we sense our need. Secrets block us from others and thus from God too. The messages we need to hear, the guidance offered by God, can't be received when we close ourselves off from the caring persons in our lives. They are the carriers of God's message.

How freeing to know we share the same fears, the same worries. Offering our story to someone else may be the very encouragement she needs at this time. Each of us profits from the sharing of a story. We need to recognize and celebrate our "sameness." When we share ourselves, we are bonded. Bonding combines our strength.

Silence divides us. It diminishes our strength. Yet all the strength we need awaits us. I will let someone else know me today.

There is no such thing as conversation. It is an illusion. There are interesting monologues, that is all.
—Rebecca West

How often we want to be heard, to be truly listened to by our spouse, our children, friends and co-workers. And we deserve to be fully attended to. So do the other persons in our lives who come to us to be heard. We let our minds wander in the midst of important messages. And we may miss the very phrase that we need to hear—the answer to a problem, perhaps. Our minds wander, randomly, looking for a place to light, unconsciously searching for peace, the serenity promised by the Twelve Steps.

Living fully in the present, soaking up all the responses of the life we are immersed in for the moment, is the closest we can get to our higher power, our God. Being there—fully—is conversation with God. How can we know all that God intends for us to know if we don't take advantage of God's many messages? Every moment of every day offers us information, divine information. Each time we turn our minds to self-centered thoughts, we're refusing the chance to grow.

As I come together with friends and family today, I will remember to listen for God's message. I will hear what I need to hear if I will but listen.

I want to do it because I want to do it. Women must try to do things as men have tried. When they fail, their failure must be but a challenge to others.
—Amelia Earhart

Fear of failure plagues many women, not just those who get into trouble with drugs, alcohol, food. Those of us in this recovery program may still fear failure. Halting our addiction doesn't solve all our problems, but it does allow us to realistically take stock of our assets. Knowing our assets and accepting them provides the confidence we need to attempt a project, to strive for a goal.

Another plus of this recovery program is the help available from our groups and our higher power. All things become possible when we understand we are not alone. Seeing other women strive and succeed or strive, fail, and strive again, undefeated, creates an energy flow that can spur us on, if we choose. Feeling good about others' accomplishments can motivate each of us.

Today, I will pay particular attention to the accomplishments of other women, those close to me and those I read or hear about. I will believe their example and feel the forward push.

*. . . How much bondage and suffering a woman
escapes when she takes the liberty of being her own
physician of both body and soul.*
                                    —Elizabeth Cady Stanton

If we listen to ourselves, to the innermost voice of our
Spirits, we know that we have the power to heal ourselves.
Self-healing begins with making our own decisions—about
what we wear, what we do, who we are—and deciding that
we will be true to ourselves. With the help of our spiritual
guide, we can resist the temptations to betray ourselves, for
these temptations are born of fear; the fear that we are not
good enough to be our "own physicians."

To give away our powers binds us and causes us to suffer. But we can go to others for help without losing our own
strength.

---

*Today and every day, I will pray for the wisdom to choose wise
counselors and the strength to love and heal myself.*

*If you attach yourself to one person, you ultimately
end up having an unhealthy relationship.*
                                    —*Shirley MacLaine*

Needing people in our lives is healthy, human, and
natural. Needing a single person to love at a very deep level
is also soothing to the soul's well-being. Love and attachment are not synonymous, however. They are close to being
opposites. If we "attach" ourselves to others, our movements
as separate individuals are hampered. Attachment means
dependency; it means letting our movements be controlled
by the one we are "hooked" to.

Dependency on mood-altering chemicals, on food, on
people, means unmanageability in our individual lives.
Many of us in this recovery program, though abstinent, still
struggle with our dependency on a certain person or a
certain friend.

The tools we are learning apply in all cases of dependency. It is healthy independence we are striving for—
taking responsibility for our own lives—making choices
appropriate for our personal selves. Loving others means
letting them make their own choices unhampered by our
"attachment."

---

*Are my relationships attachments or are they based on love? I
will take an inventory of them today.*

I have a simple philosophy. Fill what's empty. Empty what's full. And scratch where it itches.
—Alice Roosevelt Longworth

All too often, we complicate our lives. We can wonder and worry our way into confusion; obsession or preoccupation it's often called. "What if?" "Will he?" "Should I?" "What do you think?" We seldom stop trying to figure out what to do, where to do it, how to meet a challenge, until someone reminds us to "keep it simple."

What we each discover, again and again, is that the solution to any problem becomes apparent when we stop searching for it. The guidance we need for handling any difficulty, great or small, can only come into focus when we remove the barriers to it, and the greatest barrier is our frantic effort to personally solve the problem. We clutter our minds; we pray for an answer and yet don't become quiet enough, for long enough, to become aware of the direction to go, or the steps to take. And they are always there.

Inherent in every problem or challenge is its solution. Our greatest lesson in life may be to keep it simple, to know that no problem stands in our way because no solution eludes a quiet, expectant mind.

I have opportunities every day to still my mind. And the messages I need will come quietly. My answers are within me, now.

Mental health, like dandruff, crops up when you least expect it.
                                                    —Robin Worthington

We're responsible for the effort but not the outcome. Frequently, a single problem or many problems overwhelm us. We may feel crazy, unable to cope and certain that we have made no progress throughout this period of recovery. But we have. Each day that we choose sobriety, that we choose abstinence from pills or food, we are moving more securely toward mental health as a stable condition.

We perhaps felt strong, secure, on top of things last week, or yesterday. We will again tomorrow, or maybe today. When we least expect it, our efforts pay off—quietly, perhaps subtly, sometimes loudly—a good belly-laugh may signal a glimmer of our mental health.

No one achieves an absolute state of total mental health. To be human is to have doubts and fears. But as faith grows, as it will when we live the Twelve Steps, doubts and fears lessen. The good days will increase in number.

Meeting a friend, asking for a raise, resolving a conflict with my spouse, or friend, will be handled more easily, when I least expect it. Looking forward with hope, not backward, is my best effort—today.

Often God shuts a door in our face, and then subsequently opens the door through which we need to go.
                                        —*Catherine Marshall*

We try and try to control the events of our lives. And not seldom the events in others' lives, too. The occasions are frequent when our will conflicts with God's. Then for a time we feel at a loss. Our direction is uncertain. But always, always, another door opens. A better way beckons. How stubborn we are! And how simple life would be were we to daily, fully, turn our will and our lives over to the care of God. God's help and direction in all things are always available. Turning a deaf ear is like trying to find a seat in a darkened movie theater unaided by the usher.

Every experience is softened when we face it accompanied by our higher power. Any past struggle, any present fear, is a testament to our attempts to do it alone. Too frequently we forge ahead, alone, only to have our way blocked. The detours need never be there. No door closes unless there is a better way. Divine order will prevail.

There is no need to struggle today. I will breathe deeply and take my higher power with me wherever I go. And the doors will be open for as far as I can see.

Joy fixes us to eternity and pain fixes us to time. But desire and fear hold us in bondage to time, and detachment breaks the bond.

—Simone Weil

We live both in the material realm and the spiritual. In our material dimension we seek material pleasures, inherent in which is pain. Our human emotions are tied to our material attachments, and joy, at its fullest, is never found here. Real joy lies outside of the material dimension and lives fully within us in the secret, small place inside where we always know that all is well.

We are on a trip in this life. And our journey is bringing us closer to full understanding of joy with every sorrowful circumstance. When we are one with God, have aligned our will with the will of God, we know joy. We know this, fully, that all is well. No harm can befall us.

Each circumstance in the material realm is an opportunity for us to rely on the spiritual realm for direction, security, understanding. As we turn within to our spiritual nature we will know joy.

Every day in every situation I have an opportunity to discover real joy. It's so close and so ready for my invitation.

I am convinced, the longer I live, that life and its blessings are not so entirely unjustly distributed [as] when we are suffering greatly we are so inclined to suppose.

—Mary Todd Lincoln

Self-pity is a parasite that feeds on itself. Many of us are inclined toward self-pity, not allowing for the balance of life's natural tragedies. We will face good and bad times—and they will pass. With certainty they will pass.

The attitude "Why me?" hints at the little compassion we generally feel for others' suffering. Our empathy with others, even our awareness of their suffering, is generally minimal. We are much too involved in our own. Were we less self-centered, we'd see that blessings and tragedies visit us all, in equal amounts. Some people respond to their blessings with equanimity, and they quietly remove the sting from their tragedies. We can learn to do both.

Recovery is learning new responses, feeling and behaving in healthier ways. We need not get caught by self-pity. We can always feel it coming on. And we can let it go.

Self-pity may beckon today. Fortunately, I have learned I have other choices.

> . . . in silence might be the privilege of the strong, but
> it was certainly a danger to the weak. For the things I
> was prompted to keep silent about were nearly always
> the things I was ashamed of, which would have been
> far better aired . . .
>
> —Joanna Field

It has been said, "We are only as sick as the secrets we
keep." Our emotional health as recovering women is hindered, perhaps even jeopardized, each time we hold something within that we need to talk over with others.

Sharing our fears, our hurts, our anger, keeps open our
channel to God. Secrets clutter our mind, preventing the
stillness within where our prayers find answers. Secrets
keep us stuck. Our health, emotional and spiritual, depends
on our commitment to shared experiences.

Every secret we have and tell someone frees that person also to be herself and to grow. Sharing experiences
relieves us of our shame and invites the forgiveness we
must allow ourselves.

Steps Four and Five facilitate the process of sharing those
secrets that block our path to God and to one another.
Never can we be fully at peace with secrets left untold. Self-
revelation cleanses the soul and offers us life.

*I will be alert to the opportunities to share myself and cherish the
freedom offered.*

It's quite uncomfortable to be an adolescent at age thirty-two.

—Peggy Cahn

Our lives are in process every moment, which means change is ever-present. As new information is sorted and acquired, old habits are discarded. We don't let go of some old behaviors easily, however. They are like comfortable shoes. They may be worn thin, and they probably embarrass us in certain company, but we slip them on unconsciously—and then it's too late.

Maturity is an "as if" behavior, initially. Emotional development was stunted, for most of us, with the onset of our addictive behavior, thus, we often respond to situations like adolescents. Application of the "as if" principle will result both in new personal attitudes and unfamiliar, yet welcome, responses from others. Acting as if we are capable, strong, confident, or serene will pave the way for making those behaviors real, after a time. If we believe in ourselves and our ability to become the women we strive to be, we can then move forward confidently.

When my behavior embarrasses or shames me, I will accept the responsibility for changing it. Changing it offers immediate rewards. The people around me will react in refreshing ways, and I'll feel more fully alive.

Humor is such a strong weapon, such a strong answer.
Women have to make jokes about themselves, laugh
about themselves, because they have nothing to lose.
—Agnes Varda

Laughter can cure a physical condition; it can and will
positively affect an emotional illness as well. Laughter
ushers in a new perspective which gives vent to a changed
attitude. And our attitude toward any situation, any individual, is all-powerful.

A negative, critical attitude toward our financial situation, toward our disease, toward our boss, or spouse, or
children, determines how we feel moment by moment. In
like manner, when we raise our sights, look at the world
with lightness in our hearts, expecting to enjoy the day, the
people, the activity, we'll succeed.

Finding humor in a situation, any situation, prevents us
from succumbing to feelings of powerlessness. Feeling
powerless, behaving as victims, came easily for many of us
before we chose this program and the Twelve Steps to live
by. Choosing a humorous response, opting to laugh at our
situation, at any point in time, keeps our personal power
where it belongs—with ourselves.

My emotional health depends on my active involvement in
deciding who I am, right now. Deciding to chuckle rather than
snarl will give me an unexpected emotional boost.

*No one can build (her) security upon the nobleness of
another person.*

—Willa Cather

Where do we look for our security? Do we look to our
husbands or our lovers? Do we look to a parent or our
children? Perhaps we seek our security in our jobs. But
none of these avenues brings lasting contentment, as we've
each probably discovered, just as pills, alcohol, or maybe
food failed to give us lasting security.

Security of the spirit is with us from our birth. It's just
that we haven't tapped into the source. Perhaps we don't
even know the source, but it's been with us always, awaiting
our realization of it.

No step do we ever take alone. Each breath we take is in
partnership with the eternal source of strength and security
within us. We have the choice to accept this partnership
any time. And this guarantee of security in all things at all
times is the gift of freedom.

Our desire for security is God-given. The security we
desire is also given by God to us. We are secure today and
every day.

*Each step I take is in concert with my higher power. I need
experience nothing alone. I can breathe in and tap the plentiful
source of strength awaiting me, now.*

One doesn't recognize in one's life the really important moments—not until it's too late.
—Agatha Christie

Every moment is special and offers us an opportunity—to let an experience change us in an important way, to invite another person into our life, to nurture the growing, changing woman within. Life's events move so rapidly we seldom relish the moments individually, but each day teems with tiny gifts divinely designed for our well-being. The woman smiled at in the grocery store yesterday or the man acknowledged on the bus last week felt special. And we were softened, too, by our expression.

We change, and we change our world when we acknowledge one another's presence in it. The wonderful reality is that we are in another's world because of the special qualities we each have and are able to share with one another.

For many of us, in times past, no moment felt important. The days were simply long and painful. But now, we can relish even the past pain for what it taught us. We know now that we can look to this day before us with expectation. We can be conscious of every moment, thankful for every experience and every person we encounter.

In this inner game of life, I share the court, and I will have my turn to serve. To really live, I must participate fully.

There are really only two ways to approach life—as victim or as gallant fighter—and you must decide if you want to act or react, deal your own cards or play with a stacked deck. And if you don't decide which way to play with life, it always plays with you.
—Merle Shain

Being the victim is, or was, uncomfortably familiar to many of us. Perhaps some of us are only now realizing we have choices, that we need not let life happen to us. Becoming responsible to ourselves, choosing behavior, beliefs, friends, activities, that please us, though unfamiliar at first, soon exhilarates us. The more choices we make, the more alive we feel. The more alive we feel, the healthier our choices.

Our aim is recovery. Recovering means participating fully in our lives. It means self-assessment and self-direction. It means trusting to move forward, step-by-step, choice-by-choice, knowing all the while that no thoughtful action can trouble us.

Many opportunities to make choices will present themselves today. The choices I make will satisfy me; they will move me toward my goal of recovery.

Peace, she supposed, was contingent upon a certain disposition of the soul, a disposition to receive the gift that only detachment from self made possible.
—Elizabeth Goudge

Self-centeredness, egocentrism, and selfishness are familiar to most of us. We have judged our world and all the situations and people in it in terms of how their existence affects our own. We have become tied to him or to her or to a situation just as surely as an anchor to a boat. Most of us learned in very early childhood to read others' behaviors. And we determined our own worth accordingly.

As adult women we still struggle, trying to read another's actions, hoping to find acceptance. Which means we are always vulnerable, exposing our "self" to the whims of other, equally vulnerable "selves." What we search for is peace and security. We think if others love and accept us, we'll be at peace. We'll know serenity. A most important lesson for us to learn in this life is that peace is assured when we anchor ourselves to our God. Peace, well-being, serene joy will accompany our every step when we expose our vulnerable selves to God's care and only God's care. We'll no longer need to worry about the self we try to protect. It will be handled with care.

Peace awaits me today. I will look to God, and only God, to know that all is well, that I am all that I need to be.

*. . . that is what learning is. You suddenly understand
something you've understood all your life, but in a
new way.*

—Doris Lessing

As we are changed by our experiences, that which we
know also changes. Our experiences foster growth and
enlightenment, and all awarenesses give way to new understandings. We are forever students of life blessed with
particular lessons designed only for us. There is joy in
knowing that learning has no end and that each day offers
us a chance to move closer to becoming the persons we are
meant to be.

To understand something more deeply requires that we
be open to the ideas of others, willing to part with our
present opinions. The program offers us many opportunities to trade in the understandings we've outgrown.
Throughout our recovery we have discovered new inter-
pretations of old ideas. And we will continue to expand
our understanding.

Every situation, every person, every feeling, every idea
has a slightly different hue each time we encounter it. The
wonder of this is that life is forever enriched, forever fresh.

---

*Each moment offers me a chance to know better who I am and
to understand more fully the real contribution that is mine to
make in this life. I will let the anticipation of my changing ideas
excite me.*

Women like to sit down with trouble as if it were knitting.

—Ellen Glasgow

How often we turn minor challenges into monumental barriers by giving them undue attention, forgetting that within any problem lies its solution! However, the center of our focus must be off the problem's tangle if we are to find the solution's thread. The best remedy for this dilemma is the Serenity Prayer.

We cannot change our children, our husbands or partners, not even the best friends who we know love us. But with God's help we can change the attitude that has us blocked at this time. A changed attitude, easing up on ourselves, lessening our expectations of others, will open the door to the kind of relationships we seek, the smooth flowing days we long for.

We need not take life so seriously. In fact, we shouldn't take it so seriously. We can measure our emotional health by how heartily we laugh with others and at ourselves. The 24 hours stretching before us at this time promises many choices in attitude. We can worry, be mad, depressed, or frustrated, or we can trust our higher power to see us through whatever the situation. So, we can relax. It is our decision, the one decision over which we are not powerless.

I will be in control of my attitude today. I can have the kind of day I long for.

Of course, fortune has its part in human affairs, but conduct is really much more important.
—*Jeanne Detourbey*

It's not infrequent that we are faced with a dilemma; what is the best action to take in a certain situation? We can be guided, rightly, in every situation if we but turn inward and let our conscience direct our behavior. We have often heard it said at meetings that when we long for a message from God we will hear it, either through our conscience or in the words of our friends. Thus we can never really be in doubt; our conduct can always be above reproach if we but listen.

Right behavior leads to fortunate opportunities for those who look for them. Behavior that we're proud of seems to attract blessings in our lives. One's good fortune is really God-given and in proportion to one's willingness to act well toward others in all situations.

Simply, what goes around, comes around. Our behavior comes back to us, manyfold. In our encounters with others today, we'll have numerous occasions to decide about the best behavior for the particular circumstance. We must not forget that our behavior elicits the responses we receive.

I will invite blessings today. I will also shower blessings on my friends.

No one can make you feel inferior without your consent.

—*Eleanor Roosevelt*

We are competent women. We made a wise choice for ourselves when we decided to recover. Each day that we continue working this program our Spirits are strengthened. And our gifts will multiply.

Feeling inferior can become a habit. Being passive and feeling inferior go hand-in-hand, and they prepare us for becoming dependent on alcohol, pills, food, and people. We didn't understand, instinctively, that we are just who we're meant to be. We grew up believing we were not smart enough, not pretty enough, not capable enough. We grew up too distant from the source of our real strength.

How wonderful for us that we found the program! How lucky we are to have, for the taking, all the strength we'll ever need to face any situation, to handle any problem, to resolve any personal relationship conflict. Feeling inferior can be only a bad memory. The choice is ours. The program promises a better life. The Steps promise the strength to move forward. Our friends promise us outstretched hands.

I will look forward to the challenges of today with hope and strength and know that I am able to meet them.

*I have listened to the realm of the Spirit. I have heard
my own soul's voice, and I have remembered that love
is the complete and unifying thread of existence.*
—Mary Casey

The act of loving someone else brings us together, closes
whatever the gap between us. It draws us into the world of
another, making richer the world we call our own. Love is
the great equalizer.

We no longer wish to conquer or dominate those whom
we love. And our love for one increases our capacity for
loving others. Love heals another, and love heals ourselves,
both giving it and receiving it.

Love from another acknowledges our existence, assuring
us that we do count, that our presence is valued by someone else. It is human to need these reminders, these as-
surances. But our need for them is lessened each time we
acknowledge another person in our midst.

Where love is absent, people, even in a crowd, feel alone,
forgotten, unimportant. No doubt we can each recall times
of quiet desperation—moments of alienation. We must
reach out to someone and send thoughts of love to someone
who may need to be remembered. Our loving thoughts for
persons close and far away always reach their destination.
They do unify us.

*Love is powerful. It can change the complexion of the universe. It
will change the direction of my life.*

*. . . those interested in perpetuating present conditions
are always in tears about the marvelous past that is
about to disappear, without having so much as a smile
for the young future.*

—Simone de Beauvoir

Hanging on to any moment, once it's gone, deadens us to
the joys and lessons of the present. We must learn to let go,
to let go of persons, painful situations, even meaningful
experiences. Life goes on, and the most fruitful lesson
before us is to move with the vibrations, to be in tune
with them.

Being open to the present is our only chance for growth.
These experiences today in our lives beckon us forward
along the path meant for us. We are not guaranteed only joy
today. But we are promised security. We may not be free of
twinges of fear or confusion, but we can learn to trust even
in the midst of adversity. We can remember that power
greater than ourselves whenever and wherever our steps are
uncertain.

Dwelling, as we are wont to do, on our rebuffs, our
rejections, invites further criticism. But neither should we
dwell on past joys. Attention to now and to the persons
here, now, is the only rightful response to life. Not being
here, now, invites others to turn away, just as we have
turned away.

*I will celebrate the thrill of the present, squeeze the moments of
today, and trust the outcome to God.*

The trouble is not that we are never happy—it is that happiness is so episodical.

—Ruth Benedict

Happiness is our birthright. The decision to be happy is ours to make, every day, when confronted with any experience. Too many of us grew up believing that life needed to be a certain way for us to be happy. We looked for the right lover, the right job, the right dress. We looked outside of ourselves for the key to happiness. In time, we even looked to alcohol, drugs, food perhaps—to no avail.

Happiness lies within. We must encourage it to spring forth. But first we need to believe that happiness is fully within our power. We must trust that the most difficult circumstances won't keep it from us when we have learned to tap the source within.

Life is a gift we are granted moment by moment. Let us be in awe of the wonder of it, then revel in it. We can marvel at creation for a moment and realize how special we are to be participants. Happiness will overcome us if we let it. We can best show our gratitude for the wonder of this gift by smiling within and without.

That I am here is a wonderful mystery to which joy is the natural response. It is no accident that I am here.

Through spontaneity we are reformed into our-
selves. Freed from handed-down frames of reference,
spontaneity becomes the moment of personal freedom
when we are faced with a reality, explore it, and
act accordingly.

—Viola Spolin

Living in the here and the now opens up untold possibilities for new growth. Our inner self is enticed in new
directions when our attention is fully in the present. When
our minds are still on last night's argument or tomorrow's
board meeting, we wear blinders to the activity at hand.
And God, as our teacher and protector, resides in *this* experience, in the hearts of *these* people present.

Every single moment has something for us. Maybe a new
piece of information. A piece that solves a problem that's
been puzzling us. Perhaps a chance to make a new friend,
one who will be there in a time of need.

Letting go of yesterday frees us. We need not be burdened. It is gone. Our lives could be eased, so much, if we
kept our focus on the experience at hand, where the problems we ponder have their solutions. Always.

I will greet today, skipping, smiling, ready for the answers, the
truths, the directions meant only for me. The wonders of today
will bless me.

If I can stop one heart from breaking, I shall not live in vain; If I can ease one life the aching, Or cool one pain, Or help one fainting robin Into his nest again, I shall not live in vain.

—Emily Dickinson

The gift of attention to each other is "passing on" the love of God. In order to feel love, we have to give it away. We will know love when we give love.

Our attachment to the world, the sense of belonging most of us longed for the many years prior to recovery, awaits us, is showered upon us even as we reach out to someone else. We are no longer alone, scared, alienated when we let others know they are not alone. We can heal one another. The program opens the way for our healing.

Each day, each one of us can ease the pain of a friend, a co-worker, a child. The beauty of the program, the beauty of God's plan for us all, is that our own pain is relieved in the process of easing the pain of another. Love is the balm. Loving others makes our lives purposeful.

No day is lived in vain, if I but cherish someone else's presence.

I have come to believe in the "Sacrament of the Moment," which presupposes trust in the ultimate goodness of my creator.

—Ruth Casey

The moment, realized, is like a bud blossoming. The day unfolds and with each minute we are moved along to the experiences right for us at this place and this time. Our resistance to certain experiences and particular people creates the barrier that blocks the good in store for us.

We can rest assured, our higher power is caring for us. Each breath we take is Spirit-filled, and the plan for our lives is an accumulation of necessary experiences that are helping us to grow and develop our special talents. What we often forget is that the difficult periods of our lives stretch us, enlighten us, ready us to be the women we desire within to be.

This moment is sacred. All moments are sacred. They will not come again. What is offered this moment for us to grow on will not be offered in exactly this way again. Our higher power knows our needs and is caring for them. We can trust the goodness of today.

Whatever situation I encounter today, I will believe in its goodness. It is right for me. It may stretch my patience rather than elicit laughter, but it is right for me at this time.

The problem is not merely one of woman and career, woman and the home, woman and independence. It is more basically: how to remain whole in the midst of the distractions of life; how to remain balanced, no matter what centrifugal forces tend to pull one off center; how to remain strong, no matter what shocks come in at the periphery and tend to crack the hub of the wheel.

—Anne Morrow Lindbergh

Before getting into this recovery program, many of us didn't cope with life's distractions except with the help of our addiction. We had no sense of wholeness and were constantly bouncing from one crisis to another. We may still feel pulled. The crises may still trip us up. But we have a center now that we are beginning to understand and rely upon. That center is our spiritual selves.

Slowing down, going within to our center, listening to the message therein, unravels our problem, smooths the waves of the storm. The strength to go forward awaits us.

We can absorb the shocks that "crack the hub of the wheel" and be enriched by them. Each moment we are weaving our tapestry of life. Each experience colors our design. Our pain and sorrow and joy give the depth that one day will move us to say, "I see, I understand."

I will be grateful for the experiences today that give my tapestry its beauty.

Have the courage to act instead of react.
—Darlene Larson Jenks

Taking the time to be thoughtful about our responses to the situations we encounter offers us the freedom to make choices that are right for us. Impulsive behavior can be a thing of our past, if we so choose. It seldom was the best response for our well-being.

Decision-making is morale boosting. It offers us a chance to exercise our personal powers, an exercise that is mandatory for the healthy development of our egos. We need to make careful, thoughtful choices because they will further define our characters. Each action we take clearly indicates the persons we are becoming. When we have consciously and deliberately chosen that action because of its rightness for us, we are fully in command of becoming the persons we choose to be.

Our actions reveal who we are, to ourselves and others. We need never convey an inaccurate picture of ourselves. We need only take the time and risk the courage necessary to behave exactly as we choose. We will know a new freedom when we are in control.

I will exercise my power to act and feel the fullness of my being.

At fifteen life had taught me undeniably that surrender, in its place, was as honorable as resistance, especially if one had no choice.

—Maya Angelou

We had to surrender to a power greater than ourselves to get to where we are today. And each day, we have to turn to that power for strength and guidance. For us, resistance means struggle—struggle with others as well as an internal struggle.

Serenity isn't compatible with struggle. We cannot control forces outside of ourselves. We cannot control the actions of our family or our co-workers. We can control our responses to them. And when we choose to surrender our attempts to control, we will find peace and serenity.

That which we abhor, that which we fear, that which we wish to conquer seems suddenly to be gone when we decide to resist no more—to tackle it no more.

The realities of life come to us in mysterious ways. We fight so hard, only to learn that what we need will never be ours until the struggle is forsaken. Surrender brings enlightenment.

Life's lessons are simple once I give up the struggle.

It is ironic that the one thing that all religions recognize as separating us from our Creator—our very self-consciousness—is also the one thing that divides us from our fellow creatures.

—Annie Dillard

Getting outside of ourselves, moving beyond our own egos, opens the door to real communication with the people we'll meet today. We have to learn to look with loving appreciation into the soul of that person or child who stands before us. We have to practice being concerned with their needs before our own, and in time our concern will be genuine. The separation between us will exist no more.

This division from others, the barrier that keeps us apart, comes from our individual insecurities. We have grown accustomed to the quick comparisons of ourselves with those we meet. We determine them to be either inferior or superior to ourselves. Whatever gifts we have to offer each other are left unwrapped, at least for now.

Let's come together, truly together, with someone we've been holding off until now. We can trust that the people who have come into our lives are there by design. We are equal to them, and they to us. We need what they have to offer us, and their growth needs our gifts, too.

I will appreciate the design of my life today. I will draw myself close to the day.

*I wake each morning with the thrill of expectation
and the joy of being truly alive. And I'm thankful for
this day.*

—*Angela L. Wozniak*

Being open to the day's offering, all of it, and looking for
the positive experiences therein, become habits only after a
firm commitment and dedicated practice. Today is special
for each of us.

These next twenty-four hours will be unlike all others.
And we are not the persons we were, even as recently as
yesterday. Looking forward to all of the day's events, with
the knowledge that we are in the care of our higher power,
in every detail, frees us to make the most of everything
that happens.

We have been given the gift of life. We are survivors. The
odds against survival in our past make clear we have yet a
job to do and are being given the help to do it. Confidence
wavers in all of us, but the strength we need will be given to
each of us.

*In this day that stands before me, I can be certain that I'll have
many chances for growth, for kindness to others, for developing
confidence in myself. I will be thoughtful in my actions today.
They are special and will be repeated no more.*

How I relate to my inner self influences my relationships with all others. My satisfaction with myself and my satisfaction with other people are directly proportional.

—*Sue Atchley Ebaugh*

Hateful attitudes toward others, resistance to someone's suggestions, jealousy over another woman's attractiveness or particular abilities are equally strong indications of the health of our spiritual programs. Our security rests with God. When that relationship is nurtured, the rewards will be many and satisfactions great.

Our inner selves may need pampering and praise. They have suffered the abuse of neglect for many years, no doubt. In many instances we have chided ourselves, perhaps shamed ourselves. Learning to love our inner selves, recognizing the value inherent in our very existence, takes effort, commitment, patience—assets we may only just now be developing in this recovery program.

Our inner selves are the home of our Spirit wherein our attachment to all strength, all courage, all self-esteem, all serenity resides. Our Spirit is one with our higher power. We must acknowledge the presence and utilize the comforts offered.

My relationships with others are as healthy and fulfilling as my communication with God.

For this is wisdom; to live,
To take what fate, or the Gods, may give.

—Laurence Hope

We can't control the events of our lives, but we do have mastery over our attitudes. The chances will be many, today, to react negatively or positively to circumstances we find ourselves in. We can consider that each circumstance has something special in it for us.

Positive expectations regarding the planned as well as spontaneous activities of the day will influence the activity's flow, our involvement with it, and our interactions with the other people involved. A positive attitude seems to breed positive experiences. In other words, we attract into our lives that which we expect. How often do we get up angry, feeling behind when the day has only begun, short-tempered with our children, "ready" for a tough one at work? And we generally find it.

The Serenity Prayer offers us all the knowledge, all the wisdom we'll ever need. We can accept what has to be, change what we can, and not get confused between the two. We can inventory our attitude. Are we taking charge of it? Our attitude is something we can change.

I won't get trapped today by a negative attitude. I will accept the challenge of turning my day around.

. . . The idea has gained currency that women have often been handicapped not only by a fear of failure— not unknown to men either—but by a fear of success as well.

—*Sonya Rudikoff*

It was our practice, before coming to this program, to eat, drink, and smoke our fears away. What we came to realize, profoundly, was that the fears couldn't be escaped even while high. This program is helping us to understand that fears are human, normal and survivable when we let God and our friends in the program lend a helping hand.

Drugs and alcohol distorted our perceptions. Our fears, whether large or small, were distorted. And we still distort those fears, on occasion, because we move away from the spiritual reality of our lives. Remember, we are confronted with no situation too big to handle, no experience for which we are unprepared, if we but turn to that greater power that the program offers us.

We cannot fail in whatever we try today. The outcome of any task attempted is just as it should be. And however we succeed today, we will be shown the steps, at the right time, to make use of that success.

I shall not fear failure or success. I am not alone in experiencing either; both are stepping stones on my life's journey.

I have a clear choice between life and death, between reality and fantasy, between health and sickness. I have to become responsible—responsible for mistakes as well as accomplishments.

—Eileen Mayhew

Choosing to participate actively in our own lives ushers in joy and sometimes fear. We are energized by our conscious involvement; making thoughtful choices regarding our development heightens our sense of well-being. But occasionally we may fear potential failure. About as frequently, we may fear probable success.

Not every day do we want the responsibility for our lives; but we have it. On occasion we only want the loving arms of a caretaker. The beauty of our lives at this time is that we do have a caretaker at our beck and call, a caretaker who has demonstrated repeatedly a concern for our safety, a caretaker who will help us shoulder every responsibility we face.

Clearly, our coming to this program shows that we have chosen to act responsibly. And just as clearly, every day that we ask for the guidance to live to the best of our abilities, we will be helped to accomplish the tasks right for us in this stage of our lives.

All I have to do is make the right choices. I will always know which they are, when I ask for guidance.

We want the facts to fit the preconceptions. When they don't, it is easier to ignore the facts than to change the preconceptions.

—Jessamyn West

To live fully and creatively, to contribute what is only ours to give, requires that we be receptive, wholly, to the reverberations of each present moment. Even anticipation of what may transpire next can prejudice our minds, our level of awareness. Preconceptions cloud our senses. They prevent the actual situation from being fully realized. And it is only in the *now*, as sensed moment by moment, that we find our cues to proceed along the path chosen for us.

As we grow more comfortable with Step Three, daily turning our lives and wills over to the care of God, we'll see how much more rewarding our experiences are. We'll see, too, how much greater are our own contributions. Preconceptions of any situation, persons, anticipated experience, dulls the magic, the depth of the moment. And only when we attune ourselves to the invitation of the moment do we give of ourselves, wholly. Our partnership with God lives now, as we go forth in this moment.

I will look to each moment with child-like eyes. I'll find joy and contentment.

To keep a lamp burning we have to keep putting oil in it.

—*Mother Teresa*

Our spiritual nature must be nurtured. Prayer and meditation lovingly kindle the flame that guides us from within. Because we're human, we often let the flame flicker and perhaps go out. And then we sense the dreaded aloneness. Fortunately, some time away, perhaps even a few moments in quiet communion with God, rekindles the flame.

For most of us, the flame burned low, or not at all, for many years. The flickering we may feel today, or tomorrow, or felt yesterday, will not last, so we may put away our fears. We can listen to the voice of our higher power in others. We can listen, too, as we carry the message. Prayer surrounds us every moment. We can fuel our inner flame with the messages received from others. We can let our spirit spring forth, let it warm our hearts and the hearts of others.

We each have a friend whose flame may be flickering today. I will help her and thus myself. A steady flame can rekindle one that's flickering.

The beauty of loving someone is the feeling of "wholeness" that I experience. The need for that individual in my life, the "I'm part of you and you're part of me" feeling that connects two people and makes them necessary to each other.
—Kathleen Andrus

All that is asked of us by our Creator is that we love one another. Where love doesn't flow easily, perhaps we can just decide to not hurt someone. If we each avoided hurting all people, for just one day, lives would be transformed. We'd each see the world with a fresh perspective.

The more we love others, any others, the deeper our love will grow for all others. Loving lifts our hearts and lightens our burdens. Every day's tribulations can become triumphs when we carry love in our hearts. Love fills us up, and the more we share it, the fuller we become.

We are connected—each of us to one another, all of us together. Our contributions to the whole are necessary. Its completion is made perfect by our presence.

As I pass a friend today, I will be grateful for her contribution to my wholeness, too.

Harmony exists in difference no less than in likeness,
if only the same key-note governs both parts.
—Margaret Fuller

Harmony exists everywhere, as an entity of itself. Our personal attitudes bring the disharmony to a situation. An attitude of love can bless all situations and all people.

The converse is likewise true. We all desire harmony in our relationships. And we will find it, every time we bring an attitude of honest gratitude into a situation.

How we feel, today, about this person or that situation, reflects the strength of our relationship with God. When we experience life in the company of our higher power, we will let life flow. We will observe harmony, then, even in the midst of difference.

All of life's elements are moving toward a state of total and perfect harmony. We need not fear. We can trust the company of our higher power and know that every situation, no matter how adverse its appearance, is contributing to a harmonious outcome if we'd but lend a trusting attitude.

Harmony is everywhere. I will celebrate it. I will trust the present. I will trust the future.

It is the creative potential itself in human beings that is the image of God.

—Mary Daly

God's presence is within us, now and always, even though we feel alone, alienated, scared, and forgotten much of the time. We often overlook God's presence because we don't recognize it. Our talents, our desires, and our pursuits are the evidence—all the evidence we'll ever need once we understand it—that God is present within and about us all the time.

The creative potential goes unrealized among so many of us, perhaps because we have a rigid definition of what creativity is. We are creative. We are all, each of us, creative. We must be because God's presence is here now. When we choose to let it guide us, we'll be able to offer our own unique gifts to the world of friends around us. Encouraging creativity, our own and someone else's, may mean breaking old habits. It surely does mean stepping out of our own way. It also means giving ourselves fully to the experience of the moment and trusting that God's presence will prompt the deliverance of our special gift.

In the moment lives God within us. In the moment I am creative, blessed with gifts like no other. I will stay in the moment and offer them, guided by the God within.

Love doesn't just sit there like a stone, it has to be made, like brick; re-made all the time, made new.
                                        —Ursula K. LeGuin

We love to be loved; we love to be held; we love to be caressed. A show of appreciation we love too. And we love to know we've been heard. The friends, the spouses, the children in our lives want the same from us. Like a garden that needs water, sun, weeding to nurture the growth, so does love need attending to. To become whole and healthy women, we need tender nurturing. And we also need to give away what we get. Those we nurture will bless our growth.

Love is dynamic, not static. It is always changing, and it always changes those it enfolds. Since coming into this program where the sharing of oneself, the open expression of love, is profoundly evident, we each have changed. And our presence has changed others. We have learned to accept love and give it. But better yet, we have learned that we deserve love.

I will look around me today at others, and I will remember, my growth and theirs depends on loving and being loved. I will reach out. I can make love new.

The secret of seeing is to sail on solar wind. Hone and spread your spirit, till you yourself are a sail, whetted, translucent, broadside to the merest puff.
—Annie Dillard

Our progress today, and certainly our serenity, is enhanced by our willingness to accept all that we are blessed with today. Not only to accept, but to celebrate, trusting that these events are moving us toward our special destiny.

Flowing with the twists and turns in our lives, rather than resisting them, guarantees smooth sailing, helps us to maximize our opportunities, increases our serenity. Accepting our powerlessness over all but our own attitude is the first step we need to take toward finding serenity.

Resistance, whether it is against a person or a situation in our lives, will compound the problem as we perceive it. We can believe in the advantages for growth that all experiences offer. We can sail with our experiences. We can be open to them so they can carry us to our destination. We can trust, simply trust, that all is well and in our favor, every moment.

———————

My serenity is in my control today. I will look to this day with trust and thanksgiving. And my Spirit will soar.

Though we be sick and tired and faint and worn—
Lo, all things can be borne!
                                    —Elizabeth Chase Akers

What bothered us most a year ago? A month ago? Even a week ago? It's probable that whatever it was, we were obsessed with it, certain that our futures were ruined, that there was no reasonable solution. It's also probable that we feared we simply couldn't survive the complexity of the situation. But we did. And we always will be able to survive any and all difficulties. We are never, absolutely never, given more than we can handle. In fact, we are given exactly what we need, at any given time.

We have many lessons to learn. Fortunately, we have the structure of the Twelve Steps to guide us through the lessons. We need mainly to remember what we are powerless over, that there is a power greater than ourselves, and that life will become simple; we'll need no extra homework when we've turned it over to the care of God.

Whatever my problem today, I will let God have it. A solution is in the making. I'll see it just as quickly as I can let go of the problem.

All that is necessary to make this world a better place to live is to love—to love as Christ loved, as Buddha loved.

—Isadora Duncan

To be unconditionally loved is our birthright, and we are so loved by God. We desire just such a love from one another, and we deserve it; yet, it's a human quality to look for love before giving it. Thus many of us search intently for signs of love.

Too many of us are searching, rather than loving. Truly loving another means letting go of all expectations. It means full acceptance, even celebration of another's personhood. Not easy, but so rewarding, to ourselves as well as to the one who is the focus of our love.

Love is a balm that heals. Loving lightens our burdens, whatever they are. It invites our inner joy to emerge. But most of all, it connects us, one with another. Loneliness leaves. We are no longer alienated from our environment. Love is the mortar that holds the human structure together. Without the expression of love, it crumbles. This recovery program has offered us a plan for loving others, as well as ourselves. Love will come to us, just as surely as we give it away.

Each and every expression of love I offer today will make smooth another step I take in this life.

Let me tell thee, time is a very precious gift of God; so precious that it's only given to us moment by moment.
—Amelia Barr

Where are our minds right now? Are we focused fully on this meditation? Or are our minds wandering off to events scheduled for later today or tomorrow perhaps? The simple truth is that this moment is all God has allowed right now. It's God's design that we will live fully each moment, as it comes. Therein lies the richness of our lives. Each moment contributes to the full pattern that's uniquely our own.

We must not miss the potential pleasure of any experience because our thoughts are elsewhere. We never know when a particular moment, a certain situation, may be a door to our future. What we do know is that God often has to work hard getting our attention, perhaps allowing many stumbling blocks in order to get us back on target.

Being in tune with now, this moment, guarantees a direct line of communication to God. It also guarantees a full, yet simple life. Our purpose becomes clear as we trust our steps to God's guidance. How terribly complicated we make life by living in the past, the present, and many future times, all at once!

One step, one moment, and then the next step and its moment. How the simple life brings me freedom!

The bottom line is that I am responsible for my own well-being, my own happiness. The choices and decisions I make regarding my life directly influence the quality of my days.

—Kathleen Andrus

There is no provision for blaming others in our lives. Who we are is a composite of the actions, attitudes, choices, decisions we've made up to now. For many of us, predicaments may have resulted from our decisions to not act when the opportunity arose. But these were decisions, no less, and we must take responsibility for making them.

We need not feel utterly powerless and helpless about the events of our lives. True, we cannot control others, and we cannot curb the momentum of a situation, but we can choose our own responses to both; these choices will heighten our sense of self and well-being and may well positively influence the quality of the day.

I will accept responsibility for my actions, but not for the outcome of a situation; that is all that's requested of me. It is one of the assignments of life, and homework is forthcoming.

They sicken of the calm, who knew the storm.
—Dorothy Parker

Variety in experiences is necessary for our continued growth. We mistakenly think that the "untroubled" life would be forever welcome. It's the deep waves of life that teach us to be better swimmers.

We don't know how to appreciate the calm without the occasional storm that pushes us to new limits of ourselves. The calm following the storm offers us the time we need to become comfortable with our new growth. We are ever changing, refining our values, stepping gingerly into uncharted territories. We are forever in partnership in these new territories, let us not forget.

We long for challenge even in the midst of the calm that blesses us. Our inner selves understand the journey; a journey destined to carry us to new horizons; a journey that promises many stormy seasons. For to reach our destination, we must be willing to weather the storms. They are challenges, handpicked for us, designed to help us become all that we need to be in this earthly life.

The mixture of the calm with the storm is not haphazard. Quite the contrary. My growth is at the center of each. I will trust its message.

To have one's individuality completely ignored is like being pushed quite out of life. Like being blown out as one blows out a light.

—Evelyn Scott

We need to know that we matter in this life. We need evidence that others are aware of our presence. And thus, we can be certain that others need the same attention from us. When we give it, we get it. So the giving of attention to another searching soul meets our own need for attention as well.

Respectful recognition of another's presence blesses her, ourselves, and God. And we help one another grow, in important ways, each time we pay the compliment of acknowledgment.

We're not sure, on occasion, just what we have to offer our friends, families, co-workers. Why we are in certain circumstances may have us baffled, but it's quite probably that the people we associate with regularly need something we can give them; the reverse is just as likely. So we can begin with close attention to people in our path. It takes careful listening and close observation to sense the message another soul may be sending to our own.

I will be conscious of the people around me. I shall acknowledge them and be thankful for all they are offering me.

I'm a most lucky and thankful woman. Lucky and thankful for each morning I wake up. For three wonderful daughters and one son. For an understanding and very loving husband with whom I've shared 52 blessed years, all in good health.
—Thelma Elliott

Gratitude for what's been offered us in our lives softens the harsh attitudes we occasionally harbor. Life presents us with an assortment of blessings; some bring us immediate joy; some invite tears; others foster fear. What we need help in understanding is that all experiences are meant for our good, all bless us in some manner. If we are able to see the big picture, we'd greet all situations, large and small, with a thankful heart.

It's so very easy to wish away our lives, never finding satisfaction with our families, our jobs, our friends. The more we find fault with life, the more fault we are guaranteed to find. Negative attitudes attract negative experiences, while positive attitudes lighten whatever burden we may be learning from.

The years pass so quickly. Our chances to enjoy life pass quickly too. We can grab what comes our way and be grateful. We are never certain that this experience offered now might not be our last.

Each morning I awake is blessing number one.

For me, stopping smoking wasn't a matter of will power, but being will-less.

—Joan Gilbertson

Most of us have struggled, willfully, with untold numbers of addictions; liquor, uppers, downers, sugar, chocolate, cigarettes, men. The more we became determined to control our use or to abstain, the greater the compulsion felt for one drink, one bite, one puff. Giving in completely was the turning point.

This recovery program helps each of us find relief from our primary addiction once we humble ourselves, accept our powerlessness, and ask for help. It can help us equally effectively, every day, with any problem we are willfully trying to control. Is a family member causing us grief? Is a co-worker creating anxiety? Has a close friend pulled away? We expend so much energy trying to manage outcomes! In most cases, our attempt to control will invite even more resistance.

The program offers the way out of any frustrating situation. We can be mindful of our powerlessness and cherish the opportunities offered by our higher power. We can turn over whatever our problem to God and quietly, trustingly, anticipate the resolution. It's guaranteed.

How much easier I will find life's experiences if I will let go of my willful ways. The right outcome in all cases will more quickly surface.

*. . . the growth of understanding follows an ascending
spiral rather than a straight line.*
—Joanna Field

We each are traveling our own, very special path in this
life. At times our paths run parallel to each other. On
occasion they may intersect. But we do all have a common
destination: knowledge of life's meaning. And we'll arrive at
knowledge when we've arrived at the mountain's summit,
separately and yet together.

We do not go straight up the side of the mountain on
this trip. We circle it, slowly, carefully, sometimes losing our footing, sometimes backtracking because we've
reached an impasse. Many times we have stumbled, but as
we grow in understanding, as we rely more and more on
our inner strength, available for the taking, we become
more sure-footed.

We have never needed to take any step alone on this trip.
Our troubles in the past were complicated because we did
not know this; but now we do. Our lifeline is to our higher
power. If we hang on to it, every step of the way will feel
secure. The ground will be stable under us.

---

*I am on a path to full understanding. I am learning to trust
the lifeline offered by the program and God and my friends. As
I learn, my footing is less tentative, and it supports me
more securely.*

Imagination has always had powers of resurrection that no science can match.
—Ingrid Bengis

In the imagination are transmitted messages, from God to us. Inspiration is born there. So are dreams. Both give rise to the goals that urge us forward, that invite us to honor this life we've been given with a contribution, one like no other contribution.

Our imagination offers us ideas to ponder, ideas specific to our development. It encourages us to take steps unique to our time, our place, our intended gifts to the world. We can be alert to this special "inner voice" and let it guide our decisions; we can trust its urgings. It's charged with serving us, but only we can decide to "listen."

The imagination gives us another tool: belief in ourselves. And the magic of believing offers us strength and capabilities even beyond our fondest hopes. It prepares us for the effort we need to make and for handling whatever outcome God has intended.

―――――

My imagination will serve me today. It will offer me the ideas and the courage I need to go forth.

When a woman has love, she is no longer at the mercy of forces greater than herself, for she, herself, becomes the powerful force.

—*Veronica Casey*

The need for love is universal. Each of us longs for the affirmation that assures us we are needed, appreciated, desired. We are strengthened by the strokes others give us, and when no strokes are forthcoming, we sometimes falter.

With emotional and spiritual maturity comes the understanding that we are loved, unconditionally, by God. And the awareness of that love, the realization of its abiding presence, will buoy us up when no other love signals to us. Most of us still lose our connection to the omnipresent God, however. Thus, our buoyancy is tentative.

Until that time when we are certain about our value, about the presence of God's love, we'll need to practice self-affirmation. But learning how to nurture ourselves, how to be gentle and caressing to the woman within, may be painstaking. Patience will ease the process. Unconditionally loving ourselves will become natural in time. In fact, we'll sense our inner person growing, changing. Our wholeness will become apparent to others as well as to ourselves.

Love breeds love. I will shower it upon myself and others and relish the growing sense of self that emerges.

Anything forced into manifestation through personal will is always "ill got" and has "ever bad success."
—Florence Scovel Shinn

The main thrust of our recovery is to attune ourselves to God's will, struggling no longer to impose our own. The pain we've endured in past years was often of our own making. We controlled situations until we managed to force the outcome we desired, only to realize it didn't offer happiness. It was, instead, a bitter ending to the struggle.

When we want something or someone to play by our rules, we can expect barriers. And when the barriers don't give way with a gentle push, we should consider it a clue that we are off course. When we want what God wants for us, the barriers, if any, will fall away.

What God wants for us at every moment is growth and happiness. When we step away from our ego and develop a selfless posture toward life, we'll find serenity in the midst of any turmoil. Serenity is God's promise. When we get in line with God's will, we'll find peace.

I will know God's will if I will listen to my inner voice. I will do what feels right, and peace will be my reward.

Often when we're being tough and strong, we're scared. It takes a lot of courage to allow ourselves to be vulnerable, to be soft.

—Dudley Martineau

We've developed defenses for protection because we have felt the need for protection from the abuses of others, parents on occasion, bosses, spouses, even strangers. And in certain situations, our defenses served us well for a time. However, they have taken their toll. Hiding behind them for long makes them habitual, and we move farther and farther away from our center, from the woman each of us needs and wants to be.

Exposing who we really are invites judgment, sometimes rejection, oftentimes discounting. It's a terribly hard risk to take, and the rewards are seldom immediate. But with time, others respect us for our vulnerability and begin to imitate our example. We are served well by our integrity, in due time.

Letting others see who we really are alleviates confusion, theirs and ours. We no longer need to decide who we should be; we simply are who we are. Our choices are simplified. There is only one appropriate choice to every situation—the one that is honest and wholly reflective of who we are at that moment.

Rewards will be forthcoming when I am honest.

Life does not need to mutilate itself in order to be pure.

—*Simone Weil*

How terribly complicated we choose to make life's many questions. Should we call a friend and apologize or wait for her call? Are the children getting the kind of care they must, right now? That we "Came to believe in a power greater than ourselves" is often far from our thoughts when we most need it.

Our need to make all things perfect, to know all the answers, to control everything within our range, creates problems where none really exist. And the more we focus on the problem we've created, the bigger it becomes.

Inattention relieves the tension; last week's problems can seldom be recalled. The one we are keeping a problem with our undivided attention can be turned loose, at this moment. And just as quickly, the turmoil we've been feeling will be beyond recall too.

The program offers us another way to approach life. We need not mutilate it or ourselves. We can learn to accept the things we cannot change, and change the things we can . . . with practice.

I will pray for wisdom today. I shall expect wisdom, not problems, and the day will smoothly slip by.

Love is a force. It is not a result; it is a cause. It is not a product; it produces. It is a power, like money, or steam or electricity. It is valueless unless you can give something else by means of it.
                                    —Anne Morrow Lindbergh

Love and feeling loved—how often both elude us! We have taken the first step, though. Let's be grateful for our recovery; this is an act of love. We have chosen to love ourselves, and the program opens the way to our loving others. Love and loving are balms for the soul sickness we experience. We are being healed. We are healing one another.

Loving others means going beyond our own selfish concerns, for the moment, and putting others' concerns first. The result is that others feel our love. They feel a caring that is healing. And our spiritual natures are likewise soothed.

We find God and ourselves through touching the souls of one another. Our most special gift is being loved and giving love. Every moment we spend with another person is gift-giving time.

Every day is a gift-giving holiday, if I will but make it so.

Life is not always what one wants it to be, but to make the best of it as it is, is the only way of being happy.
—*Jennie Jerome Churchill*

We are generally so certain that we know what's best for ourselves. And we are just as often certain that what we think is best will guarantee happiness. Perhaps we should reflect on all the times in the past when our wishes didn't come true—fortunately.

Did any one of us expect to be doing, today, what we each are doing? We may have expected children, a particular kind of home, a certain career, but did we really anticipate all that life has wrought? Addiction, and then recovery from it, was probably not in our pictures. But it does fit into the big picture. The happiness we experience today probably doesn't visit us in the way we anticipated a few years back. But it is measured out according to our needs. The choice to be happy with what is, is ours to make, every moment.

I can take life as it is, and trust that it is just right, just what it needs to be. The big picture guarantees me lasting happiness. Today's experiences will move me a step closer.

Today was like a shadow. It lurked behind me. It's now gone forever. Why is it that time is such a difficult thing to befriend?

—Mary Casey

Each passing minute is all that we are certain of having. The choice is ever present to relish the moment, reaping fully whatever its benefits, knowing that we are being given just what we need each day of our lives. We must not pass up what is offered today.

Time accompanies us like a friend, though often a friend denied or ignored. We can't recapture what was offered yesterday. It's gone. All that stands before us is here, now.

We can nurture the moment and know that the pain and pleasures offered us with each moment are our friends, the teachers our inner selves await. And we can be mindful that this time, this combination of events and people, won't come again. They are the gift of the present. We can be grateful.

We miss the opportunities the day offers because we don't recognize the experiences as the lesson designed for the next stage of our development. The moment's offerings are just, necessary, and friendly to our spiritual growth.

I will take today in my arms and love it. I will love all it offers; it is a friend bearing gifts galore.

. . . to have a crisis and act upon it is one thing. To dwell in perpetual crisis is another.
—Barbara Grizzuti Harrison

Exaggerating the negative element in our lives is familiar behavior for all too many of us. But this obsession is our choice. We can stop at any moment. We can decide to let go of a situation that we can't control, turn it over to God, and be free to look ahead at the possibilities for happiness.

Perhaps we can learn to accept a serious situation in our lives as a special opportunity for growth first of all, but even more as an opportunity to let God work in our lives. We learn to trust by giving over our dilemmas to God for solutions. With patience, we will see the right outcomes, and we will more easily turn to God the next time.

Crises will lessen in number and in gravity in direct proportion to the partnership we develop with our higher power. The stronger our dependence on that power, for all answers and all directions, the greater will our comfort be in all situations.

Serenity is the gift promised when we let God handle our lives. No crisis need worry us. The solution is only a prayer away.

I will take action against every crisis confronting me—I will turn to God. Each crisis is an invitation to serenity.

*Everything in life that we really accept undergoes
a change. So suffering must become love. That is
the mystery.*

—Katherine Mansfield

Acceptance of those conditions that at times plague us
changes not only the conditions but, in the process, ourselves. Perhaps this latter change is the more crucial. As
each changes, as we all change into more accepting women,
life's struggles ease. When we accept all the circumstances
that we can't control, we are more peaceful. Smiles more
easily fill us up.

It's almost as though life's eternal lesson is acceptance,
and with it comes life's eternal blessings.

*Every day offers me many opportunities to grow in acceptance
and thus blessings. I can accept any condition today and
understand it as an opportunity to take another step toward
serenity, eternal and whole.*

With each new day I put away the past and discover
the new beginnings I have been given.
—Angela L. Wozniak

We can't recapture what is no more. And the minutes or hours we spend dwelling on what was or should have been only steal away from all that presently is. Today stands before us with promise. The opportunities for growth are guaranteed, as is all the spiritual help we need to handle any situation the day offers.

If today offers us a challenge, we can be grateful. Our challenges are gifts. They mean we are ready to move ahead to new awarenesses, to a new sense of our womanhood. Challenges force us to think creatively; they force us to turn to others; they demand that we change. Without challenges, we'd stagnate, enjoying life little, offering life nothing.

We each are making a special contribution, one that only we can make, each time we confront a new situation with courage. Each time we dare to open a new door. What we need to do today is to close the door on yesterday. Then we can stand ready and willing to go forward.

This day awaits my full presence. I will be the recipient of its gifts.

We're only as sick as the secrets we keep.
                    —*Sue Atchley Ebaugh*

Harboring parts of our inner selves, fearing what others would think if they knew, creates the barriers that keep us separate, feeling different, certain of our inadequacies.

Secrets are burdens, and they weigh heavily on us, so heavily. Carrying secrets makes impossible the attainment of serenity—that which we strive for daily. Abstinence alone is not enough. It must come first, but it's not enough by itself. It can't guarantee that we'll find the serenity we seek.

This program of recovery offers self-assurance, happiness, spiritual well-being, but there's work to be done. Many steps to be taken. And one of these is total self-disclosure. It's risky, it's humbling, and it's necessary.

When we tell others who we really are, it opens the door for them to share likewise. And when they do, we become bonded. We accept their imperfections and love them for them. And they love us for ours. Our struggles to be perfect, our self-denigration because we aren't, only exaggerates even more the secrets that keep us sick.

Our tarnished selves are lovable; secrets are great equalizers when shared. We need to feel our oneness, our sameness with other women.

Opportunities to share my secrets will present themselves today. I will be courageous.

Were our knowledge of human relationships a hundredfold more reliable than it is now, it would still be foolish to seek ready-made solutions for problems of living in the index of a book.
—Mirra Komarovsky

The problems each of us experience have within their own parameters the solutions most fitting. And we each must discover those solutions, understand their appropriateness, and absorb them into the body of information that defines who we are and who we are becoming.

We learn experientially because only then is our reality significantly affected. Others' experiences are helpful to our growth and affirm how similar is our pain, but each of us must make our own choices, take responsible action in our own behalf.

How fortunate that we are now in a position to make healthy decisions about our relationships! No longer the victim, we have the personal power to choose how we want to spend our time and with whom. Through active participation in all our relationships, we can discover many of the hidden elements in our own natures and develop more fully all the characteristics unique to our personhood. Our growth as recovering women is enhanced in proportion to our sincere involvement within the relationships we've chosen.

I can inform myself about who I am within my relationships. Therein lie the solutions to my problems.

There were many ways of breaking a heart. Stories were full of hearts broken by love, but what really broke a heart was taking away its dream—whatever that dream might be.

—Pearl S. Buck

No new door is opened without the inner urge for growth. Dreams guide us, encourage us, stretch us to new heights—and leave us momentarily empty when they are dashed.

Recovery has given us resilience and a multitude of reasons for living. We have come to understand that when one dream serves us no longer, it is making way for an even better one. Our dreams are our teachers. When the student is ready, a new one comes into focus.

Dreams in our earlier years often come to nought. They couldn't compete for our attention as effectively as the self-pity. The direction they offered was lost. Each day that we look forward with positive anticipation, we put the wreckage of the past farther from our minds.

Our dreams are like the rest areas on a cross-country trip. They refresh us, help us to gauge the distance we've come, and give us a chance to consider our destination.

Today's dreams and experiences are points on the road map of my life. I won't let them pass unnoticed.

In soloing—as in other activities—it is far easier to start something than it is to finish it.

—*Amelia Earhart*

Procrastination plagues us all, at one time or another. But any activity that is worthy of our effort should be tackled by bits and pieces, one day at a time. We are too easily overwhelmed when we set our sights only on the accomplished goal. We need to focus, instead, on the individual elements and then on just one element at a time. A book is written, word by word. A house is built, timber by timber. A college degree is attained, course by course.

By the time we got to this program, most of us had accumulated a checkered past, much of which we wanted to deny or forget. And the weight of our past can stand in the way of the many possibilities in the present.

Our past need not determine what we set out to do today. However, we must be realistic: We can't change a behavior pattern overnight. But we can begin the process. We can decide on a reasonable, manageable objective for this 24-hour period. Enough days committed to the completion of enough small objectives will bring us to the attainment of any goal, large or small.

I can finish any task I set my sights on, when I take it one day at a time. Today is before me. I can move forward in a small way.

*A woman who has no way of expressing herself and of
realizing herself as a full human has nothing else to
turn to but the owning of material things.*
                                —Enriqueta Longeaux y Vasquez

Each of us struggling with these Twelve Steps is finding
self-expression and self-definition. Introspection, coupled
with self-revelation through sharing with others, affords us
the awareness of how like others we are. How human we are.
And what we receive from others who respond to our vulnerability diminishes our need for "things" to fill our lives.

The love that we receive freely from a trusting, caring
friend or group fills up the empty places in our souls, the
places we used to try filling up with alcohol or cookies or
sex. New clothes, maybe even a new home or a different job
served their terms as void fillers too. Nothing succeeded for
long, and then the program found us.

The program is the filler for all times. Of this we can be
certain. Time will alleviate any doubts we may have. All that
is asked of us is openness, honesty, and attention to others'
needs as well as our own.

---

*I can share our likenesses and relish whatever differences may
surface. The chain of friendship I've created makes me the proud
owner of my wholeness. I am a succeeding woman who is moving
forward with courage and self-awareness on this, my road of life.*

Acceptance is not submission; it is acknowledgment of the facts of a situation. Then deciding what you're going to do about it.

—*Kathleen Casey Theisen*

Recovery offers us courage to make choices about the events of our lives. Passive compliance with whatever is occurring need no longer dominate our pattern of behavior. Powerlessly watching our lives go by was common for many of us, and our feelings of powerlessness escalated the more idle we were.

Today, action is called for, thoughtful action in response to the situations begging for our attention. Recovery's greatest gift is the courage to take action, to make decisions that will benefit us as well as the people who are close to us. Courage is the byproduct of our spiritual progress, courage to accept what we cannot change, believing that all will be well, courage to change in ourselves what we do have control over.

An exhilaration about life accompanies the taking of action. The spell that idleness casts over us is broken, and subsequent actions are even easier to take. Clearly, making a choice and acting on it is healthful. The program has given us the tools to do both.

Decisions will be called for today. I will be patient with myself, and thoughtful. I will listen closely to the guidance that comes from those around me.

There are sounds to seasons. There are sounds to places, and there are sounds to every time in one's life.
—Alison Wyrley Birch

Live is rich and full. Your life. My life. Even when the day feels flat or hollow, there's a richness to it that escapes our attention. We see only what we choose to see. We hear selectively, too. Our prejudgment precludes our getting the full effects of any experience. Some days we hear only the drum of the humdrum.

But the greater our faith in the program and a loving God, the clearer our perceptions become. We miss less of the day's events; we grow in our understanding of our unfolding, and we perceive with clarity the role others are playing in our lives.

We can see life as a concert in progress when we transcend our own narrow scope and appreciate the variety of people and situations all directed toward the same finale. The more we're in tune with the spiritual activity surrounding us, the more harmoniously we will be able to perform our parts.

I will listen to the music of today. I will get in tune, in rhythm. I am needed for the concert's beauty.

Life is either a daring adventure or nothing.
                                        —*Helen Keller*

The next 24 hours are guaranteed to excite us, to lift us to new levels of understanding, to move us into situations with others where we can offer our unique contributions. All that is asked of us is a willingness to trust that we will be given just what we need at each moment.

We can dare to live, fully, just for today. We can appreciate the extraordinariness of every breath we take, every challenge we encounter. Within each experience is the invitation for us to grow, to reach out to others in caring ways, to discover more fully the women we are capable of being. We must not let a single moment go by unnoticed.

When we withdraw from life, we stunt our growth. We need involvement with others, involvement that perturbs us, humors us, even stresses us. We tap our internal resources only when we have been pushed to our limits, and our participation in life gifts us, daily, with that push. How necessary the push!

None of us will pass this way again. What we see and feel and say today are gone forever. We have so much to regret when we let things slip away unnoticed or unappreciated.

A special series of events has been planned for me today. I shall not miss it.

*I like my friend for what is in her heart, not for the
way she does things.*
—Sandra K. Lamberson

We find good in situations, experiences and people when
we look for it. Generally we find just what we expect to
find. The power attaching to our attitudes is awesome.
Often it is immobilizing; too seldom is it positive.

We each create the personal environment that our soul
calls home, which means that at any moment we have the
power to change our perspective on life, our response to
any particular experience and most of all, our feelings about
ourselves. Just as we will find good in others when we
decide to look for it, we'll find good in ourselves.

We are such special women, all of us. And in our hearts
we want joy. What the program offers is the awareness that
we are the creators of the joy in our hearts. We can re-
linquish the past and its sorrows, and we can leave the
future in the hands of our higher power. The present is
singular in its importance to our lives, now.

---

*Behavior generally reveals attitudes which are of the mind and
frequently in conflict with the heart. I will strive for congruence. I
will let my heart lead the way. It will not only find the good in
others, it will imitate it.*

Tears are like rain. They loosen up our soil so we can grow in different directions.

—Virginia Casey

Full self-expression softens our being, while self-reservation makes us brittle. Our wholeness is enhanced each time we openly acknowledge our feelings and share our many secrets. The tears that often accompany self-disclosure, self-assessment, or the frustration of being "stuck" seem to shift whatever blocks we have put in our paths.

At each stage of our lives, we are preparing for yet another stage. Our growth patterns will vary, first in one direction, and then another. It's not easy to switch directions, but it's necessary. We can become vulnerable, accept the spiritual guidance offered by others and found within, and the transition from stage to stage will be smooth.

Tears shed on the rocky places of our lives can make tiny pebbles out of the boulders that block our paths. But we also need to let those tears wash away the blinders covering our eyes. Tears can help us see anew if we're willing to look straight ahead—clearly, openly, and with expectation of a better view.

Tears nurture the inner me. They soften my rootedness to old behavior. They lessen my resistance to new growth.

Success can only be measured in terms of distance traveled.

—*Mavis Gallant*

We are forever moving from one experience to another, one challenge to another, one relationship to another. Our ability to handle confidently all encounters is a gift of the program, and one that accompanies us throughout every day, providing we humbly express gratitude for it. Success is ours when we are grateful.

We are not standing still. No matter how uneventful our lives may seem, we are traveling toward our destiny, and all the thrills and tears, joys and sorrows, are contributing to the success of our trip. Every day, every step, we are succeeding.

We can reflect on yesterday, better yet, on last week or even last year. What were our problems? It's doubtful we can even remember them. We have put distance between them and us. They were handled in some manner. We have succeeded in getting free of them. We have succeeded in moving beyond them.

How far we have come! And we will keep right on traveling forward. As long as we rely on the program, we are assured of success.

I can do whatever I need to do, today, with success, when I humbly accept the program's gifts.

If I had to describe something as divine it would be what happens between people when they really get it together. There is a kind of spark that makes it all worthwhile. When you feel that spark, you get a good feeling deep in your gut.

—June L. Tapp

How lucky we are, that we can experience that divine spark with one another, and with all recovering women. The program offers us the chance, every moment of our lives from this day forward, to experience divinity. All we are asked to do is be there, for one another, to share fully who we are. Vulnerability gets easier as we learn that we can trust each other, that we can share pain, that it's okay to pull and prod and follow, first you and then me and then her.

What a thrill it is to leave our competition behind! The program bonds us together, and the bond will strengthen each of us, but it can elude us, too. It often does when we forget to be there, in one another's presence, when the opportunity comes.

I need these sparks to nurture my growth, singly and collectively. I will be part of a divine experience today.

*. . . satisfaction is a lowly thing, how pure a thing
is joy.*

—Marianne Moore

Our perfectionism generally dashes all hopes of self-satisfaction. But the program is here to show us that we can make progress. We can learn to believe that we are doing any task as well as we need to do it, at this time. Our job is the effort. The outcome is part of a larger plan, one that involves more than ourselves.

We'll find joy when we find acceptance of ourselves and our efforts and the belief that we are spiritual beings whose lives do have purpose and direction.

The wisdom that accompanies spiritual growth offers us security, that which we have sought along many avenues. And when we feel secure, we can trust that the challenges confronting us are purposeful and to our advantage.

One day at a time, one small prayer at a time, move us ever closer to spiritual security. We can look with glad anticipation at our many responsibilities and activities today. They are our opportunities for spiritual security. We can trust our growing inner resources by simply asking for guidance and waiting patiently. It will find us.

*I must exercise my prayers if I want the spiritual security where
I can find joy. I will ask for guidance with every activity today.*

For all the sadness of closure, there is a new and joyful unfolding in the process of becoming.
                                        —Mary Casey

We must let go of people, places, memories, and move on to new experiences. The doors of the past must be closed before we can enter those that are opening to us today. However, no experience is gone forever. All of our experiences are threaded together, each one contributing to the events that claim our attention now.

Recovery has offered us a chance to be aware of our process of becoming. With each day, each experience, each new understanding, we are advancing along the path of personal growth. Let us remember that each of us has a particular path, like no other. Thus, our experiences are ours alone. We need not envy what comes to someone else.

Life is unfolding for us. The pain of the present may be necessary for the pleasure of tomorrow. We can accept the unfolding. Our inner selves have a goal; experiences of the past must be left in the past; experiences at hand will lead us to our destination today.

I am moving and changing and growing, at the right pace. The process can be trusted. What is right for me will come to me. I will let the joy of becoming warm me.

Pity is the deadliest feeling that can be offered to a woman.

—Vicki Baum

We must move forward with confidence, trusting that the strength we need will be given us, having faith in our visions to guide us. Problems need not daunt us. Rather, they can spur us on to more creative activity. They challenge our capabilities. They insist that we not stand still.

Pity from others fosters inaction, and passivity invites death of the soul. Instead, our will to live is quickened through others' encouragement. All else dampens the will. Pity feeds the self-pity that rings the death knell.

We can give strokes wherever we are today and know that we are helping someone live. And each time we reach out to encourage another, we are breathing new life into ourselves, new life that holds at bay the self-pity that may appear at any moment.

We can serve one another best, never by commiserating with sadnesses, but by celebrating life's challenges. They offer the opportunities necessary to our continued growth.

Someone needs a word of encouragement from me. I will brighten her vision of the future.

We can build upon foundations anywhere if they are well and firmly laid.

—Ivy Compton-Burnett

Recovery is a process, one which rebuilds our lives. And the Twelve Steps provide the foundation to support our growth as healthy, productive women. But each Step must be carefully and honestly worked, or the whole foundation will be weakened.

How lucky we are to have found this program and the structure it offers. We looked for structure in our past. We searched, maybe for years, running from one panacea to another, hoping to find ourselves. Booze—pills—food—lovers—causes; none gave us the security we longed for. We couldn't find ourselves because we hadn't defined ourselves. At last we've come home. Self-definition is the program's guarantee. Not only can we discover who we are, now, but we can change, nurture those traits that we favor, diminish those that attract trouble.

My actions today are the key. They tell who I am at this moment. Who I become is up to me. I will pick a Step and reflect before I move ahead. The strength of my foundation depends on it.

*Remember your good memories, but live for today
and keep the memories behind you.*
                                        —Jodi K. Elliott

The stuff of our memories comprise who we have become. Each recollection is akin to an ingredient in a simmering pot of stew. The full flavor of our lives is enhanced by each additional experience, whether it be painful or joyful.

Our experiences have a way of dovetailing, of grouping themselves, perhaps even tailoring themselves, to provide us the best advantage. So human is our tendency to linger in thought on past times that we fail to take advantage, to be fully present in the moment which is assuredly making a necessary contribution to the total panorama of our lives.

Who are we to judge the value of any single experience? It's how all experiences have mingled, that we must trust. We can be certain, in retrospect, that those situations that created the most inner turmoil also offered us the most as growing, developing women.

The experiences offered today, in the 24 hours ahead, are significant because they are unique. I will cherish them for the addition they are making to my total person.

It's astonishing in this world how things don't turn out at all the way you expect them to!

—Agatha Christie

Probably every day of our lives, a plan goes awry. Often we have counted heavily on a particular outcome. We generally assume we have all things under control and know exactly what's best for us, and everyone else as well. But such is not the case. There is a bigger picture than the one we see. The outcome of that picture is out of our hands.

Our vision is limited, and again divinely so. However, we are able to see all that we need to see, today. And more important, if we can trust our inner guidance regarding the events of today, we'll begin to see how each day fills in a shade more of the bigger picture of our lives. In retrospect we can see how all events have contributed, in important ways, to the women we are becoming. Where today's events are leading we can't know, for certain, but we can trust the divine plan.

I will anticipate with faith what lies ahead today. All experiences carry me forward to fulfill my goal in life. I will be alert for the nudge.

*I do not want to die . . . until I have faithfully made
the most of my talent and cultivated the seed that was
placed in me until the last small twig has grown.*
—Käthe Kollwitz

There's so much to do before we rest . . . so much to do.
We each are gifted with talents, similar in some respects to
others' talents, but unique in how we'll be able to use them.
Do we realize our talents? We need only to dare to dream,
and there they'll be.

It's so easy to fall into the trap of self-pity, thinking we
have no purpose, fearing we'll take life nowhere, dreading
others' expectations of us. But we can turn our thinking
around at any moment. The choice is ours. We can simply
decide to discover our talents, and nurture them and enrich
the lives of others. The benefits will be many. So will the joys.

We have a very important part to play, today, in the lives
we touch. We can expect adventure, and we'll find it. We
can look for our purpose; it's at hand. We can remember,
we aren't alone. We are in partnership every moment. Our
talents are God-given, and guidance for their full use is part
of the gift.

I will have a dream today. In my dream is my direction.

It isn't for the moment you are struck that you need courage, but for the long uphill climb back to sanity and faith and security.
—Anne Morrow Lindbergh

Most of us are on a long uphill climb at this moment. It is a climb we are making together, and yet a climb we can't do for each other. I can reach out my hand to you, and you can grasp my hand in return. But my steps are my own, just as you, too, can only take one step at a time.

For brief periods we skip, even run, along the uphill path. The rocks and the occasional boulder momentarily trip us up. We need patience and trust that the summit is still achievable. We can help one another have patience. We can remind one another to trust.

We look back at the periods that devastated us so long ago. And now we are here. We have climbed this far. We are stronger, saner, more secure. Each step makes easier the next step—each step puts us on more solid ground.

I may run into some rocks or even a boulder today. I have stepped around them in the past. I will do so again.

I used to think I'd never know the difference between serenity and depression because depression subdued me.

—S.H.

Depression is familiar to us all, and less incapacitating than it used to be. We have made progress, we can be assured. "This too shall pass" is not an empty slogan.

Each of us can recall, with ease probably, a period we thought we'd never survive. Maybe our problem was family-related, or a tough on-the-job situation. Or maybe we felt inadequate and lacking in strength to cope with all situations. But we managed. Here we are today, taking charge of our lives and moving forward in search of serenity.

Serenity no doubt eludes us, again and again, throughout the day. But we can let our minds rest. We can give our thoughts to the wind, and serenity will find us. Serenity's peace nurtures us, strengthens us to withstand the turmoil ahead. There is always turmoil ahead. Life's lessons are found there. The irony is that a life with no problems doesn't offer the opportunities we must have if we are to grow.

I will let the serene moments wash over me. I will cherish them. They soften me. And the blows of today's tumultuous storm will be lessened.

*No person is your enemy, no person is your friend,
every person is your teacher.*
—Florence Scovel Shinn

We can open ourselves to opportunities today. They
abound in our lives. No circumstance we find ourselves in
is detrimental to our progress. No relationship with someone at work or at home is superfluous to our development.
Teachers are everywhere. And as we become ready for a
new lesson, one will appear.

We can marvel at the wonder of our lives today. We can
reflect on our yesterdays and be grateful for the lessons they
taught. We can look with hopeful anticipation at the days
ahead—gifts, all of them. We are on a special journey, serving a special purpose, uniquely our own. No barrier, no difficult person, no tumultuous time is designed to interrupt
our progress. All experiences are simply to teach us what we
have yet to learn.

Trusting in the goodness of all people, all situations, all
paths to progress will release whatever our fears, freeing us
to go forth with a quicker step and an assurance that eases
all moments.

The Twelve Steps help us to recognize the teachers in our
lives. They help us clear away the baggage of the past and
free us to accept and trust the will of God, made known to
us by the teachers as they appear.

---

*I am a student of life. I can learn only if I open my mind to
my teachers.*

Nobody told me how hard and lonely change is.
—Joan Gilbertson

Pain, repeatedly experienced, indicates a need for self-assessment, an inventory of our behavior. Honest self-appraisal may well call for change, a change in attitude perhaps, a change in specific behavior in some instances, or maybe a change in direction. We get off the right path occasionally, but go merrily on our way until barriers surface, doors close, and experiences become painful.

Most of us willingly wallow in our pain a while, not because we like it, but because its familiarity offers security. We find some comfort in our pain because at least it holds no surprises.

When our trust in God is high, we are more willing to change. And we open ourselves to the indications for movement in a new direction. Each of us must find our own willingness. Each of us must develop attentiveness to the signs that repeatedly invite changes in our behavior. But most of all, each of us has to travel the road to change, singly. Changes we must find the courage to make will never be exactly like someone else's changes.

Courage to change accompanies faith. My fears are telling me to look within to the spiritual source of strength, ever present but often forgotten.

What a strange pattern the shuttle of life can weave.
—Frances Marion

How shortsighted is our judgment about today's experiences! We'll see with clarity where they may lead us only after we've reached our destination. Of one thing we can be certain: Today's experiences, in concert with yesterday's and all that's gone before, are combining to weave an intricate life design, unique, purposeful, and for our ultimate good.

We need not feel remorse over lost chances or unproductive behavior in the past. Our destination remains the same, and our arrival is guaranteed. Our actions and decisions are never wrong. We may veer off course for a time, but the design for our lives will pull us back on the track.

The program is part of the design for our lives. It's helping us to stay on course. In fact, when we're working the Steps, we're at ease with our direction, and we trust the outcome of our efforts to the power of the program. We will add to the richness of our design, today, just as we have every day of our lives. We can anticipate today's experiences with an excited heart.

There is something special going on in my life today. I will give everybody and every event my full attention.

When our myths, dreams, and ideals are shattered,
our world topples.
—Kathleen Casey Thiesen

The act of "becoming" topples our world, and rightly so. We outgrow yesterday's ideals, and we have begun realizing, in our unfolding, the dreams of last year. Now new dreams call us. Recovery has toppled our world. Hallelujah!

In our abstinence, each day offers us fresh opportunities to "create" new realities to replace the outworn, outgrown myths of the using days. But letting go of the old takes patience, persistence, and strength. The old comforted us when there was little else.

Perhaps we need reminding that were it not for the shattered myths of last year or last week, we'd not be progressing, unfolding, as the bigger picture calls us. We have a part to play in this life, as do our sisters, our friends, our children. New dreams and ideals will lead us on our way. Old dreams served us yesterday, and the past is gone. They can't direct our present.

I will look with excitement at my toppling world. It signifies growth—intellectual, emotional and spiritual. Old ideals will bind me—I will dare to dream new dreams and go where they lead with confidence.

I long to speak out the intense inspiration that comes to me from lives of strong women.

—Ruth Benedict

Each day that we thoughtfully make choices about our behavior and our attitudes, we offer ourselves as examples to others—examples of strength.

As women on recovery paths, we find encouragement from one another's successes. No one of us met our experiences very successfully before discovering this program. In most cases we lacked the structure that comes with the Steps. Direction was missing from our lives. Too often we passively bounced from man to man, job to job, drunk to drunk.

When working the Steps, we are never in doubt about the manner for proceeding in any situation. The Steps provide the parameters that secure our growth. They help us to see where we've been and push us toward the goals which crowd our dreams.

We have changed. We will continue to-grow. The past need haunt us no more. The future can be faced with confidence. Whatever strength is needed to fulfill our destinies will find us. And our forward steps will make the way easier for the women who follow.

What a blessing these Steps are! They answer my every question. They fulfill my every need.

Desire and longing are the whips of God.
—*Anna Wickham*

Our dreams and desires inspire us to reach beyond our present stopping-place. That which we can achieve will draw our attention, and with certainty, a partner is on hand to help us chart the steps for realizing the goal.

Before our introduction to the Twelve Steps, we experienced desires and set many goals. Some we attained. What we often lacked was confidence, and then our commitment wavered. The program is helping us realize that all pure desires are attainable when we invite the program's structure into our daily planning.

Our lives are purposeful. Each of us is fulfilling a necessary role. The longings that tug at us, longings that bring no harm to ourselves or others, push us to realize our full potential.

Courage and strength, ability and resourcefulness are never lacking when we follow the guidance within and trust in its direction. All the wisdom necessary for succeeding at any task, completing any goal, charting any desire, is as close as our attention is to God.

I will pay heed to my desires today. I will pray for the wisdom to fulfill them. All doors will open and my steps will be guided, when the desire is spiritually sound.

The future is made of the same stuff as the present.
                                        —Simone Weil

The moment is eternal. It is unending. When we move with the moment, we experience all that life can offer. Being fully awake to right now guarantees rapture even when there's pain, because we know we are evolving, and we thrill with the knowledge. We are one with all that's going on around us. Our existence is purposeful and part of the whole of creation, and we can sense our purpose.

Nothing is—but now. And when we dwell on what was, or what may be, we are cut off from life—essentially dead. The only reality is the present, and it's only in the present that we are invited to make our special contribution to life; perhaps at this moment our special contribution is to reach out to another person, an act that will change two lives, ours and hers.

We must cling to the present or we'll miss its invitation to grow, to help a friend perhaps, to be part of the only reality there is. The present holds all we need and all we'll ever need to fulfill our lives. It provides every opportunity for our happiness—the only happiness there is.

Abstinence offers me the gift of the present. I will cherish it, be grateful, relish it.

. . . concern should drive us into action and not into depression.

—Karen Horney

The role of victim is all too familiar to many of us. Life *did* us injustices—we thought. And we passively waited for circumstances to change. With the bottle we waited, or maybe the little white pills. Nothing was our fault. That we were willing participants to victimization is an awareness not easily accepted, but true nonetheless.

Victims no more, we are actors, now. And since committing ourselves to this program, we have readily available a willing and very able director for our role in life. Every event invites an action, and we have opted for the responsible life.

Depression may be on the fringes of our consciousness today. But it need not become our state of mind. The antidote is and always will be action, responsible action. Every concern, every experience wants our attention, our active attention.

Today stretches before me, an unknown quantity. Concerns will crowd upon me, but guidance regarding the best action to take is always available to me.

Anger conquers when unresolved.

—*Anonymous*

Emotions need recognition. But not only attention; they also need acceptance as powerful dimensions of who we are. Their influence over who we are capable of becoming is mighty.

Respectful attention to and willing acceptance of our emotions, whether fear or anger or hateful jealousy, take away their sting. We can prevent them from growing larger than they are. Like a child who screams and misbehaves more and more fiercely until attention is won, our emotions grow larger and more intense the longer we deny their existence.

Our emotions bless us, in reality. They enrich our experiences. They serve as guideposts on the road we're traveling. How we "feel" at any single moment flags the level of our security, how close we are to our higher power, the level of our commitment to the program. Our emotions serve us well when they are acknowledged. On the other hand, when ignored or denied, they can immobilize us, even defeat us.

My feelings frequent my being, always. They steer my behavior They reflect my attitudes. They hint at my closeness to God.

Who will I be today? The "Cosmopolitan" woman, the little girl, the scholar, the mother? Who will I be to answer the needs of others, and yet answer the needs of me?

—*Deidra Sarault*

We wear many hats. One aspect of our maturity is our ability to balance our roles. It's often quite difficult to do so; however, the program offers us many tools for balancing our lives.

Fulfilling some of the needs of significant others in our lives brings us joy. Our own needs must be given priority, though. We cannot give away what we don't have, and we have nothing unless we give sincere attention and love to ourselves.

In years gone by, we may have taken too little care of others, or we overdid it. In either case, we probably neglected ourselves. Most of us starved ourselves spiritually, many of us emotionally, a few physically. We were all too often "all-or-nothing" women.

Today we're aware of our choices. We've been making a number of good ones lately: We're abstinent. We're living the Steps. And we're choosing how to spend our time, and what to do with our lives. But no choice will turn out very well if we haven't taken care of ourselves.

I will center on myself. I will nurture the maturing woman within and then reach out.

Woman must not be awed by that which has been built up around her; she must reverence that woman in her which struggles for expression.
—Margaret Sanger

Let us not stifle ourselves any longer. Let us dare to dream and realize those dreams. Let us dare to take risks, having faith that to advance in any respect implies taking risks. Fortunately, we have the support of the program and one another to cushion the fall, if it should come. But more important, we have one another's example to inspire us as we contemplate our own agenda for self-expression.

Many of us for far too long passively watched others move forward. No longer need we be passive observers, but the familiarity of no action, no choice-making, and irresponsibility, makes passivity attractive at times. We must remember responsible choices, for only those make possible our very special contributions.

Not every day do we awaken with the strength needed to "do our part." But the strength will be available just as quickly as we call for it. Alone, we are strugglers; however, we have a ready partnership, and it guarantees us guidance, wisdom, and strength when we ask for it.

I have so much to offer other women. And I need another's example. Every expression of my strength will boost another woman's strength. I will give.

. . . we do not always like what is good for us in this world.
— *Eleanor Roosevelt*

Most of us can look back and recall how we fought a particular change. How certain we were that we wouldn't survive the upheaval! Perhaps we lost a love or were forced to leave a home or a job. Retrospect allows us to see the good of the change, and we can see the necessary part each change has played in our development as recovering women. We've had to change to cover the distances we've traveled. And we'll have to continue changing.

The program and its structure, and our faith in that structure, can ease the harsh consequences of change. Our higher power wants only the best for us, of that we can be sure. However, the best may not always "fit" when first we try it. Patience, trust, and prayer are a winning combination when the time comes for us to accept a change. We'll know when it's coming. Our present circumstances will begin to pinch.

Change means growth. It's a time for celebration, not dread. It means I am ready to move ahead—that I have "passed" the current test.

Why is life so tragic, so like a little strip of pavement over an abyss? I look down; I feel giddy; I wonder how I am ever to walk to the end.

—*Virginia Woolf*

As we look toward the hours ahead, we can be thankful that we need be concerned with only a single day's worth of hours. No more. What may come tomorrow, a decision that might be necessary next week, a big change in our lives coming next year, all will be handled with ease, when the time is right.

How fortunate we are, those of us who share this program for living! Our worries about the future are over, if we want them to be. We need to take only one step at a time. One day at a time. And always in the care of God. Relief from our lives of worry is immediate when we live the axiom, "Let go and let God."

Life does present us with tragedies, and we learn from them. They need not detour us, however. In fact, they strengthen us and encourage personal growth. And no experience will ever be more than we and our higher power can handle.

I will turn to the program and everything it offers today. Just today, and no more, is my concern.

The wisdom of all ages and cultures emphasizes the tremendous power our thoughts have over our character and circumstances.

—Liane Cordes

"As we think, so we are." We are gifted with the personal power to make thoughtful choices and thus decide who we are. Our actions and choices combine to create our character, and our character influences the circumstances of our lives.

Our personal mind power will work to our advantage when we think positively, or it will contribute to our disadvantage. Imagining our good fortunes will prepare us for them. Imagining the successful completion of a task heightens and strengthens the commitment we must make daily to it. Imagining the steps necessary to the successful accomplishment of any goal directs our efforts so we don't falter along the way. Our minds work powerfully for our good. And just as powerfully to our detriment, when fears intrude on all our thoughts.

The program has given me positive personal power; it lies in the relationship I have with my higher power. My outlook and attitude toward life reveal the strength of my connection to God. I will work with God and imagine my good fortune today.

I can honestly say that I was never affected by the question of the success of an undertaking. If I felt it was the right thing to do, I was for it regardless of the possible outcome.

—Golda Meir

Living a principled life is what the inner self desires. It's what God desires. And it's what the healthier ego desires. Living the program's principles is giving each of us practice in living a principled life, one that is free of guilt for our shortcomings.

Having principles assures direction. We need not ponder long how to proceed in any situation, what decision to make regarding any matter, when we are guided by principles. They offer us completeness. They help us define who we are and who we will be, in any turn of events.

As women, particularly as recovering women, we have struggled with self-definition. Often we were as others defined us, or we merely imitated those close by. Sometimes we may slip into old behavior and lose sight of who we are and how we want to live. It's then that the program's principles come immediately to our aid.

There is no doubt about how today should be lived. I will do it with confidence and joy.

Female friendships that work are relationships in which women help each other to belong to themselves.
—*Louise Bernikow*

To have anything worth giving to a friend, we must belong to ourselves. Are we someone we like? Does our behavior agree with our beliefs? Do our friends share our values, and when we are together do we support one another?

If we don't like our own company, we will try to hide our real selves. The more we hide, the further we are running from wholeness and health. We can assess ourselves, calmly and lovingly, so that we can keep on becoming the women we want to be. The more congruent are our behavior and our beliefs, the more we belong to ourselves. The better we like ourselves, the better friends we can be.

The love and sympathy of my women friends can help me in my spiritual journey toward serenity, and I can help theirs. Today, I will accompany others on their journey, and thus find company for my own.

Birds sing after a storm; why shouldn't people feel as free to delight in whatever remains to them?
—Rose Fitzgerald Kennedy

We choose the lives we lead. We choose sadness or happiness; success or failure; dread or excited anticipation. Whether or not we are conscious of our choices, we are making them every moment.

Accepting full responsibility for our actions is one of the requirements of maturity. Not always the easiest thing to do, but necessary to our further development. An unexpected benefit of accepting our responsibility is that it heightens our awareness of personal power. Our well-being is within our power. Happiness is within our power. Our attitude about any condition, present or future, is within our power, if we take it.

Life is "doing unto us" only what we allow. And it will favor us with whatever we choose. If we look for excitement, we'll find it. We can search out the positive in any experience. All situations present seeds of new understanding, if we are open to them. Our responses to the events around us determine whatever meaning life offers. We are in control of our outlook. And our outlook decides our future.

This day is mine, fully, to delight in—or to dread. The decision is always mine.

Women are often caught between conforming to existing standards or role definitions and exploring the promise of new alternatives.
—*Stanlee Phelps and Nancy Austin*

This is a time of exploring for many of us. Recovery means change in habits, change in behavior, change in attitudes. And change is seldom easy. But change we must, if we want to recover successfully.

We do have support for trying our new alternatives. We have support from our groups and our higher power. Perhaps we want a career or more education. Perhaps we want to develop a hobby or try a sport. Sharing that desire and then looking for support guarantees some guidance. This program has given us a chance to start fresh—to become our inner desire.

We are only caught in an old pattern if we assent to it. The going won't always be easy, but support and guidance are available and free if we but look for them.

Today I will consider my alternatives. Do I want to make a change?

Fortunate are the people whose roots are deep.
—Agnes Meyer

Deep roots offer strength and stability to an organism. They nourish it plentifully. They anchor it when the fierce winds blow. We each are offered the gifts of roots when we give ourselves fully to the program.

We are never going to face, alone, any difficult situation after discovering recovery. Never again need we make any decision in isolation. Help is constant. Guidance through companionship with others and our contacts with God will always be as close as our requests. The program anchors us; every prayer we make, every step we take, nourishes the roots we are developing.

Becoming rooted in the program, with daily attention to the nourishment we need, offers us sanity and hope. We discover that all things can be handled; no situation is too much for us. Strength, confidence, freedom from fear are the benefits of our deepening roots. We will be anchored if we do what needs to be done by us. The program's gifts are ours, only if we work the program.

I won't neglect my roots today. I will nourish them so they in turn can fill me up with confidence when my need is there.

Ambiguity means admitting more than one response to a situation and allowing yourself to be aware of those contradictory responses. You may want something and fear it at the same time. You may find it both beautiful and ugly.

—Tristine Rainer

Flexibility is a goal worth the striving. It eases our relations with others, and it stretches our realm of awareness. Letting go of rigid adherence to what our perceptions were yesterday assures us of heightened understanding of life's variables and lessons.

Being torn between two decisions, feeling ambivalent about them, need not create consternation, though it often does. Hopefully, it will encourage us to pray for direction, and then to be responsive to the guidance. And we must keep in mind that no decision is ever wrong. It may lead us astray for a time, but it will also introduce us to uncharted territories which offer many opportunities for flexibility.

Our contradictory responses, which we may express to others or to ourselves, keep us on our toes, lend an element of excitement to our lives, and push us to think creatively about our perceptions. Growth and change are guaranteed.

I will be in tune with myself today. I will let my perceptions guide me.

*If I love with my Spirit, I don't have to think so hard
with my head.*

—*Peggy Cahn*

Love smooths all ruffles. All situations are calmed, all
tension is eased. The expression of love is a balm on all
wounds, particularly our own. Feeling love toward the people
in our lives today will boost our spirits; our personal difficulties will lessen. We'll discover resolution. The answers
we've been searching for become known to us when we
concentrate less on our problems and more on the gift of
love we can give to the travelers we encounter today.

The solutions to our problems are seldom found in our
heads. They burst forth from our hearts. We suddenly seem
to know what to do. Perhaps someone else's words or behavior will trigger the inspiration we've longed for. We can
let our concern today be on the moment and the experience. We can let its power wash over us, and in the wake
we'll find the answers we search for.

When we're brittle, cold to others, we close off whatever
messages are being directed to us. Our love for others softens
us, making it possible for the words and ideas we await to
permeate us.

*If I am in need today, if I have a problem that wants a solution,
I will reach out to others with love. They'll hand me my answer
in return.*

Sometimes I think I'm the luckiest person in the world. There's nothing better than having work you really care about. Sometimes I think my greatest problem is lack of confidence. I'm scared, and I think that's healthy.
—*Jane Fonda*

We each vacillate between feeling confident on some days, lucky on others, and yet frequently scared on others. It's very human to vacillate. We need not be anxious because our emotions refuse to stand still.

Changing emotions are part of the process of normal living. And changing emotions reflect an involvement with the moment. Situations do touch us, as they should. They do invite responses, as they should. And our responses will reveal our emotional involvement, as they should. We can cherish the variety of our emotions. They enrich us. But they may also create problems, if they go unchecked.

We need to maintain a balance. Confidence, certainly desirable, can become overconfidence and thus complacency. Confidence needs humility to temper it. Fear makes us cautious, and that's good; but too much can immobilize us. Being in charge of our emotions makes them work for us.

Emotions can energize me and keep me involved with the moment. They can also control me. It's my decision to be in charge.

Many people are living in an emotional jail without recognizing it.

—*Virginia Satir*

Each of us is blessed with an internal guide, a source able to direct our actions if we but acknowledge it. Never are we in doubt for long about what path to take. The courage to take it might not be immediately forthcoming; however, it, too, is one of the gifts with which we've been blessed. Courage is ours for the asking. Right direction is ours for the taking.

Trusting our inner selves takes practice, followed by attention to the results of our risks. Before recovery, many of us passively waited for others to orchestrate our behavior, our feelings, our attitudes. Stepping forward as the leading lady, with our own script in hand, is quite a change, but one we are being coached, daily, to make.

The Steps help us to know who we are. More importantly, they help us become the women we long to be. But most important, they offer us the spiritual strength to risk listening to the message within and the strength to go forth as directed.

Right results, again and again, are elicited by right action. And my knowledge of the right action is always, and forever, as close as myself.

There is a divine plan of good at work in my life. I will let go and let it unfold.

—Ruth P. Freedman

We are never certain of the full importance or the eventual impact of any single event in our lives. But of one thing we can be sure: Each experience offers something valuable to our overall development. We must not discount the experiences that are long gone. They contributed to all we've achieved at the present. And wherever today takes us will influence what tomorrow will bring.

Perhaps our greatest difficulty as recovering women is not trusting that life is a process and one that promises goodness. That growth and change are guaranteed. That our lives have design, and we're blessed therein. Trusting isn't easy. But we can learn, and we'll discover freedom.

Letting go of the outcome of every experience, focusing instead on our efforts, making them as good as possible, validates our trust in the ultimate goodness of life. Our frustrations diminish when our efforts, only, are our concern. How much easier our days go when we do our work and leave the outcome where it belongs.

I will know a new freedom when I let go and trust that "my plan" is unfolding as it must. I will do my part, and no more.

The great creative power is everything. If you leave out one whole chunk of it, by making God only masculine, you have to redress the balance.
—Martha Boesing

What a blessing, to be part of God! For many of us, invoking God with a male pronoun put an obstacle in the path of our spiritual growth. We felt left out. Worship of something called "He" or "Him" didn't jibe with our spirituality. When we pray, we pray to a spiritual source that includes everything, that leaves nothing out: both sexes, all races, all ages and conditions.

Some of us had no trouble understanding that God is everything, no matter how God is invoked. But whatever our path to spirituality, the Twelve Step program has enriched our understanding. Before we practiced the Twelve Steps, we had allowed ourselves to forget the strength and nurture that are always at hand, and now we are grateful to be reminded that God is with us, within us, and all is well.

One woman says, "When I feel far from God, I ask myself: Who moved?" God is always there. Today I will pray for the wisdom to stay close to my spiritual source, the Creator Spirit.

When all of the remedies and all of the rhetorical armor have been dropped, the absence of love in our lives is what makes them seem raw and unfinished.
　　　　　　　　　　　　　　　　　　—Ingrid Bengis

Love soothes, encourages, inspires. It enhances our wholeness, both when we give it and when we receive it. Without the expression of love we are severed from our family and friends. It's the bond that strengthens each of us, giving us the courage to tackle what's lying ahead.

We need not wait for someone else's expression of love before giving it. Loving must be unconditional. And when it is, it will be returned tenfold. Loving attracts itself, and it will heal us, soften the hard edges of our lives, and open us up to receive the blessings that others' gratitude will foster.

It's such a simple thing asked of us—to love one another. Unconditional love of our sisters, our lovers, our children breaks down the barriers to our achievements and theirs. Loving frees us to enjoy life. It energizes us and makes all goals attainable. We carry God's message through our love of one another.

I am charged with only one responsibility today: to love someone, dearly and wholly.

Sometimes it's worse to win a fight than to lose.
                                        —Billie Holiday

Our struggles with other people always take their toll on us. They often push us to behavior we're not proud of. They may result in irreparable rifts. They frequently trigger an emotional relapse. No battle is worth the damage to the psyche that nearly any battle can cause. Nonresistance is the safer way to chart our daily course.

Bowing with the wind, flowing with the tide, eases the steps we need to take, the steps that will carry us to our personal fulfillment. Part of the process of our growth is learning to slide past the negative situations that confront us, coming to understand that we are in this life to fulfill a unique purpose. The many barriers that get in our way can strengthen our reliance on God if we'll let them. We need never be thwarted by people or situations. We will profit from taking all experiences in our stride. The course we travel is the one we chart. The progress we make toward our life goals is proportionate to the smoothness of our steps.

I will flow with the tide. It will assuredly move me closer to my destination.

Be still and listen to the stillness within.
                              —*Darlene Larson Jenks*

No answer eludes us if we turn to the source of all answers—the stillness within. Prayer accompanied by meditation will always provide the answers we need for the situations facing us. The answers we want are not guaranteed, however. We must trust that we will be directed to take the right steps. Our well-being is assured if we let go of being the one in control and turn our wills over to the care of God, our messenger within.

How comforting to know that all answers are as close as our quiet moments. God never chooses to keep the answers from us. We simply fail to quiet our thoughts long enough to heed them. Our minds race, obsessively, all too often. We jump from one scenario to another, one fear to another, one emotion to another. And each time our thoughts capture a new focus, we push the answer we seek further into the background.

The process is simple, if I want to follow it. The answers await me if I truly want them. I need only sit quietly and ask God to offer the guidance I need. And then I will sit quietly some more.

. . . there are two entirely opposite attitudes possible in facing the problems of one's life. One, to try and change the external world, the other, to try and change oneself.

—Joanna Field

God grant us the courage to change what we can—ourselves. How difficult it is to let go of our struggles to control and change someone else. How frequently we assume that everything would be fine if only someone else would change. All that needs to change is an attitude, our own.

Taking responsibility for improving one's own life is an important step toward emotional health. Blaming another for our circumstances keeps us stuck and offers no hope for improved conditions. Personal power is as available as our decision to use it. And it is bolstered by all the strength we'll ever need. The decision to take our lives in hand will exhilarate us. The decision each day to be thoughtful, prayerful, and wholly responsible for all that we do will nourish our developing selves. Each responsible choice moves us toward our wholeness, strengthening our sense of self, our well-being.

I will change only who I can today: myself.

Never turn down a job because you think it's too small; you don't know where it can lead.

—Julia Morgan

How short is our vision of where an invitation might take us! Any invitation. Of one thing we can be certain, it offers an opportunity for making a choice, which means taking responsibility for who we're becoming. Choice-making is growth-enhancing because it strengthens our awareness of personal power.

Our lives unfold in small measures, just as small as they need to be for our personal comfort. It's doubtful that we could handle everything the future has in store, today; however, we will be prepared for it, measure by measure, choice by choice, day by day. We need not fear; what is meted out to us in the invitations offered is for our benefit. We are on a pathway to goodness.

The thrill of making choices is new to many of us when we enter this program. We'd opted for the passive life, all too often, and we became increasingly aware of, and often depressed by, our self-imposed powerlessness. Free at last! We are free at last to fully participate in our lives.

I will be grateful for the many options to act tugging at me today. Every choice I make strengthens my womanhood.

The balance between mind and spirit comes hard for me. The eternal split. Two entities, perfectly aware and yet perfectly unwilling to cooperate.

—Mary Casey

The program directs our spiritual growth, a human aspect that had atrophied, if ever it had existed, for most of us before abstinence. And the process of developing our spiritual nature is painstaking. Living by our wits, or the fervent application of "situational analysis," had been our survival tools for months or years.

To return repeatedly to the old tools for quick solutions to serious situations is second nature. Learning to rely on spiritual guidance for solutions and to use it to sharpen our analytical focus takes patience and continual effort.

Within our spiritual realm we find our connection to God. We have been given the wisdom; all the knowledge we need is at our fingertips. The confidence to move ahead and offer our special talent to others comes from our Spirit. We are all that we need to be. Our mind and our Spirits, in concert, can tackle any challenge and succeed.

My mind and my Spirit can become compatible entities with the development of my trust in each. Knowledge plus courage can move mountains. I have been given both.

Character contributes to beauty. It fortifies a woman as her youth fades.

—Jacqueline Bisset

How common it is for us to be overly concerned with our looks. The culture encourages it through our families, our friends, the media. Many of us anguished over our looks in years past, and the pain of fading youth haunts some even now.

Perhaps it's time for us to take special note of the women we admire for their achievements. We should emulate them, honor them, and celebrate their particular beauty—a beauty generally enhanced by dignity, perseverance, courage.

We can cultivate our special interests. They'll contribute to our achievements, which will add depth to our soul—the home of true beauty. Mature persons who acknowledge this true beauty are those we wish to attract into our lives. How fickle is the beautiful face! And even more fickle is the one who can see no deeper.

Youth and its beauty are fleeting. Not so the beauty of the developing character; time strengthens it. The program makes character development not only possible but simple. Each of the Twelve Steps, any Step, offers us an opportunity to take charge of our lives, right now.

I will remember, it's who I am inside that truly counts in the lives of others.

History provides abundant examples of . . . women whose greatest gift was in redeeming, inspiring, liberating, and nurturing the gifts of others.
—Sonya Rudikoff

Part of our calling as members of the human community is to unconditionally love and support the people emotionally close to us. We have been drawn together for purposes wonderful but seldom readily apparent. We need one another's gifts, compassion, and inspiration in order to contribute our individual parts to the whole.

Not only do we need to nurture and to inspire others, but our personal development, emotionally and spiritually, demands that we honor ourselves in like fashion. Self-love, full self-acceptance, is necessary before we can give anything of lasting value to someone else. We must selflessly give to others if, indeed, our love and support are meant to serve, and giving anything selflessly is evidence of healthy self-love.

Selfless love liberates the giver and the recipient. Giving selflessly reveals our personal contentment, and it means we are free to nurture our own gifts.

It's good and right that I should encourage someone else today. I will pay the same respect to myself, too.

*Pride, we are told, my children, "goeth before a fall"
and oh, the pride was there, and so the fall was not
far away.*

—*Wilhelmina Kemp Johnstone*

Requesting help. Admitting we are wrong. Owning our
mistake in either a big or small matter. Asking for another
chance or someone's love. All very difficult to do, and yet
necessary if we are to grow. The difficulty is our pride, the
big ego. We think we need to always be right. If we're
wrong, then others may think less of us, look down on us,
question our worth. "Perfectionism" versus "worthlessness."

If we are not perfect (and of course we never are), then
we must be worthless. In between these two points on the
scale is "being human." Our emotional growth, as women,
is equal to how readily we accept our humanness, how able
we are to be wrong. With humility comes a softness that
smooths our every experience, our every relationship. Pride
makes us hard, keeps us hard, keeps others away, and sets
us up for the fall.

I will let myself be human today. It will soften my vision of life.

When people bother you in any way, it is because their souls are trying to get your divine attention and your blessing.

—Catherine Ponder

We are in constant communication with one another and, in the spiritual realm, with God. No matter how singular our particular course may appear, our path is running parallel to many paths. And all paths will intersect when the need is present. The point of intersection is the moment when another soul seeks our attention. We can be attentive and loving to the people seeking our attention. Their growth and ours is at stake.

We can be grateful for our involvement with other lives. We can be mindful that our particular blessing is like no one else's and that we all need input from the many significant persons in our lives. There is no insignificant encounter in our passage through life. Each juncture with someone else is part of the destiny of both participants.

I will look carefully and lovingly at the people around me today and bless them, one and all. They are in my life because they need to be. I, likewise, need them.

One of the conclusions I have come to in my old age is the importance of living in the ever-present now. In the past, too often I indulged in the belief that somehow or other tomorrow would be brighter or happier or richer.

—Ruth Casey

How easily our minds jump from the present to the foibles of the past or our fears about the future. How seldom are our minds on this moment, and only this moment.

Before we picked up this book, where were our thoughts? We need to practice, with diligence, returning our minds to whatever the experience is at hand. A truly creative response to any situation can only be made when we are giving it our undivided attention. And each creative response initiates an even more exciting follow-up experience.

All we have of life, all that it can offer us is here, now. If we close our minds to the present, this present, we'll only continue to do so when the tomorrow we dream of now becomes the present. There are no tomorrows.

I will let go of the past and the future. My only reality is here, now. God's gifts are here, today, right now.

. . . You don't get to choose how you're going to die.
Or when. You can only decide how you're going to
live. Now.

—Joan Baez

How thrilling to contemplate that we can choose every
attitude we have and every action we take. We have been
gifted with full responsibility for our development. What
will we try today? It's our personal choice. How will we
decide on a particular issue? Our options are only limited
by our vision.

Every situation in life offers us a significant opportunity
for making a decision that will, of necessity, influence the
remaining situations we encounter. Just as we are interdependent, needing and influencing one another in all instances that bring us together, likewise our decisions are
never inviolate. Each is singly important; however, its impact is multiplied by the variety of other decisions triggered.

The choice is ours for living fully today, for taking advantage of all the opportunities that present themselves. Our
personal growth, our emotional and spiritual development,
are in our hands. God will provide us with the guidance,
and the program offers us the tools. The decision to act is
ours, alone.

I will exercise my personal power. My choices determine
my development.

The strength of the drive determines the force required to suppress it.

—Mary Jane Sherfey

We are all struggling to succeed. And each day of our lives we'll be confronted with major or minor adversities that might well interfere with our success. Adversities don't have to hinder us, however. They can strengthen us, if we incorporate them as opportunities for growth.

For many of us, the ability to handle adversity is a fairly recent phenomenon. And not always can we do it securely and with ease. But we are coming to believe that a power greater than ourselves is at hand and will guarantee us all the strength we'll ever need. Knowing that action is always possible, that passive acceptance of any condition need never be necessary are unconditional gifts of living the Twelve Step program.

Our path forward is as certain as our commitment to it, our belief in the strength of the program, and our faith that all is well even when times are troubled. No one ever promised that our new way of life would be always easy. But we have been promised that we'll arrive at our proper destination if we do the footwork and let God do the navigating.

Success is at hand. I will apply what I'm learning, and I'll meet it.

Children awaken your own sense of self when you see
them hurting, struggling, testing; when you watch
their eyes and listen to their hearts. Children are gifts,
if we accept them.

—Kathleen Tierney Crilly

Children look to us and their world with fresh eyes, uncynical attitudes, open hearts. They react spontaneously to the events in their lives; what they feel is who they are.

Close observation of children can help us. See how complex we have made our lives! Their simple honesty can serve us well. To look at the world, once again, with wonder, is a by-product offered us when we live the principles of this program.

So many gifts await us when we accept the program and its principles. We dispense with the baggage of the past. We learn to live this day only. And we come to believe that there is a power greater than ourselves that has us and everything in our lives under control. Children instinctively trust those who take care of them. We can learn to trust, once again, when we apply the Steps of this program to our lives.

I will look to this day with wonder and trust. Everything is okay.
I am in the care of a power greater than myself.

. . . words are more powerful than perhaps anyone suspects, and once deeply engraved in a child's mind, they are not easily eradicated.

—May Sarton

How burdened we became, as little girls, with the labels applied by parents, teachers, even school chums. We believe about ourselves what others teach us to believe. The messages aren't always overt. But even the very subtle ones are etched in our minds, and they remind us of our "shortcomings" long into adulthood.

Try as we might to forget the criticisms, the names, they linger in our memories and influence our self-perceptions as adults. The intervening years have done little to erase whatever emotional scars we acquired as children.

Our partnership with God will help us understand that we are spiritual beings with a wonderful purpose in this life. And we are as lovely, as capable, as successful as we perceive ourselves to be. Our own thoughts and words, our own labels can become as powerful as those of our youth. It takes practice to believe in ourselves. But we can break the past's hold on us.

My higher power will help me know the real me. I am all that I ever needed to be; I am special, and I will come to believe that.

*The universal human yearning [is] for something
permanent, enduring, without shadow of change.*
—Willa Cather

The specter of change builds dread in most of us. We
fear the effects on our personal lives. We lack faith that the
impending change will benefit us. Only time can assure us
of that. And it will, just as every change we've survived up
to now has done.

Changes are gifts, really. They come as hallmarks to our
present attainments. They signify successful growth. And
they announce our readiness for more growth. How we
struggle to understand this, and how quickly we forget it
once we have adapted to the change. The struggle is then
repeated the next time change visits us.

We long for permanence, believing it guarantees security,
not realizing the only real security available to us comes with
our trust in God, from whom all change comes as a blessing
on the growth we've attained. If we were to experience total
lack of change, we'd find death. Life is challenge, continued
change, always endurable and growth-enhancing. We can
reflect on what's gone before, and trust that which faces
us now.

Change means I am progressing, on course.

Love has the quality of informing almost everything—
even one's work.

—Sylvia Ashton-Warner

We are changed through loving and being loved. Our attitudes are profoundly and positively affected by the presence of love in our lives. Each time we offer a loving response to a friend, co-worker, even a stranger, we powerfully influence the dynamics of the interaction between us.

Every response we make to someone changes us while it informs them. When we treat others with disdain, we invite the same. When we express only criticism of others, our self-assessment is equally negative. The beauty of a loving posture is that it calls forth love in response. The more love we give away, the more we receive.

Any task before us is lessened when we carry love in our hearts. Love is more powerful than fear. Love helps to open the channel to God, assuring us of the strength, the understanding, the patience needed to complete any assignment confronting us.

I am loved, unconditionally, by God. And I will experience the reality of that love the more I give it away. Love wants to change me—and it can.

My life has been a tapestry of rich and royal hue,
An everlasting vision of the ever-changing view.
                                        —*Carole King*

Every event of our lives is contributing a rich thread to our personal tapestry. Each of us is weaving one unique to ourselves, but all of our tapestries are complementary. We need others' rich designs in order to create our own.

We seldom have the foresight to understand the worth, the ultimate value of a particular circumstance at its beginning. But hindsight offers us clarity. It's good to reflect on the many circumstances that failed to thrill us; in all cases we can now see why we needed them. As our trust in God and the goodness of all experiences grow, we'll more quickly respond with gladness when situations are fresh. No experience is meant for harm. We are coming to understand that, even though on occasion we forget.

Practicing gratitude will help us more fully appreciate what has been offered us. Being grateful influences our attitude; it softens our harsh exterior and takes the threat out of most new situations.

If I greet the day, glad to be alive, I will be gladdened by all the experiences in store for me. Each is making a necessary contribution to my wholeness.

Problems have only the size and the power that you give them.

—*S. H.*

We will not be free from all difficulties today, or during any period of our lives. But we have the personal power to eliminate the threat, the sting of any challenge. But it's our vision of circumstances that gives them their interpretation.

At this moment, we are defining our experience. We are labeling events good or bad, valuable or meaningless. And our growth, particularly this day, is greatly influenced by the value judgments we attach to our experiences.

As we grow stronger emotionally and spiritually, we learn that all difficulties are truly opportunities for exceptional growth and increased awareness of the truth of existence. All experiences can be taken in stride if we are trustful of their intended blessing.

We are sharing this life, every moment of it, with a power greater than ourselves. We need not worry about any circumstance. Always we are watched over. We never need struggle alone.

We can let go of our problems. It's ourselves and the attitude we have cultivated that make any situation a problem. We can turn it loose and therein discover the solution.

I will not make mountains out of the molehills of my life.

The most elusive knowledge of all is self-knowledge.
　　　　　　　　　　　　　—Mirra Komarovsky

Discovering who we are is an adventure, one that will thrill and sometimes trouble us and will frequently occupy our thoughtful reflections. We are growing and changing as a result of our commitment to the program. And it's that process of commitment that heightens our self-awareness.

We learn who we are by listening to others, by sensing their perceptions of us, by taking an honest, careful inventory of our own behavior. The inner conversations that haunt us while we're interacting with others are poignant guidelines to self-knowledge, self-definition. Just when we think we've figured out who we are and how to handle our flaws, a new challenge will enter our realm of experiences, shaking up all the understandings that have given us guidance heretofore.

It is not an easy task to discover who we really are. It's an even harder job to love and accept the woman we discover. But too many years went by while we avoided or denied or, worse yet, denounced the only person we knew how to be. The program offers us the way to learn about and love fully the person within. Nor will we find the way easy every day. But there's time enough to let the process ease our investigation.

I will be soft and deliberate today as I listen to myself and others.

Let your tears come. Let them water your soul.
—Eileen Mayhew

Letting down our guard, releasing the tension that keeps us taut, often invites our tears, tears that soften us, melt our resistance, reveal our vulnerability, which reminds us that we are only human. So often we need reminding that we are only human.

Perfectionism may be our bane, as it is for so many of us in this program. We've learned to push, push harder, and even harder yet, not only ourselves but those around us. We must be better, we think, and we tighten our hold on life. The program can teach us to loosen our grip, if we'll let it. The magic is that when we loosen our grip on this day, this activity, this person, we get carried gently along and find that which we struggled to control happening smoothly and naturally. Life is a series of ironies.

We should not hide from our tears. We can trust their need to be present. Perhaps they need to be present for someone else, as well as ourselves. Tears encourage compassion; maybe our assignment in life, today, is to help someone else experience compassion.

My tears will heal. And the wounded are everywhere.

Intuition is a spiritual faculty and does not explain,
but simply points the way.
—Florence Scovel Shinn

Should we make this move? Should we change jobs? Should
we talk to others about our feelings? We are seldom short on
prayers when we're filled with fear and indecision. We are,
however, short on answers. Our worries block them out.

No prayer ever goes unanswered. Of this we can be certain. On the other hand, the answer may not be what we'd
hoped for. In fact, we may not recognize it as the answer
because we are expecting something quite different. It takes a
willingness on our part to be free of our preconceptions—free
to accept whatever answers are offered.

Our answers come unexpectedly, a chance meeting on
the street, a passage in a book or newspaper, a nagging feeling within. God speaks to each of us throughout the day.
Our prayers are answered, our problems find solutions, our
worries are eased, if we but attune ourselves to the messages. They are all around.

I will be attentive to all the signs from God today. Whatever
answer I seek is finding its way to me.

It's a simple formula; do your best and somebody might like it.

—Dorothy Baker

We're never guaranteed success by others' standards. However, if we do our best according to the standards we think God has in mind, we'll be successful. And from God we'll always receive unconditional love and acceptance.

In the past many of us were haunted by fears that our best wasn't good enough. And not infrequently those fears hindered our performance, thus validating our fears. We can slip back into those immobilizing fears if we don't attend, with vigilance, to the program and its suggestions.

Our higher power will help us do whatever task lies before us. And no task will be ours except those for which we've been readied. Our job is simply to go forth, taking God as our partner, and set about completing the task. We will not falter if we remember where our strength rests, where the guidance lies.

Self-esteem is one of the by-products of a job done with God's help. An additional by-product is that we learn more quickly to rely on God's direction and strength the next time, thus reducing the time we give to fear.

I can be successful today, in every endeavor, if I let God manage my moves.

For to be a woman is to have interests and duties, raying out in all directions from the central mother-core, like spokes from the hub of a wheel.
    —Anne Morrow Lindbergh

It is sometimes easy to get overwhelmed by our duties, forgetting that our interests fit the scheme of our lives. They are inspired by our lives and flow from them. Our interests round us out; they beckon us to become our better selves.

Our duties have their places as well. In our careers, with our families and friends, we have responsibilities. People need to be able to count on us for our part in completing their particular scheme for life.

Finding the right balance between our duties and our interests takes daily attention. It is perhaps our greatest struggle. Feeling duty-bound is common among women; putting a low value on our interests is a familiar trick we play on ourselves.

We need reminding that our interests will cull out our better, inner selves. We must stretch to become all we are meant to be. Our interests entice us to live up to God's expectations.

Each day I need to pay heed to interests as well as duties. I will let no day go by without heeding an interest.

Love and the hope of it are not things one can learn; they are a part of life's heritage.

—Maria Montessori

Love is a gift we've been given by our Creator. The fact of our existence guarantees that we deserve it. As our recognition of this grows, so does our self-love and our ability to love others.

High self-esteem, stable self-worth were not our legacies before finding this program. We sought both through means which led nowhere. These Steps and our present relationships are providing the substance and direction needed in our lives to discover our worthiness.

Had we understood that we were loved, in all the years of our youth, perhaps we'd not have struggled so in the pain of alienation. We were always at the right hand of God, never apart, loved and watched over. But we didn't recognize the signs. The signs are everywhere present now. Each Step is a constant reminder. Every human contact is a message from God. Any desire we are eager to make manifest is a beckoning from God for growth.

I will look for the signs of my benefactor today. They're present everywhere.

It is the calm after the storm. I feel a rainbow where there once were clouds, and while my Spirit dances in gratitude, my mind speculates on the next disaster. Duality.

—Mary Casey

Our growth as women is contingent on our ability to flow with the dualities, the contradictions inherent in one's lifetime, not only to flow with them but to capitalize on them.

We are not offered a painless existence, but we are offered opportunities for gathering perspective from the painful moments. And our perspectives are cushioned by the principles of the program. The rough edges of life, the storms that whip our very being, are gifts in disguise. We see life anew, when the storm has subsided.

We can enjoy the calm, if that surrounds us today. We deserve the resting periods. They give us a chance to contemplate and make fully our own that which the recent storm brought so forcefully to our attention. We are powerless over the storm's onslaught. But we can gain from it and be assured that the storm gives all the meaning there is in the calm.

I will be glad today for the clouds or the rainbows. Both are meant for my good. And without both, neither has meaning.

Beginnings are apt to be shadowy.
—Rachel Carson

When we embark on a new career, open an unfamiliar door, begin a loving relationship, we can seldom see nor can we even anticipate where the experience may take us. At best we can see only what this day brings. We can trust with certainty that we will be safely led through the "shadows."

To make gains in this life we must venture forth to new places, contact new people, chance new experiences. Even though we may be fearful of the new, we must go forward. It's comforting to remember that we never take any step alone. It is our destiny to experience many new beginnings. And a dimension of the growth process is to develop trust that each of these experiences will in time comfort us and offer us the knowledge our inner self awaits. Without the new beginnings we are unable to fulfill the purpose for which we've been created.

No new beginning is more than we can handle. Every new beginning is needed by our developing selves, and we are ready for whatever comes.

I will look to my new beginnings gladly. They are special to the growth I am now ready for.

Perhaps this very instant is your time . . .
—Louise Bogan

The only lessons that matter for our lives at this time will come to us today. Just as what we needed and were ready for yesterday came yesterday, tomorrow ensures more of the same. Concerning ourselves with any other moment but the present prevents us from responding when "the teacher appears."

In years gone by, we perhaps hung on to yesterday's problems. We may still struggle to hang on to them. Or perhaps we try to see too far ahead. But we are learning that there is a right time for all growth. A right time for all experiences. And the right time may not fit our timetable. What doesn't come our way today, will come when the time is right. Each day we are granted just what is needed. We need not worry about the future. It will offer us whatever rightly comes next, but it can't do so until we have experienced these 24 hours before us.

There is wonder and joy awaiting me, each day. The growth I experience is just what is needed at this time. I am a student, and the teacher will appear.

Of course fortune has its part in human affairs, but conduct is really much more important.
—Jeanne Detourbey

Behaving the way we honestly and sincerely believe God wants us to behave eliminates our confusion. When we contribute in a loving manner to the circumstances involving us, we carry God's message; and that's all that's expected of us in this life.

This recovery program has involved us in the affairs of many other people. We are needed to listen, to guide, to sponsor, to suggest. Each time we have an opportunity to make an impact on another person, it's to our benefit, and hers too, to let God direct our conduct.

Too often God's message is missed due to our selfish concerns, but it's never too late to begin listening for it. God is forever at hand, awaiting our recognition. We can be mindful that the ease of our lives is directly proportional to the recognition we offer.

Right conduct is never a mystery to us. We may not always choose to do it, but we never fail to know what should be done.

I will trust my conscience to be my guide every moment.

. . . we will be victorious if we have not forgotten how to learn.

—Rosa Luxemburg

For most of us the struggle was long, painful and lonely to the place where we are now. But survive we have, and survive we will. The times we thought we could go no further are only dimly recalled. The experiences we were certain would destroy us fit ever so neatly into our book of memories.

We have survived, and the program is offering us the means for continued survival. Step by Step we are learning to handle our problems, build relationships based on honesty, and choose responsible behavior. We are promised serenity if we follow the Steps.

Gratitude for our survival is best expressed by working the program, setting an example for others, helping those women who haven't yet attained victory. We must give away what we have learned to make way for our own new growth. There are many victories in our future if we keep pressing forward, opening new doors, and trusting in the process of the program and its promises.

I am still willing to learn or I wouldn't be here, now. There are victories in my future. I will look for a victory today. It's certain to accompany responsible action on my part.

As in the physical world, so in the spiritual world, pain does not "last forever."
—Katherine Mansfield

Each of us struggles with pain and its repercussions; some of us more than others. At times pain seems unending. Sometimes we hang on to the pain in our lives, maybe because we fear even more what's on the other side. The unknown so easily controls us. Right at this moment, each of us can look back on other painful times and feel thankful for what they taught us. The puzzle pieces take on a deeper meaning when we enjoy the gift of perspective. The pain at this moment fits, too, in the bigger picture of our lives. And it will pass. It is passing.

The wisdom of the past tells us that pain enriches us, prepares us to better serve others. We come to know who we are and the specialness of our gifts through the despair that at times encumbers us. An old, wise saying, is, "We are never given more than we can handle."

My pain today is bringing me closer to the woman I'm meant to be. With each breath I'll remember that.

On any journey, we must find out where we are before we can plan the first step.
—Kathy Boevink

Our lives in all aspects are a journey toward a destination, one fitting to our purpose, our special gifts, our particular needs as women. Each day contributes to our journey, carrying us closer to our destination. However, we often take a circuitous route. We get stranded or waylaid by our selfish desires, by the intrusion of our controlling ego.

We can reflect on the progress we've made toward our destination, the steps we've taken that have unknowingly contributed to our journey. Our easiest steps have been the ones we took in partnership with God. It's in God's mind that our path is well marked.

We are just where we need to be today. The experiences that we meet are like points on the map of our journey. Some of them are rest stops. Others resemble high-speed straightaways. The journey to our destination is not always smooth, but the more we let God sit in the driver's seat, the easier will be our ride.

I will plan my journey today with God's help, and my ride will be smooth.

Because society would rather we always wore a pretty face, women have been trained to cut off anger.
—Nancy Friday

Anger is an emotion. Not a bad one, nor a good one; it simply exists when particular conditions in our lives are not met as we'd hoped.

We can get free of our anger if we choose to take action appropriate to it. Anger can be a healthy prompter of action. But when no action is taken, anger turns inward, negatively influencing our perceptions of all experiences, all human interaction.

We need to befriend all of our emotions. We need to trust that they all can serve us when we befriend them, learn from them, act in healthy concert with them. Our emotions reveal the many faces of our soul. And all are valid, deserving respect and acceptance. They are all representative of the inner self.

Because we are less at home with anger, it becomes more powerful. When we deny it, it doesn't disappear. It surfaces in unrelated circumstances, complicating our lives in unnecessary ways. We can learn to enjoy our anger by celebrating the positive action it prompts. We can cherish the growth that accompanies it, when we take the steps we need to.

It's okay for me to be angry today. It's growthful, if I use it for good.

Life has got to be lived—that's all there is to it. At 70 I would say the advantage is that you take life more calmly. You know that, "This, too, shall pass!"
—Eleanor Roosevelt

Wisdom comes with age, but also with maturity. It is knowing that all is well in the midst of a storm. And as our faith grows, as we trust more that there is a power greater than ourselves which will see us through, we can relax, secure that a better time awaits us.

We will come to understand the part a difficult circumstance has played in our lives. Hindsight makes so much clear. The broken marriage, the lost job, the loneliness have all contributed to who we are becoming. The joy of the wisdom we are acquiring is that hindsight comes more quickly. We can, on occasion, begin to accept a difficult situation's contribution to our wholeness while caught in the turmoil.

How far we have come! So seldom do we stay caught, really trapped, in the fear of misunderstanding. Life must teach us all we need to know. We can make the way easier by stretching our trust—by knowing fully that the pain of the present will open the way to the serenity of the future.

I know that this too shall pass.

*Fantasies are more than substitutes for unpleasant
reality; they are also dress rehearsals, plans. All acts
performed in the world begin in the imagination.*
—Barbara Grizzuti Harrison

Our minds mold who we become. Our thoughts not only
contribute to our achievements, they determine the posture
of our lives. How very powerful they are. Fortunately, we
have the power to think the thoughts we choose, which
means our lives will unfold much as we expect.

The seeds we plant in our minds indicate the directions
we'll explore in our development. And we won't explore
areas we've never given attention to in our reflective moments. We must dare to dream extravagant, improbable
dreams if we intend to find a new direction, and the steps
necessary to it.

We will not achieve, we will not master that which goes
unplanned in our dream world. We imagine first, and then
we conceive the execution of a plan. Our minds prepare us
for success. They can also prepare us for failure if we let our
thoughts become negative.

---

*I can succeed with my fondest hopes. But I must believe in my
potential for success. I will ponder the positive today.*

My Declaration of Self-Esteem:

I am me. In all the world there is no one else exactly like me. There are persons who have some parts like me, but no one adds up exactly like me. Therefore, everything that comes out of me is authentically mine because I alone chose it.

—Virginia Satir

Feeling special, feeling worthy and unique in the contribution we make to our surroundings is perhaps not a very familiar feeling to many of us in this recovery program. We may have recognized our differences from others, but not in a positive way. We may well have figured that to be our problem. "If only I were more like her . . ." To celebrate our specialness, the unique contribution we make to every situation we experience, is one of the gifts of recovery.

It's spiritually moving to realize the truth of our authenticity. To realize that no other choice will ever be just like our choice—to realize that no other contribution will be just like our contribution. Our gift to life is ourselves. Life's gift to us is the opportunity to realize our value.

Today, I will be aware of my gifts, I will offer them and receive them thankfully.

Pain is inevitable. Suffering is optional.
—Kathleen Casey Theisen

How awesome is our power, personally, to choose our attitudes and our responses to any situation, to every situation. We will feel only how we choose to feel, no matter the circumstance. Happiness is as free an option as sorrow.

Perceiving our challenges as opportunities for positive growth rather than stumbling blocks in our path to success is a choice readily available. What is inevitable—a matter over which we have no choice—is that difficult times, painful experiences will visit us. We can, however, greet them like welcome guests, celebrating their blessings on us and the personal growth they inspire.

No circumstance demands suffering. Every circumstance has a silver lining. In one instance you may choose to feel self-pity; in the next, gladness.

We do not always feel confident about our choices, even when we accept the responsibility for making them. How lucky for us that the program offers a solution! Prayer and meditation, guidance from our higher power, can help us make the right choice every time.

I will relish my freedom to choose, to feel, to act. I and only I can take it away.

*Zeal is the faculty igniting the other mind powers into
the full flame of activity.*

—*Sylvia Stitt Edwards*

When enthusiasm is absent in our lives, no activity appears inviting. In fact, most situations foster fear. We're ever so familiar with fear. The program we're committed to relieves us of all fear, when we work it. And it offers us the enthusiasm that will guarantee positive outcomes for our efforts, when we look to our higher power for the right attitude.

An open, trusting, sincere relationship with our higher power equals enthusiasm about life. But that relationship takes work on our part. When we've done our homework we discover that no lesson will baffle us. Prayer and meditation make all things understandable and guarantee that we will "pass the course" on life.

I will begin this day, and every day, looking to God for the gift of zeal to live fully every moment, to give fully what I have to give, and to glory fully in all that I receive. My attitude of gratitude will increase my happiness manyfold. I will look to this day with zeal.

Rigidity is prevented most of the time as love and compassion mesh us into tolerant human beings.
—Kaethe S. Crawford

Looking outward with love, offering it freely to our friends and family, makes fluid, flowing, and fertile our existence. Each expression of love engenders more love, keeping tender our ties to one another, encouraging more ties.

The more flexible our lives, the more easily we'll be attracted to an unexpected opportunity. And flexibility is fostered by a loving posture. As we approach the world, so it greets us. We are not mere recipients of life's trials and tribulations. We find what our eyes are wanting to see. When our focus is rigid and narrow, so are our opportunities.

The Steps are leading us to be freer with our love, more tolerant in our expectations. The level of our compassion, fully felt and fully expressed, is the measure of our emotional health. Rigid attitudes, rigid behavior, rigid expectations of others recede as the level of our emotional health rises. Our approach to life changes and so do the results we meet.

I will love others. It's my only assignment in life, and it guarantees the security I crave.

I think happiness is like the effect on an audience (when acting), if you think of it all the time you will not get it, you must get lost in the part, lost in your purposes and let the effect be the criterion of your success.

—Joanna Field

Happiness is a gift that accompanies every instance of our lives if we approach each situation with gratitude, knowing that what's offered to us is special to our particular needs. The experiences we meet day to day are honing our Spirit, tempering our hard edges. For these we should offer gratitude.

Our well-being is the gift. Deciding what will make us happy, in fact, what we must have to be happy, prevents us from grasping the unexpected pleasure of the "chance" events of the moment. When we intently look for what we think we need, we may well be blind to more beneficial opportunities God has chosen for us.

Our self-centeredness hinders every breath we take. It prejudices every encounter. It stifles our creative potential. And most of all, it blocks any chance for a spontaneous reaction to the moment. Spontaneity is the breeding ground for creative living. And happiness is the by-product.

Happiness is my decision, every moment.

Do not compare yourself with others, for you are a unique and wonderful creation. Make your own beautiful footprints in the snow.

—Barbara Kimball

Comparisons we make of ourselves to other women do destruction far greater than our conscious minds are aware of. Positioning ourselves or her on the "beloved pedestal" prevents the equality of sisterhood that offers each woman the freedom to be solely herself.

Comparisons in which we are the losers darken the moment, cut us off from the actual rhythms of that moment. The consequences can be grave. Within any moment might be the opportunity we've awaited, the opportunity to achieve a particular dream. We must not miss our opportunities.

Each life is symbolized by a particular set of footprints in the snow. How wonderful and how freeing to know that we each offer something uniquely our own. We need never compete to be noticed. Each of us is guaranteed recognition for what we contribute, because it is offered by us alone.

Envy eats at us; it interferes with all of our interactions. It possesses all of our thoughts, caging us, denying us the freedom to achieve that can be ours.

I will look with love on my sisters. I will free them and myself to be all we are capable of becoming.

Experience is a good teacher, but she sends in terrific bills.

—Minna Antrim

It is not by chance but by design that the sorrows we experience throughout our lives are countered by equal servings of joy. One offsets the other. And we are strengthened by their combination.

Our longing for only life's joys is human—also folly. Joy would become insipid if it were our steady diet. Joyful times serve us well as respites from the trying situations that push our growth and development as women.

Laughter softens the cutting edges of the lessons we seek or are cornered by. It offers perspective when the outlook is bleak. And for those of us who are recovering, wallowing in the bleaker times used to be acceptable behavior. But no more. The reality is that each day will present both occasions for anguish and ones inviting easy laughter. Both are valuable. Neither should dominate.

Joy and sorrow are analogous to the ebb and flow of the ocean tide. They are natural rhythms. And we are mellowed by their presence when we accept them as necessary to our very existence.

Any pain today guarantees an equal amount of pleasure, if I willingly accept them both.

*Continuous effort—not strength or intelligence—is
the key to unlocking our potential.*

—Liane Cordes

Perseverance may well be our greatest asset. As we forge
ahead on a project, it loses its power over us. Our confidence and abilities grow in concert with our progress on
the project, preparing us to tackle the next one too.

We have something special, uniquely our own to offer in
this life. And we also have the potential to offer it successfully. However, we don't always realize our potential.
Many of us stifled our development with fears of failure,
low self-worth, assumed inadequacies. The past need plague
us no longer.

Help is readily available for us to discover our capacities
for success. Abilities stand ready to be tapped, goals and
projects await our recognition. Any commitment we make
to a task that draws our interest will be reinforced by God's
commitment to our efforts. We have a partner. Our efforts
are always doubled when we make them—truly make them.

*I will not back away from a project today. I will persevere and
find completion. I'll feel completed.*

. . . as awareness increases, the need for personal secrecy almost proportionately decreases.
—Charlotte Painter

We hang on to secrets when we're unsure of ourselves and the role we're asked to play—secrets about our inner thoughts, our dreams and aspirations, our feared inadequacies.

Because we strive for perfection, assume it's achievable, and settle for no less in all our activities, we are haunted by our secret fears of not measuring up. The more committed we become to this program, the greater is our understanding of the fallacy of this way of thinking. And as our awareness increases, the more accepting we become of our human frailty, and the less need we have to cover it up. Our mental health is measurable by the openness we offer to the world. Secrets belie good health and heighten the barriers to it.

The program's Fourth and Fifth Steps are the antidotes to being stuck in an unhealthy state of mind. They push us to let go of our secrets, freeing us from the power they wield. Practicing the principles of the program offers the remedy we need for the happiness we deserve.

I will share a secret today and be free of its power over my life.

*All of the fantasies in your life will never match those
I once tried to attain. Now older, it's more important
reaching the more realistic goals, and having them
come true.*

—Deidra Sarault

Simply knowing that we are important creatures of the
universe offers too little security for most of us. We do have
a role to play; our talents are special and unique to each
of us. Using them in a well-planned manner will benefit
us emotionally and spiritually. Others will profit from our
talents as well.

Fantasies have their place in our lives, too. They often
tempt us to even greater heights. We can't always collar our
fantasies, but we can take the necessary steps to realize the
goals that our fantasies have birthed.

Recovery is freeing us to achieve those goals we'd only
dreamed of or perhaps feared tackling in the past. The defects that we hid behind before are, with patience, giving
way to positive behavior. We can accomplish our heart's
pure desires. We need not let the fear of failure trap us again
as it did so many of us for so long.

---

*I will set my sights high and trust the program to coach my
progress. My goals are attainable. It only takes one small step at
a time.*

When you send out real love, real love will return to you.

—Florence Scovel Shinn

Real love is selfless love. It expects nothing in return. It is not conditional. It doesn't keep score. It is too seldom given. Many of us came into the program hurting, feeling unloved, looking desperately for love, unable to love selflessly. But we are learning.

We are climbing the same mountain, all of us. Our particular paths will cross the paths of many others before reaching the top, where we will find full enlightenment. And any path we cross has a special contribution to make to our own progress. We can be grateful for all intersecting paths, no matter how adverse they seem at the time. We can offer all our fellow travelers real love, and our own trip will benefit manyfold.

We need not be ashamed of our desire for love. Nor need we feel shame that we've bargained for it. But we do need to understand that the kind of love we seek can only be gained when we quit searching for it and simply offer it to all the people in our midst.

I will look into the hearts of all the people I encounter today and offer them love. I'll receive that which I give.

"If onlys" are lonely

—*Morgan Jennings*

The circumstances of our lives seldom live up to our expectations or desires. However, in each circumstance we are offered an opportunity for growth or change, a chance for greater understanding of life's heights and pitfalls. Each time we choose to lament what isn't, we close the door on the invitation to a better existence.

We simply don't know just what's best for us. Our vision is limited. Less so today than yesterday, but limited still. The experiences we are offered will fail to satisfy our expectations because we expect so much less than God has planned for us in the days ahead.

We get what we need, in the way of relationships, adventures, joys and sorrows, today and every day. Celebrating what we get and knowing there is good in it eases whatever trial we are undergoing. We are cared for, right now. We need not lament what we think we need. We do have what we need. We will always get what we need, when we need it.

I will breathe deeply and relax. At this moment my every need is being attended to. My life is unfolding exactly as it should.

Change occurs when one becomes what she is, not when she tries to become what she is not.
—Ruth P. Freedman

Learning self-acceptance, and then loving the selves we are, present perhaps our two biggest hurdles to the attainment of emotional and spiritual health. Fortunately, they are not insurmountable hurdles. The program offers ready assistance.

Women everywhere are making great strides in self-love and self-acceptance. We are learning self-love. And we are changing. The support we can give our sisters, and the support we receive, multiplies many times the healthy energy created—healthy energy that touches us all.

Emotional and spiritual health are gifts promised by the program, when we work it. We must move beyond our perfectionism and relish our humanness, and the Steps are the way. We must learn humility and develop faith, and the Steps are the way. Learning to love all our parts, the qualities we like and the traits that discouragingly hang on, offers a new freedom. A freedom that invites change. A freedom that safeguards the emotional and spiritual well-being that we strive for.

Confidence will come with my healthy self-acceptance.

We are all held in place by the pressure of the crowd around us. We must all lean upon others. Let us see that we lean gracefully and freely and acknowledge their support.

—Margaret Collier Graham

We did not come into this world alone. And our voyage through this life is in concert with many others: some who directly aid us, while others seem to hinder our paths. We don't have full knowledge, however. We can't determine the many ways we are being helped to take the right steps, even by those who block our way for the moment.

Likewise, our presence is helping to pave the way for both the friends and the strangers we will encounter today, at work, on the street, at the meeting perhaps. We have all been charged, in this life, with a similar responsibility—to help one another fulfill our destinies. Our impatience with one another, our wavering love and acceptance of each other, at times our disavowal of our brothers and sisters comes because we fail to understand the necessary part we each play in the drama of one another's life.

In my personal drama, I am sharing the stage with everyone else I encounter today. I need a supporting cast. And I need applause. I will give it freely today.

Limited expectations yield only limited results.
—*Susan Laurson Willig*

Schoolchildren perform according to the expectations their teachers have of them. Likewise, what we women achieve depends greatly on what we believe about ourselves, and too many of us have too little belief in ourselves. Perhaps we grew up in a negative household or had a nonsupportive marriage. But we contributed, too, in our negative self-assessment. The good news is that it no longer needs to control us.

We can boost our own performance by lifting our own expectations, even in the absence of support from others. It may not be easy, but each of us is capable of changing a negative self-image to a positive one. It takes commitment to the program, a serious relationship with our higher power, and the development of positive, healthy relationships with others.

It's true, we can't control other people in our lives. And we can't absolutely control the outcome of any particular situation. But we can control our own attitudes. Interestingly, when we've begun seeing ourselves as competent and capable, instead of inadequate, we find that other people and other situations become more to our liking, too.

———

I will be fair with myself. I can do what I need to do wherever I am today. Only I can hold myself down.

The idea of God is different in every person. The joy of my recovery was to find God within me.
—*Angela L. Wozniak*

The program promises peace. Day by day, step by step, we move closer to it. Each time we clearly are touched by someone else, and each time we touch another, carries us closer to a realization of God's presence, in others, in ourselves, in all experiences. The search for God is over, just as soon as we realize the Spirit is as close as our thoughts, our breath.

Coming to believe in a greater power brings such relief to us in our daily struggles. And on occasion we still fight for control to be all-powerful ourselves, only to realize that the barriers we confront are of our own making. We are on easy street, just as soon as we choose to let God be our guide in all decisions, large and small.

The program's greatest gift to us is relief from anxiety, the anxiety that so often turned us to booze, or pills, or candy. Relief is felt every time we let go of the problem that's entrapped us and wait for the comfort and guidance God guarantees.

God's help is mine just as quickly as I fully avail myself of it. I will let go of today's problems.

Faith is like the air in a balloon. If you've got it you're filled. If you don't, you're empty.

—Peggy Cahn

Being faith-filled takes effort, not unlike becoming a good writer, tennis player, or pianist. Faith grows within our hearts, but we must devote time to foster this growth. Daily discussions with God are required, frequent quiet times to hear God's messages to us—just as practice on the court hitting balls or sitting for extended periods at the typewriter or a piano are necessary to attain these other goals.

Life's difficulties are eased when we have faith. The most frightening situation, a job interview, an evaluation with our boss, a showdown with a friend, can be handled confidently when we let our faith work for us. But, we must first work for it, work to attain it and work to keep it. Like any skill, it gets rusty with lack of use.

I will make sure to add to my reserves today. We never know when we may need to let our faith direct our every action. I will make a friend of my higher power, and that partnership will carry me over any troubled time.

Doubt indulged soon becomes doubt realized.
—*Frances Ridley Havergal*

We are powerless over our addictions, whether liquor, pills, people, food. We are powerless over the outcome of all events involving us. And we are powerless over the lives of our friends and family members. We are not powerless, however, over our own attitudes, our own behavior, our own self-image, our own determination, our own commitment to life and this simple program.

Power aplenty we have, but we must exercise it in order to understand its breadth. We'll find all the day's activities, interactions, plans decidedly more exciting when we exercise control over our responses. We don't have to feel or respond except in the way that pleases us. We have total control and we'll find this realization exhilarating.

Our recovery is strengthened each time we determine the proper behavior, choose an action that feels right, take responsibility where it is clearly ours to take. The benefits will startle us and bring us joy.

I will take charge of my life today.

And it isn't the thing you do, dear,
It's the thing you leave undone
Which gives you a bit of a heartache
At the setting of the sun.
—*Margaret Sangster*

A quality we all share, a very human quality, is to expect perfection from ourselves, to expect the impossible in all tasks done. We must rejoice for the good we do. Each time we pat ourselves on the back for a job well done, our confidence grows a little bit more. Recovery is best measured by our emotional and spiritual health, expressed in our apparent confidence and trust in "the process."

We need to recognize and celebrate our strong points, and they'll gain even more strength. Likewise, we need to practice prayer and listening to guidance first to develop our ties to God, but more importantly to be able to acknowledge when help is at hand. We can do all we need to do with God's help.

Having goals but keeping them realistic, for the day or the year, is a sign of emotional health. Not dwelling on those that can't be accomplished, at the moment, is another sign. A change of attitude is all most of us need to move from where we are to a better place emotionally.

There's never a better time than right now for rejoicing over what I've done.

The old woman I shall become will be quite different from the woman I am now. Another I is beginning . . .
—George Sand

Change is constant. And we are always becoming. Each chance, each feeling, each responsibility we commit ourselves to adds to the richness of our womanhood. We are not yesterday's woman, today. Our new awarenesses have brought us beyond her. And we can't go back without knowing, somehow, that she no longer meets the needs of today.

We can look forward to our changes, to the older woman we are becoming. She will have the wisdom that we still lack. She will have learned to live and let live. She will have acquired, through years of experiences, a perspective that lends sanity to all situations.

The lessons we are learning today, the pain that overwhelms us now and again, are nurturing the developing woman within each of us. If only we could accept the lessons and master them. If only we could trust the gift of change that accompanies the pain.

I am becoming. And with the becoming, comes peace. I can sense it today. I know where I was yesterday.

Sometimes, sisters have the same journey in their hearts. One may help the other or betray her. Will they cross over? Will the ship sail without them?
—Louise Bernikow

Other women share our struggle. When we treat our women friends as sisters and fellow pilgrims, we find great joy in our mutual help. We pray for the wisdom to let go our feelings of insecurity and rivalry with other women.

Rivalry is not good for us. It leads us to forget our own unique qualities. We each are the best person in the world at one thing: being ourselves. When we compete, we need to retain a balanced perspective and to think well of ourselves whether we win or lose. We run the best race we can; therefore, let us not regard other women as rivals. They are our sisters, and they, too, are doing the best they can.

Today, I will pray for the serenity that will let me see when my sisters have the same journey in their hearts as I.

I want to feel myself part of things, of the great drift and swirl; not cut off, missing things, like being sent to bed early as a child.

—Joanna Field

Feeling apart from the action and always looking on; wanting attention, and yet afraid of being noticed; no doubt these are familiar memories to most of us. We may still struggle with our self-perception, but we can celebrate that we no longer drown our moods. Connecting with the people next to us, though difficult, is no longer impossible when we rely on the program.

There is a way to be a part of the action, a way that never fails. It takes only a small effort, really. We can simply look, with love, at someone nearby today and extend our hearts in honest attention. When we make someone else feel special, we'll become special too.

Recovery can help each of us move beyond the boundaries of our own ego. Trusting that our lives are in the loving care of God, however we understand God, relieves us of the need for self-centeredness. We can let go of ourselves now that God is in charge, and we'll discover that we have joined the action.

I will open my heart, and I'll be joined to all that's around me.

It is a long baptism into the seas of humankind, my daughter. Better immersion than to live untouched.
—Tillie Olsen

We have each had days when we preferred hiding under the covers, avoiding life at all costs. And in times gone by, we did just that, sometimes too frequently. What we didn't always know, and what we still forget on occasion, is that we have a ready and willing partner who will join us in every pursuit.

The more fully we commit ourselves to one another and to all our experience, the closer we will come to the very serenity we long for. Serenity accompanies our increasing understanding of life's many mysteries. It's easy to cheat ourselves out of the prizes any day offers us. Fear fosters inertia, leaving us separate, alone, even more afraid. But we have an appointment with life. And our appointment will bring us to the place of full understanding, the place where we'll be certain, forever after, that all is well. And that life is good.

Today's appointments are part of the bigger plan for my life. I will face them, enjoy them, and reap their rewards.

Each day provides its own gifts.
—Ruth P. Freedman

We are guaranteed experiences that are absolutely right for us today. We are progressing on schedule. Even when our personal hopes are unmet, we are given the necessary opportunities for achieving those goals that complement our unique destinies.

Today is full of special surprises, and we will be the recipient of the ones which are sent to help us grow—in all the ways necessary for our continued recovery. We might not consider every experience a gift at this time. But hindsight will offer the clarity lacking at the moment, just as it has done in many instances that have gone before.

We are only offered part of our personal drama each day. But we can trust our lives to have many scenes, many acts, points of climax, and a conclusion. Each of us tells a story with our lives, one different from all other stories and yet necessary to the telling of many other stories too. The days ahead will help us tell our story. Our interactions with others will influence our outcomes and theirs. We can trust the drama and give fully to our roles.

Every day is a gift exchange. I give, and I will receive.

*Promises that you make to yourself are often like the
Japanese plum tree—they bear no fruit.*
                                        —Frances Marion

The resolve to fulfill commitments we make to ourselves
and others may be lacking until we learn to rely on the wisdom and strength offered by our higher power—strength
that will make us confident in any situation; wisdom that
will ensure our right actions. What is difficult alone is always
eased in partnership.

We promise ourselves changed behavior, new habits,
perhaps, or a positive attitude. But then we proceed to focus
on our liabilities, giving them even more power, a greater
hold over us. We can practice our assets, and they'll foster
the promises we want to keep.

No longer need we shame ourselves about unfulfilled
promises. Whatever our desires, whatever our commitments, if for the good of others and ourselves, they will
come to fruition. We can ask for direction. We can ask for
resolve, and each worthy hope and unrealized promise will
become reality.

*My assets, when strengthened through use, pave the way for
God's help. Any promise can bear fruit when I make it in
partnership with God.*

I have found that sitting in a place where you have never sat before can be inspiring.
—Dodie Smith

Repeatedly, today and every day, we will be in new situations, new settings with old friends, and old settings and situations with new friends. Each instance is fresh, unlike all the times before. And inspiration can accompany each moment, if we but recognize how special it is.

"We will never pass this way again," so the song says, which heightens the meaning of each encounter, every experience. Acknowledging that something can be gained each step along the way invites inspiration.

Inspiration moves us to new heights. We will be called to step beyond our present boundaries. Maybe today. Whenever the inspiration catches our attention, we can trust its invitation; we are ready for the challenge it offers. We need not let our narrow, personal expectations of an experience, a new situation perhaps, prevent us from being open to all the dynamic possibilities it offers.

I must be willing to let my whole self be moved, inspired. I must be willing to let each moment I experience be the only moment getting my attention.

To do nothing is failure. To try, and in the trying you make some mistakes and then you make some positive changes as a result of those mistakes, is to learn and to grow and to blossom.

—Darlene Larson Jenks

Life is a process, one that is continuously changing. And with each change, we are offered unexpected opportunities for growth. Change is what fosters our development as women. It encourages us to risk new behavior and may even result in some mistakes. Fortunately, no mistakes can seriously hinder us. In fact, most mistakes give us an additional opportunity to learn.

Where we stand today is far removed from our position last year, or even last week. Each and every moment offers us new input that influences any decision from this moment forward. The process that we're participating in guarantees our growth as long as we remain conscious of our opportunities and willingly respond to them. We can be glad that the life process is, in fact, never static, always moving, always inviting us to participate fully.

I will have the courage to make a mistake today. It's a promise of growth.

The forgiving state of mind is a magnetic power for attracting good. No good thing can be withheld from the forgiving state of mind.

—Catherine Ponder

Forgiveness fosters humility, which invites gratitude. And gratitude blesses us; it makes manifest greater happiness. The more grateful we feel for all aspects of our lives, the greater will be our rewards. We don't recognize the goodness of our lives until we practice gratitude. And gratitude comes easiest when we're in a forgiving state of mind.

Forgiveness should be an ongoing process. Attention to it daily will ease our relationships with others and encourage greater self-love. First on our list for forgiveness should be ourselves. Daily, we heap recriminations upon ourselves. And our lack of self-love hinders our ability to love others, which in turn affects our treatment of them. We've come full circle—and forgiveness is in order. It can free us. It will change our perceptions of life's events, and it promises greater happiness.

The forgiving heart is magical. My whole life will undergo a dynamic change when I develop a forgiving heart.

Occupation is essential.

—*Virginia Woolf*

Having desires, setting goals, and achieving them are necessary to our fulfillment. There is purpose to our lives, even when we can't clearly see our direction, even when we doubt our abilities to contribute. Let us continue to respond to our opportunities.

Many of us experienced the clouds of inaction in earlier periods . . . waiting, waiting, waiting, hoping our circumstances would change, even praying they would, but taking no responsibility for changing what was in our power. Inaction caged us. Stripped of power, life held little or no meaning. However, we've been given another chance. The program has changed our lives. We have a reason for living, each day, even the days we feel hopeless and worthless.

Maybe we are without a goal at this time. Perhaps the guidance is not catching our attention. We can become quiet with ourselves and let our daydreams act as indicators. We have something essential to do, and we are being given all the chances we'll need to fulfill our purpose. We can trust in our worth, our necessity to others.

I will remember, the program came to me. I must have a part to play. I will look and listen for my opportunities today.

*If I am to be remembered, I hope it is for the honesty I
try to demonstrate, the patience I try to live by, and
the compassion I feel for others.*

—JoAnn Reed

Each of us hopes we are leaving a lasting, positive impression on those we befriend and maybe even those we
encounter by chance. Having others speak well of us provides the strokes that are often necessary to our "keeping
on" when difficulties surface. What we sometimes forget is
that we are responsible for whatever lasting impression we
leave. Our behavior does influence what another person
carries away from our mutual experience.

We may have left unfavorable impressions during our
using days. On occasion, we do yet. However, it's progress,
not perfection, we're after. And each day we begin anew,
with a clear slate and fresh opportunities to spread good
cheer, to treat others with love and respect, to face head-on
and with full honesty all situations drawing our attention
and participation.

*As I look forward to the hours ahead, I will remember that I
control my actions toward others. If I want to be remembered
fondly, I must treat each person so.*

*Across the fields I can see the radiance of your smile
and I know in my heart you are there. But the anguish
I am feeling makes the distance so very far to cross.*
　　　　　　　　　　　　　　　　　—Deidra Sarault

Looking down the hallway of our lives, we sense many uncomfortable corners. And they are there. But through the discomfort comes the ease of understanding. The security that we long for, we discover has been ours all along. All we needed to do was move into the corner—with trust.

As we stand before any problems, any new task, any unfamiliar environment, dread may overwhelm us. We stand there alone. But the choice available to us now and always is to invite the spirt of God to share the space we're in. In concert with God's Spirit, no problem or task can be greater than our combined abilities to handle it.

Our lives will be eased in direct proportion to our faith that God is there, caring for our every concern, putting before us the experiences we need to grow on. We can let go of our anguish, our doubts and fears. Eternal triumph is ours for the asking.

The smiling faces I encounter today—I will let them assure me that all is well.

A theme may seem to have been put aside, but it keeps returning—the same thing modulated, somewhat changed in form.

—Muriel Rukeyser

No struggle we have is really new. It's another shade of the struggle that plagued us last week or perhaps last year. And we'll stumble again and again until we learn to quit struggling. The trying situations at work, or the personality type that irritates us, will always exist. But when we've come to accept as good and growth-enhancing all situations and all persons, we'll sense the subtle absence of struggle. We'll realize that the person we couldn't tolerate has become a friend. The situation we couldn't handle is resolved, forever.

The lessons we need to learn keep presenting themselves, until we've finished the homework. If we sense a struggle today, we can look at it as an assignment, one that is meant for our growth. We can remember that our struggles represent our opportunities to grow. Fortunately, the program has given us a tutor. We have a willing teacher to help us. We need to move on, to be open to other assignments. No problem will be too much for us to handle.

I will enjoy my role as student today. I will be grateful for all opportunities to grow. They make possible my very special contribution in this life.

Happiness is a form of freedom, and of all people I should be the freest. I've earned this happiness and this freedom.
—Angela L. Wozniak

Life is a process, and we are progressing beautifully. We are no longer abusing our bodies and minds with drugs. We are taking special time, daily, to look for guidance. We are working the Steps of the program, better and better as the abstinent days add up. We are free from past behaviors. And we can be free from our negative attitudes too.

Making a decision to look for the good in our experiences and in our friends and acquaintances frees us from so much frustration. It ushers in happiness, not only for us but for the others we are treating agreeably. Happiness is a by-product of living the right kind of life.

We can take a moment today, each time an action is called for, to consider our response. The one that squares with our inner selves and feels good is the right one. Happiness will accompany it.

_____

Happiness is always within my power. My attitude is at the helm.

To have someone who brings out the colors of life and whose very presence offers tranquility and contentment enriches my being and makes me grateful for the opportunity to share.

—Kathleen Tierney Crilly

Loneliness and isolation are familiar states to most of us. We often protected our insecurities by hiding out, believing that we'd survive if others didn't know who we really were. But we discovered that our insecurities multiplied. The remedy is people—talking to people, exposing our insecurities to them, risking, risking, risking.

Sharing our mutual vulnerabilities helps us see how fully alike we are. Our most hated shortcoming is not unique, and that brings relief. It's so easy to feel utterly shamed in isolation. Hearing another woman say "I understand. I struggle with jealousy too," lifts the shame, the dread, the burden of silence. The program has taught us that secrets make us sick, and the longer we protect them, the greater are our struggles.

The program promises fulfillment, serenity, achievement when we willingly share our lives. Each day we can lighten our burdens and help another lighten hers, too.

I will be alert today to the needs of others. I will risk sharing. I will be a purveyor of tranquility.

Give to the world the best you have, and the best will come back to you.

—Madeline Bridge

We do reap, in some measure, at some time, what we sow. Our respect for others will result in kind. Our love expressed will return tenfold. The kindness we greet others with will ease their relations with us. We get from others what we give, if not at this time and place, at another. We can be certain that our best efforts toward others do not go unnoticed. And we can measure our due by what we give.

A major element of our recovery is the focus we place on our behavior, the seriousness with which we tackle our inventories. We can look at ourselves and how we reach out and act toward others; it is a far cry from where we were before entering this program. Most of us obsessed on "What he did to me," or "What she said." And then returned their actions in kind.

How thrilling is the knowledge that we can invite loving behavior by giving it! We have a great deal of control over the ebb and flow of our lives. In every instance we can control our behavior. Thus never should we be surprised about the conditions of our lives.

What goes around comes around. I will look for the opportunities to be kind and feel the results.

Destruction. Crashing realities exploding in imperfect landings. Ouch. It's my heart that's breaking, for these have been my fantasies and my world.

—Mary Casey

We frequently aren't given what we want—whether it's a particular job, a certain relationship, a special talent. But we are always given exactly what we need at the moment. None of us can see what tomorrow is designed to bring, and our fantasies are always tied to a future moment. Our fantasies seldom correlate with the real conditions that are necessary to our continued spiritual growth.

Fantasies are purposeful. They give us goals to strive for, directions to move in. They are never as farsighted as the goals our higher power has in store for us, though. We have far greater gifts than we are aware of, and we are being pushed to develop them at the very times when it seems our world is crashing down.

We can cherish our fantasies—but let them go. Our real purpose in life far exceeds our fondest dreams. The Steps have given us the tools to make God's plan for us a reality.

How limited is my vision, my dreams. If one of mine is dashed today, I will rest assured that an even better one will present itself, if I but let it.

*My singing is very therapeutic. For three hours I have
no troubles—I know how it's all going to come out.*
—Beverly Sills

Have we each found an activity that takes us outside of
ourselves? An activity that gives us a place to focus our attention? Being self-centered and focused on ourselves accompanies the illness we're struggling to recover from. The
decision to quit being preoccupied with ourselves, our own
struggles with life, is not easy to maintain. But when we
have an activity that excites us, on which we periodically
concentrate our attention, we are strengthened. And the
more we get outside of ourselves, the more aware we
become that all is well.

It seems our struggles are intensified as women. So often
we face difficult situations at work and with children, alone.
The preoccupation with our problems exaggerates them.
And the vicious cycle entraps us. However, we don't have to
stay trapped. We can pursue a hobby. We can take a class,
join a health club. We can dare to follow whatever our
desire—to try something new. We need to experience freedom from the inner turmoil in order to know that we
deserve even more freedom.

*Emotional health is just around the corner. I will turn my
attention to the world outside myself.*

Somewhere along the line of development we discover what we really are, and then we make our real decision for which we are responsible. Make that decision primarily for yourself because you can never really live anyone else's life, not even your own child's. The influence you exert is through your own life and what you become yourself.

—*Eleanor Roosevelt*

Taking full responsibility for who we are, choosing friends, making plans for personal achievement, consciously deciding day by day where we want to go with our lives, ushers in adventure such as we've never known. For many of us, months and years were wasted while we passively hid from life in alcohol, drugs, food, other people. But we are breathing new life today.

Recovery offers us, daily, the opportunity to participate in the adventure of life. It offers us the opportunity to share our talents, our special gifts with those with whom we share moments of time.

We are becoming, every moment of time. As are our friends. Discovering who and what we really are, alone and with one another within our experiences, is worthy of celebration.

I will congratulate myself and others today.

Every person is responsible for all the good within the scope of her abilities, and no more . . .
—Gail Hamilton

We have been given the gift of life. Our recovery validates that fact. Our pleasure with that gift is best expressed by the fullness with which we greet and live life. We need not back off from the invitations our experiences offer. Each one of them gives us a chance, a bit different from all other chances, to fulfill part of our purpose in the lives of others.

It has been said that the most prayerful life is the one most actively lived. Full encounter with each moment is evidence of our trust in the now and thus our trust in our higher power. When we fear what may come or worry over what has gone before, we're not trusting in God. Growth in the program will help us remember that fact, thus releasing us to participate more actively in the special circumstances of our lives.

When we look around us today, we know that the persons in our midst need our best, and they're not there by accident but by Divine appointment. We can offer them the best we have—acceptance, love, support, our prayers, and we can know that is God's plan for our lives and theirs.

___

I will celebrate my opportunities for goodness today. They'll bless me in turn.

When action grows unprofitable, gather information;
when information grows unprofitable, sleep.
                                    —Ursula K. LeGuin

Sometimes we need to turn away from what's troubling us. Turn it over, says the Third Step. Hanging onto a situation for which no solution is immediately apparent, only exaggerates the situation. It is often said the solution to any problem lies within it. However, turning the problem over and over in our minds keeps our attention on the outer appearance, not the inner solution.

Rest, meditation, quiet attention to other matters, other persons, opens the way for God to reveal the solution. Every problem can be resolved. And no answer is ever withheld for long. We need to be open to it, though. We need to step away from our ego, outside of the problem and then listen fully to the words of friends, to the words that rise from our own hearts. Too much thinking, incessant analyzing, will keep any problem a problem.

I will rest from my thoughts. I will give my attention wholly to the present. Therein will come the solution, and when least expected.

. . . The present enshrines the past.
                                    —*Simone de Beauvoir*

Each of our lives is a multitude of interconnecting pieces, not unlike a mosaic. What has gone before, what will come today, are at once and always entwined. The past has done its part, never to be erased. The present is always a composite.

In months and years gone by, perhaps we anticipated the days with dread. Fearing the worst, often we found it; we generally find that which we fear. But we can influence the mosaic our experiences create. The contribution today makes to our mosaic can lighten its shade, can heighten its contrast, can make bold its design.

What faces us today? A job we enjoy or one we fear? Growing pains of our children? Loneliness? How we move through the minutes, the hours, influences our perception of future minutes and hours.

No moment is inviolate. Every moment is part of the whole that we are creating. We are artists. We create our present from influences of our past.

I will go forth today; I will anticipate goodness. I will create the kind of moments that will add beauty to my mosaic.

Follow your dream . . .
if you stumble, don't stop
and lose sight of your goal,
press on to the top.
For only on top
Can we see the whole view

—*Amanda Bradley*

Today, we can, each of us, look back on our lives and get a glimmering of why something happened and how it fit into the larger mosaic of our lives. And this will continue to be true for us. We have stumbled. We will stumble. And we learn about ourselves, about what makes us stumble and about the methods of picking ourselves up.

Life is a process, a learning process that needs those stumbles to increase our awareness of the steps we need to take to find our dream at the top. None of us could realize the part our stumbling played in the past. But now we see. When we fall, we need to trust that, as before, our falls are "up," not down.

I will see the whole view in time. I see part of it daily. My mosaic is right and good and needs my stumbles.

What we suffer, what we endure . . . is done by us, as individuals, in private.

—Louise Bogan

Empathy we can give. Empathy we can find, and it comforts. But our pain, the depth of it, can never be wholly shared, fully understood, actually realized by anyone other than ourselves. Alone, each of us comes to terms with our grief, our despair, even our guilt.

Knowing that we are not alone in what we suffer makes the difficulties each of us must face easier. We haven't been singled out, of that we're certain. Remembering that our challenges offer us the lessons we need in the school of life makes them more acceptable. In time, as our recovery progresses, we'll even look eagerly to our challenges as the real exciting opportunities for which we've been created.

Suffering prompts the changes necessary for spiritual growth. It pushes us like no other experience to God—for understanding, for relief, for unwavering security. It's not easy to look upon suffering as a gift. And we need not fully understand it; however, in time, its value in our lives will become clear.

I will not be wary of the challenges today. I will celebrate their part of my growth.

It is only framed in space that beauty blooms; only in space are events, and objects and people unique and significant and therefore beautiful.
— Anne Morrow Lindbergh

We must look closely, focus intently on the subjects of our attention. Within these subjects is the explanation of life's mysteries. To observe anything closely means we must pull it aside with our minds and fondle it, perhaps. We must let the richness of the object, the person, the event, wash over us and savor its memory.

Many of us only now are able to look around ourselves slowly, with care, noting the detail, the brilliant color of life. Each day is an opportunity to observe and absorb the beauty while it blooms.

I will look for beauty today, in myself, and in a friend, and I will find it.

One needs something to believe in, something for which one can have wholehearted enthusiasm.
—Hannah Senesh

Life offers little, if we sit passively in the midst of activity. Involvement is a prerequisite if we are to grow. For our lives' purposes we need enthusiasm; we need enthusiasm in order to greet the day expectantly. When we look toward the day with anticipation, we are open to all the possibilities for action.

We must respond to our possibilities if we are to mature emotionally and recover spiritually. Idly observing life from the sidelines guarantees no development beyond our present level. We begin to change once we start living up to our commitment to the program, its possibilities and our purpose, and it's that change, many days over, that moves us beyond the negative, passive outlook of days gone by.

The program has offered us something to believe in. We are no longer the women we were. So much more have we become! Each day's worth of recovery carries us closer to fulfilling our purpose in life.

I believe in recovery, my own; when I believe in success, I'll find it. There is magic in believing.

The human heart dares not stay away too long from that which hurt it most. There is a return journey to anguish that few of us are released from making.
—Lillian Smith

As the sore tooth draws our tongue, so do rejections, affronts, and painful criticisms, both past and present, draw our minds. We court self-pity, both loving and hating it. But we can change this pattern. First we must decide we are ready to do so. The program tells us we must become entirely ready." And then we must ask to have this shortcoming removed.

The desire to dwell on the injustices of our lives becomes habitual. It takes hours of our time. It influences our perceptions of all other experiences. We have to be willing to replace that time-consuming activity with one that's good and healthy.

We must be prepared for all of life to change. Our overriding self-pity has so tarnished our perceptions that we may never have sensed all the good that life daily offers. How often we see the glass as half-empty rather than half-full!

A new set of experiences awaits me today. And I can perceive them unfettered by the memories of the painful past. Self-pity need not cage me today.

Kindness and intelligence don't always deliver us from the pitfalls and traps. There is no way to take the danger out of human relationships.
—*Barbara Grizzuti Harrison*

Relationships with other people are necessary to escape loneliness; however, relationships do not guarantee freedom from pain. Nurturing a meaningful relationship with another human being takes patience, even when we don't have any. It takes tolerance, even if we don't feel it. It takes self-lessness, at those very moments our own ego is crying for attention.

Yet, we need relationships with others; they inspire us. We learn who we are and who we can become through relationships. They precipitate our accomplishments. Our creativity is encouraged by them, and so is our emotional and spiritual development.

We can look around us, attentively. We can feel blessed, even when it's a negative situation. Every situation is capable of inspiring a positive step forward. Every situation is meant for our good.

There's risk in human relationships, and it's often accompanied by pain. But I am guaranteed growth, and I will find the happiness I seek. I will reach out to someone today.

And what a delight it is to make friends with someone
you have despised!

—Colette

What does it mean to say we "despise" someone? Usually
it means that we have invested a lot of energy in negative
feelings; it means that we have let ourselves care deeply about
someone. We would never say we "despised" someone who
wasn't important to us. Why have we chosen to let negative
feelings occupy so much of our hearts?

Sometimes, in the past, that negative energy became almost
an obsession, consuming our time, gnawing at our self-
esteem. But in recovery there comes a moment of lightning
change; a moment of release from the bonds of obsession.
The other person is, after all, just another person—a seeker,
like ourselves. And, since we cared enough to devote our
time and energies to disliking her, she is probably someone
who would be rewarding to know.

Recovery has given us the opportunity to turn over many
negative feelings, to discover that "friend" and "enemy" can
be two sides of the same person.

Today, I will look into my heart and see whether I am clinging to
obsessive concerns with other people. I will resolve to let them go.

*In the process of growing to spiritual maturity, we all
go through many adolescent stages.*
—Miki L. Bowen

Progress, not perfection, is our goal in this recovery program. And many days we'll be haunted by the feeling that
we've regressed. We will display old behavior. We will
feel unable to change, to go on, to make gains once again.
But these periods will pass, and soon progress will be evident again.

We must be wary of our need for perfection. It's this need
that makes normal progress seem not good enough. And
yet, that's all we're capable of—and all we'll ever need to be
capable of. The program, its Steps and the promises offered,
provide the tools we have lacked, yet need to use in order to
accept ourselves wholly and imperfectly.

Daily attention to our spiritual side will foster the spiritual and emotional health we long for. Prayer and meditation, combined with honest inventory taking, can show us
the personal progress needed, the personal progress made.
However, we will falter on occasion. We will neglect our
program some days. But it won't ever be beyond our reach.
And each day is a new beginning.

*Today is before me, and I can make progress. I will begin with a
quiet prayer and a moment of meditation.*

THE TWELVE STEPS
OF ALCOHOLICS ANONYMOUS*

1. We admitted we were powerless over alcohol—that our lives had become unmanageable.
2. Came to believe that a Power greater than ourselves could restore us to sanity.
3. Made a decision to turn our will and our lives over to the care of God *as we understood Him.*
4. Made a searching and fearless moral inventory of ourselves.
5. Admitted to God, to ourselves, and to another human being the exact nature of our wrongs.
6. Were entirely ready to have God remove all these defects of character.
7. Humbly asked Him to remove our shortcomings.
8. Made a list of all persons we had harmed, and became willing to make amends to them all.
9. Made direct amends to such people wherever possible, except when to do so would injure them or others.
10. Continued to take personal inventory and when we were wrong promptly admitted it.
11. Sought through prayer and meditation to improve our conscious contact with God *as we understood Him*, praying only for knowledge of His will for us and the power to carry that out.
12. Having had a spiritual awakening as the result of these steps, we tried to carry this message to alcoholics, and to practice these principles in all our affairs.

---

*The Twelve Steps of A.A. are taken from *Alcoholics Anonymous*, 3rd ed., published by A.A. World Services, Inc., New York, N.Y., 59-60. Reprinted with permission of A.A. World Services, Inc.

INDEX

TODAY'S GIFT

Editor's note:

Hazelden Educational Materials offers a variety of information on chemical dependency and related areas. Our publications do not necessarily represent Hazelden or its programs, nor do they officially speak for any Twelve Step organization.

The Twelve Steps of Alcoholics Anonymous and The Twelve Steps of Al-Anon are reprinted with permission of Alcoholics Anonymous World Services, Inc. Permission to reprint the Twelve Steps of AA and Al-Anon does not mean that AA has reviewed or approved the contents of this publication, nor that AA agrees with the views expressed herein. AA is a program of recovery from alcoholism. Use of the Twelve Steps in connection with programs which are patterned after AA but which address other problems does not imply otherwise.

This book is dedicated to the memory of
J. D. Davis

ACKNOWLEDGMENTS

The following writers contributed their work to this book: Antiga, Paul Bjorklund, Cecil Carle, Liane Cordes, Paula Culp, Emilio DeGrazia, Karen Casey Elliott, Jeanne Engelmann, Patricia Hoolihan, Bonnie-Jean Kimball, Joe Klaas, Roseann Lloyd, Peter McDonald, Beth Milligan, Ann Monson, Pat O'Donnell, and Cynthia Orange.

Hazelden Publishing and Education is a division of the Hazelden Foundation, a not-for-profit organization. Since 1949, Hazelden has been a leader in promoting the dignity and treatment of people afflicted with the disease of chemical dependency.

The mission of the Foundation is to improve the quality of life for individuals, families, and communities by providing a national continuum of information, education, and recovery services that are widely accessible; to advance the field through research and training; and to improve quality and effectiveness through continuous improvement and innovation.

Stemming from that, the mission of the Publishing division is to provide quality information and support to people wherever they may be in their personal journey— from education and early intervention, through treatment and recovery, to personal and spiritual growth.

Although our treatment programs do not necessarily use everything Hazelden publishes, our bibliotherapeutic materials support our mission and the Twelve Step philosophy upon which it is based. We encourage your comments and feedback.

The headquarters of the Hazelden Foundation is in Center City, Minnesota. Additional treatment facilities are located in Chicago, Illinois; New York, New York; Plymouth, Minnesota; St. Paul, Minnesota; and West Palm Beach, Florida. At these sites we provide a continuum of care for men and women of all ages. Our Plymouth facility is designed specifically for youth and families.

For more information on Hazelden, please call **1-800-257-7800**, or access our World Wide Web site on the Internet [**http://www.hazelden.org**].

INTRODUCTION

All that is human has been preserved and shaped across thousands of generations of families. Our ability to love in a certain way, our capacity for hate, our tendencies toward envy, generosity, cruelty, and self-sacrifice are the legacy of family.

This book is meant to help us celebrate and strengthen our families. The readings are intended to inspire discussion and self-expression, and to encourage us to learn from one another no matter what our age differences are. Most of us live in families of varied interests, each member going his or her own way most of each day. Here, then, with this book, is a chance to share a few minutes with one another—to renew our mutual trust and understanding and to take advantage of the wisdom we each have to offer.

By taking part in one another's development, we can assure ourselves of the love of those who know us best when we need strength the most. We also assure that positive change will be passed on through future generations. In this way, we lay our hands lovingly on the present, and the future.

—the editor

The fragrance always stays in the hand that gives the rose.

— Hada Bejar

Nothing is more attractive than sharing with others. No trait will be admired as much as generosity. There is no surer way to gain the respect of friends and neighbors than to show by what we give that we care about others.

We can give many things besides money, shelter, clothing, or food to those in need. We can give the rich person love and understanding that money can't buy. We can sympathize with those who are troubled, even though they appear wealthier than ourselves. We can share experience, strength, and hope with those who are ill or unhappy. We can even share our suffering with others who suffer, and hold up a light for them on the road to recovery.

What do I have to give today?

Happiness is like manna; it is to be gathered and enjoyed every day.

—*Tryon Edwards*

Life is like a winding path surrounded by flowers, butterflies, and delicious fruit, but many of us spend much of life looking for happiness around the next corner. We do not bend to enjoy the happiness which is ours for the taking just at our feet.

In our desire to reach the "pot of gold," the complete and lasting happiness we all want to fill our lives, we ignore anything which doesn't seem worthy of such a large ambition, or which can't give us the whole thing all at once.

Happiness is all around us, but it often comes in small grains. When we gather it grain by grain, we soon have a basketful.

What small pieces of my happiness surround me right now?

Time is a dressmaker specializing in alterations.
—Faith Baldwin

Change surrounds us. It lies within us, too. The trees in the yard have changed. They've grown taller. Their leaves die and scatter on the ground in the fall. We don't resemble our baby pictures much anymore, either. Like trees, we've grown up. As babies, we couldn't walk. But we learned to run, ride bikes, go out alone to movies and parties.

Some changes we don't notice while they're going on. The snow melts; the birds fly south; our hair grows a little every day. Other changes startle us. A best friend moves away. Perhaps a favorite grandparent dies. These changes we wish hadn't happened, and we have to remember that change is as natural as breathing. We can't keep it from happening, but we can trust that change never means to harm us. It's a sign we're growing up.

What changes may occur today?

A tip-off to an abusive family system is a situation in which nobody ever apologizes.
—Karen Shaud

When we get a tip-off, we can open the door to a whole new way of looking at the world. The tip-off about apologies can help us learn to have a healthier family. It is hard to apologize, but with practice, it will get easier.

We are learning that we can make mistakes, and admit them, and that other people will accept our apologies. In the same way, we are learning we can accept others' apologies. Apologies are sometimes hard to make. It helps to keep in mind that we make them as much for ourselves and our own growth as for the person we apologize to. We are not worthless just because we make mistakes, but we increase our value to ourselves and others by being able to recognize them and apologize.

Is there an apology I need to make today?

. . . and, when the time comes to let it go, . . . let it go.

—Mary Oliver

If we all let go of one thing we like, and take instead each other's hand; if we let go of three minutes each day, and find instead a few perfect words for someone in the house; if we all withhold our judgments for one hour, and reveal during that time one of our own small secret sins; if we all skip the same meal each week, and spend the time together in the park; would we have less or more than what we started with?

It is one of the great and pleasing mysteries of life that we gain by giving things up. Instead of grabbing things or demanding from others if we give something up, we leave a space for something new to enter our lives.

Can I get more out of life by expecting less today?

We, too, the children of the earth, have our moon phases all through any year; the darkness, the delivery from darkness, the waxing and waning.
—Faith Baldwin

Let us think, for a moment, about the changes of the moon. In the beginning of its cycle, it is just a sliver in the darkness. Each night it grows larger until it reaches its full size. When the moon is full and rising, its orange glow fills the sky. All night its gentle light brightens everything it touches.

But this fullness is only part of the life of the moon. For a while it grows smaller, then turns its dark side toward us before reappearing as a sliver and growing again to fullness.

We are children of the earth, and we have our different moods and phases, too. There will be periods of darkness when we try to find our way by the light of the stars. Again and again we will grow to our full size, only to fade and grow again in a new way.

How does God light my way, even in dark times?

To affect the quality of the day—that is the highest of the arts.

—Henry David Thoreau

We are the sculptors of our day. We can mold it creatively into a wonderful masterpiece. We control the amount of moisture we mix into our clay. We pound it, shape it, stroke it, love it. Others can offer suggestions, and we gain new perspectives from their advice, but it is finally our own creation. Our knife may occasionally slip, or our mixture of earth may be too dry. Any great artist suffers temporary setbacks. Besides, imperfections in art often make it all the more interesting.

How creative can I be in my life today?

Deep in their roots all flowers keep the light.
—Theodore Roethke

All flowers begin with the potential to grow and blossom. Yet in winter, perennial flowers are buried under the snow. Inside the dark earth, they are patiently waiting for their time to bloom. For the flowers, faith is believing that spring will return. It is carrying the light of summer deep in their roots so that even in times of cold and dark, there is hope that they will bloom again.

When spring does return, they shoot out of the ground and burst into blossom. In times of light, they drink it deep into their roots—deep enough to sustain them through the next season of darkness.

We can do the same, keeping the memory of good times deep within us, so that when we're feeling low, it will keep our faith in the happy future strong.

What helps sustain my faith today?

Life gives us so much time to collect bizarre thoughts and feelings.

—Claire Weekes

As we go through life, we run into all kinds of negative messages: teasing on the school bus, insulting nicknames, and other put-downs.

Pretty soon we may discover that some of these messages stick in our minds, repeating themselves over and over like broken records. These messages can make us feel bad about ourselves. But when we hear one of these tapes playing inside us, we have the power to push the STOP button. Then we can record a new message. We can even say it out loud, so that our voice settles emphatically into our thoughts.

We can't make others stop saying these things, but we can stop listening to them. They only have power over us when we give it to them. We have the ability and freedom to let negative thoughts float by us, like water going downstream.

What positive message can I send to myself?

You feel the way you do right now because of the thoughts you are thinking at this moment.
—David D. Burns

Good thoughts are like bright colors in a painting. Negative thoughts are dark and dreary and drab. Each day we paint pictures of our own lives with our thoughts. If we step back and look at the canvas, we will see whether the picture is alive with bright colors or dreary and lifeless like a dark cloud.

Our thoughts have the power to bring joy or sadness our way, depending on what we expect or look for in our surroundings.

The choice of how we want our lives to be is ours. Since we paint a new picture each day, we are always free to change things when they don't please us. What better time than the present?

Is there something in my life I'd like to change today?

It does make a difference what you call things.
—Kate Douglas Wiggin

Most of us think of dandelions as weeds. We buy special tools and poisons when they crop up and complain about them as surely as we welcome the spring that brings them.

Yet is there anything more lovely than a sea of yellow dandelions by the side of the road in June? Or as remarkable in transformation as the filaments of the mature dandelion blowing on the wind?

Sometimes we let someone else define for us what are weeds and what are flowers. We don't have to. Much of the beauty of the world is that we ourselves decide what is beautiful according to our own feelings. How lucky we are that, when we choose to, we can open our eyes and see!

Can I see the beauty in those around me right now?

I held a moment in my hand, brilliant as a star,
fragile as a flower, a shiny sliver out of one hour.
I dropped it carelessly. O God! I knew not I held
an opportunity.

—Hazel Lee

Once, a famous artist was hired to put stained glass windows into a great cathedral. His eager young apprentice pleaded for the chance to design just one small window. The master artist feared an experiment on even a small window would prove costly, but the persistent young apprentice kept up his pleas. Finally, the master agreed that he could try his hand on one small window if he furnished his own materials and worked on his own time.

The enterprising apprentice began gathering bits of glass his master had discarded, and set to work. When the cathedral doors were open, people stood in groups before the small window, praising its delicate excellence.

Our lives are like this. If we take the time to gather together the moments and opportunities we too often discard and waste, we find we can weave them into something beautiful.

What can I make of moments I usually waste today?

Home is the place where, when you have to go there, they have to take you in.

—*Robert Frost*

Our home is a place of roots, a place where we can always turn in time of need. Some of us may have had the experience of being away from home and not being able to make it on our own. We know what a relief it was to reach out at last and call our family, who we knew would take us in.

We became people in our homes, we learned to eat and walk and talk there. We feel comfortable there, safe from the pressures of the outside world. It is up to us to keep it safe and healthy by growing in love and generosity there.

Home is a place to really give of ourselves and put our best into making it happy and secure. It will affect our futures more than almost anything else in our lives. It deserves our prayers of blessing. It is our foundation, the source of our first feelings for others. May we treasure our home and the people who make up our family.

What small thing can I do right now to make home a better place?

The universe is made up of stories, not atoms.
—Muriel Rukeyser

There was once a storyteller who told many people of her life. They listened and heard their own stories in hers. Hearing her story, they didn't feel so lonely anymore. Hearing about someone else who had lost things and people she loved, who had felt lonely, scared, and unsure of herself, let them feel less crazy when similar things happened to them.

Because of the healing they felt through hearing someone else's story, some of the listeners decided to become storytellers themselves. As they recounted their stories, they found that letting out secrets that had bothered them for years freed them to feel good about who they were and who they had always wanted to be.

What secrets can I share today?

Always remember that no matter what the problem may be, there is an infinity of solutions.
—Marion Weinstein

A girl named Iris was tormented by the boys at school. Whenever she walked by they would make rude noises. Sometimes, when no one was looking, they would block her way and not let her go home. She was too inexperienced at taking care of herself to realize that believing she couldn't do anything made it true. Feeling helpless kept her from thinking about what she might do.

One day she got so scared that she told her best friend what was happening. Together they began to think of all sorts of things she could do. Knowing she could do something took away the helpless feeling, and the boys noticed and stopped teasing her. It wasn't fun for them anymore.

We often feel helpless in situations that seem too much for us to handle. In fact, help is always available—through friends and family, and through God, who helps us see how we can help ourselves. All we have to do is stop being distracted by that helpless feeling and ask for what we need.

Can I see the many solutions to my problems today?

When you do something you are proud of, dwell on it a little, praise yourself for it.
—*Mildred Newman*

Each one of us is very good at something. Maybe it's baseball or tennis where we display talent. Maybe we're good in math or at giving reports. A few people are talented at being good listeners or helpful friends. To recognize our own talents we may need help from others. It's always so much easier to see our faults, or the ways we don't meet our own expectations.

But the fact is we are all skilled in many areas of our lives. To accept praise—better yet, to quietly give it to ourselves—is a sign of healthy growth.

What things have I done well lately?

Man cannot remake himself without suffering.
For he is both the marble and the sculptor.
—Alexis Carrell

A sculptor begins with an unformed piece of marble. He must be able to envision what he wants to create. Then, armed with tools and courage, he begins to chink away at the marble he does not need. Every day he examines how the piece of marble looks and what he wants it to become.

Every one of us who is trying to be a better person is like the sculptor. We envision who we want to be and what kind of qualities we believe in. Some of these qualities might be kindness, good self-esteem, the ability to love and feel loved. If we are honest, we must also look with the artist's eye at our faults. We might see some jealousy and resentment, or feelings of superiority. Our faults, human as they are, are like unwanted marble that keeps our most loving selves from taking shape. Carving away at our faults is hard work, and sometimes even hurts. Yet we do not do this work alone—we can only do it with the help of our God.

What can I chisel away today?

The stream that was locked up for the winter now ripples and gurgles along its way.
—John F. Gardner

Winter presents us with a frozen world, silent, sometimes forbidding. It seems like such a harsh time, forcing us indoors, letting us out only when we're wrapped in extra woolens, extra boots, extra hats and mittens. But beneath the snow's blanket, the earth is resting. Just as we sleep at night, the earth naps, nurturing its roots and bulbs, replenishing its moisture and minerals, refreshing itself. Spring is the earth's first stirring; it opens one eye, then another, wiggles a toe, stretches, yawns. The earth rises, shaking leaves off, brushing twigs away. It sends new shoots up to welcome the day.

We, too, are part of nature, and as such we experience our own seasons. Sometimes we are happy, full of energy, always able to handle obstacles. When we are down, when things seem to be too much for us to handle, we must remember that it is natural and proper to feel that way, and that soon, without our even trying, a new season will lift our hearts.

When I feel low, what can I do best?

A journey of a thousand miles must begin with a single step.

—Chinese proverb

Even the strongest, most loving families always have room for growth. There is no such thing as a "perfect" family. If our family is far from perfect, that's okay. It only matters that we are working at getting better. Often, runners will say they can remember many days when they just did not feel like running; however, once they started, they felt more energy and were easily able to run the distance they had set for that day.

Whatever we need to do, we can do in small acts—a chore done without being asked, a helping hand with the dishes, a soft word, a surprise gift for no reason. These are small things, easily done. Love is made of small things; what is large is the love with which they are accomplished.

When we begin to work on our relationship with our family, we will feel the new energy, and quickly we will find ourselves making progress.

What is the first thing I can do today to improve my relationship with my family?

The power of a man's virtue should not be measured by his special efforts, but by his ordinary doing.

—Blaise Pascal

The airplane kit is on the table in front of us. We have the glue, the little wooden pieces, and the instructions. We work for hours putting together each piece, step by step. A dab of glue here, a clamp there, maybe some rubber bands to hold the bigger pieces together. We work slowly, allowing the glue to set overnight, even though we want to see it fly right now.

We follow each step in order, even though we think we know how to do it on our own. Patience is the most important asset we bring to this activity—the willingness to allow each step its own time and proper place.

After we've done all the careful work and waited till the glue is firm, we take it out for a trial flight. It soars! So do we, when we allow ourselves time to learn each step of the way.

What part of my future am I assembling today?

If you realize you aren't so wise today as you
thought you were yesterday, you're wiser today.
—*Olin Miller*

Smug was a kitten who thought she knew everything. She knew how to clean herself with her sandpaper tongue, how to sleep, eat, and keep warm, and how to sharpen her tiny claws.

One day, her mother wanted to teach Smug to climb trees. I don't need to learn this, thought Smug, I already know everything I need to know.

Without much interest, Smug watched her mother climb a tall tree and come down again. When it was Smug's turn, she said, "I'll stay on the ground where it's safe." Just then, a large black dog came trotting around the corner.

Aren't we often like Smug, certain that we know all we need to know, or that we really don't need to know something another is trying to teach us? When we rid ourselves of the pride that keeps us from learning these things, we'll feel a little safer if any big black dogs come around the corner. And we will have grown smarter by recognizing our need to know more.

Am I smart enough to admit my need to learn more today?

Animals are such agreeable friends they ask no questions, they pass no criticisms.

—George Eliot

A pet is often liked by everyone and seems to have no enemies. Why is this? Pets are friendly and interested in others. They seem to get joy out of just being with us. They do not have a critical attitude. When mistreated or neglected for a while, they are quick to forgive and quickly seek once again to be by our side.

Each of us is a valuable part of the family. When we treasure one another and don't waste our time finding each other's faults, we will begin to have fewer faults. When we accept our loved ones as they are and enjoy sharing our lives with them, our lives become more enjoyable, and our family love grows because we are each more loveable.

What can I accept in others today?

Little girl, little girl, where have you been?
                                    —Mother Goose

She's been everywhere and nowhere in and around the house. She's been in her room crying with her doll, on the grass kicking her ball, on the floor big-eyed and blank in front of the TV. Her things are everywhere in the way, as if left there to block the path. She learns to be happiest alone in her room. There she can gather roses to give to the Queen and receive in return a diamond as big as a shoe. There she can wait for some prince, or dream of crossing the street without looking back.

We are all the same way, even as adults. We live with our dreams and fantasies, and our secret lives thrive in privacy.

All around us, our loved ones live out their private lives often unnoticed by us until we enter them. When we honor others' unspoken needs, when we allow others their privacy without being asked, or when we appreciate something they've done, we share the joy of living together in natural harmony.

How invisible are those in our presence every day?

Only with winter-patience
  can we bring
The deep desired, long-awaited
  spring.

—*Anne Morrow Lindbergh*

Family life requires patience. We probably realized that a long time ago. The Greek origin of the word *patience* is *pathos,* which means "suffering." In our lives together, we often suffer. Life is full of bumps and scrapes, both physical and emotional. In our search for greater family unity and harmony we need to realize that we will not be able to escape all suffering. This is why we need patience. It is a form of love.

When we suffer the bumps and scrapes and still have faith something good will come of it, we are living out our love. From this winter-patience we will surely find a reward.

How have I practiced my patience already today?

Muddy water, let stand, becomes clear.
—*Lao-tzu*

A group of friends went swimming one day and one of them lost a ring in the bottom of the lake. Everyone started diving from different directions to find it until there was so much mud and sand stirred up that no one could see anything. Finally, they decided to clear the water. They waited silently on the edge of the shore for the mud from all their activity to settle. When it finally cleared, one person dove in slowly and picked up the ring.

When we are confused about something in our lives, we will often hear answers and advice from all directions. Our friends will tell us one thing and our families another, until we feel pretty well mixed up. If we look away from our problem and let patience and time do their work, the mud inside us will settle and clear. Our answer will become visible, like the glimmer of gold in the water.

Am I overlooking the simple solution?

Nothing is more difficult than competing with a myth.

—Francoise Giroud

Sometimes we think we need to try and be something we're not. Maybe we feel pressure from friends to behave or dress like someone else. All we need to do is remember when we were younger and dressed in our parents' clothes and shoes. We pretended to be grown-ups, and it was fun for a while. Then the huge shoes on our feet grew clumsy and uncomfortable and the mountain of rolled-up sleeves kept falling down and getting in the way. Soon we grew tired of the game and stopped pretending.

Today when we start feeling the pressure to be someone else, let's remember how hard it is to play a role that doesn't fit us.

What can I do today that is most like me?

When men are rightfully occupied, then their amusement grows out of their work as the color petals out of a fruitful garden.

—John Ruskin

What do we need most in order to be happy? Certainly we all need to be loved. Yet we need even more than that. The spirit also wishes to be needed. When we are needed, no matter what age we are, we serve a purpose for others. When we are needed, we will be loved, as well as respected, imitated, and rewarded with gratitude.

Our needs are not great empty pits to be filled any way we can. They are the couplings by which we connect to those we love. Our needs also tell us what others want, and how to enrich their lives—which also enriches ours.

How do we become needed? We have only to look at our own needs and give what we need to others—love, respect, kindness, generosity. When we realize we are needed, we realize we also need others.

What do I need that I can give to another person today?

It is such a secret place, the land of tears.
—Antoine de St. Exupery

Where do tears come from? Perhaps each of us has a private well where the tears rise from. Each of has our own landscape of events that have hurt us or given us joy. And so we have our own private responses to the world around us. Something may hurt one of us that would not hurt another.

Like the oceans and rivers, sometimes our well of tears is flowing. We do not always understand all the forces affecting the oceans, or our well of tears.

The kind of bucket that draws water from a well is solid and durable, and it lowers itself deep enough to find water. Good friends and family members are like that. It is comforting to share our private well with such people.

Who will I invite to drink from my well today?

Think in terms of depletion, not depression. . . .
You can understand how a body can replenish
itself, whereas it may be difficult to understand
the way out of depression.

—*Claire Weekes*

Despair and depression may come over us suddenly, for no reason we can figure out. But if we stop and reflect, we may realize we are reacting to too much of something—too much work, too much excitement, too much fun. We may be having a letdown after holidays, after completing a project, or at the end of a school year.

When we feel a letdown coming on, we must give ourselves time. We need to take some time off and do nothing, plan nothing. Then we can ask God to help us let go of the negative feelings that come along with a letdown.

We can plan a small gift for ourselves—a walk by the lake, for instance. In our excitement with a rush of events, we often forget that we, like the infants we once were, need to take a rest and reenergize.

Do I need to do something just for myself today?

*Everyone has his own fingerprints. The white
light streams down to be broken up by those
human prisms into all the colors of the rainbow.
Take your own color in the pattern and be just
that.*

—Charles R. Brown

We are often amazed at how different members of
the same family seem to be. Contrasts are often great:
one child might be loud and funny, one might be
timid and quiet, and yet neither seems to take after the
parents.

A family is like a vegetable garden. The vegetables
respond to outside influences. The one exposed to
more sunlight will grow differently than the one growing in a damp, shady place. Vegetables growing in
crowded areas of the garden may not be as developed
as those around them, but they might be tastier.

Although we may have common roots, outside experiences and friends mold us too, making each of us
unique. We sometimes lose ourselves by comparisons
and feel as if we don't belong, but the variety of our
family garden is what makes the world so interesting!

How can I honor another person's uniqueness today?

Thou shalt not should *thyself.*

—Anonymous

When someone tells us we *should* do something, do we want to do it, or do we feel mad that someone else is telling us what we want to do? Sometimes we forget that these messages are not our own, but are the desires of others. It's important to listen to what we tell ourselves, to be aware of which messages we're giving ourselves and which come from others.

We can make a list of all our *shoulds* and identify where they came from: parent, boss, friend, self. Then we can decide which *shoulds* are *want to's,* and throw out the rest. Doing what we want to is very different from doing what we should, and we can usually do a better job of it.

Have I freed myself of shoulds *today?*

It's not enough to talk to plants, you also have to listen.

—David Bergman

Plants grow best when we pay attention to them. That means watering them, touching them, putting them in places where they will receive good light. They need people around them to notice if they are drooping at the edges or looking particularly happy in the sunlight. The more attention a plant receives, the better it will grow.

We need to be noticed in the same way. If we notice a family member or friend is drooping, perhaps we can pay some special attention to him or her. All of us need someone to care about how we are and to truly listen to us. We can share and double someone's happiness by noticing and talking about it also. We help the people around us to grow by listening to their droopy edges as well as their bright days. People need this as much as plants need light and water.

How can I help someone grow today?

Fear is the absence of faith.

— *Paul Tillich*

We all experience fear. Sometimes we fear small things that only seem large at the time, like a test in school, or meeting a new boss, or going to the dentist. Sometimes we fear big things like serious illness or death, or that someone we love will come to harm. Fear is healthy, and we all feel it. It keeps us from doing foolish things sometimes, but too much fear can also keep us from doing what we need for our growth.

If we have faith in God and in ourselves, we can turn and face whatever frightens us, believing we can, with help, do what seems impossible. And we will, and the fear will vanish. The important first step in dealing with fear is to take action—either by tackling what we fear ourselves, or by asking for help. Each time we face our fear, we gain strength, courage, and confidence in the doing.

What am I most afraid of?

In a hole in the ground there lived a hobbit. Not a nasty, dirty, wet hole . . . nor yet a dry, bare, sandy hole with nothing in it . . . it was a hobbithole, and that means comfort.
—J. R. R. Tolkien

Home is a place of comfort. When we go away and have to adjust to a different bed and someone else's cooking, we quickly discover how comfortable our own home is. Comfort in a home is more than just a familiar bed and favorite food, it is something we can give to each other. We can make home a place where we can relax and be ourselves without fear of rejection.

Each of us needs a special little place where we can come and seek refuge from the world, our own little "fort." Children are often busy making "forts," but all of us in the family need to work at making the place where we live together a fort where we can all gather for rest.

What can I add to our comfort today?

The shy man usually finds that he has been shy without cause, and that, in practice, no one takes the slightest notice of him.

—Robert Lynd

We sometimes feel self-conscious in front of others. It may be that we've just gotten braces or a new haircut and we're afraid everyone will stare at us. We stop smiling and talk with our heads bowed. Many people have worn braces and many more will. We need not be ashamed just because we feel different. By beginning to smile again we will see how many people really didn't notice our braces, or our haircuts, or anything but what they see inside us.

All we need to do is lift our heads and smile. We will be amazed to find how little even our best friends notice about the externals, the things that don't really matter. Who we are is far more noticeable and far more important than what we look like. A smile at shy times helps us accept ourselves as others do.

What makes me shy?

Let there be spaces in your togetherness.
—*Kahlil Gibran*

Sometimes it is just as important to know when to leave others alone as it is to know when to talk with them. We all need to be alone at times—to think, to work out a problem, or just to be quiet with ourselves. This is especially true in families, where we're often surrounded by others. If we tune in to our other family members, we can develop sensors that will let us know when they need some time alone. Part of good communication is knowing when *not* to talk, too.

Can I be sensitive to my family's needs for privacy today?

Pride works from within; it is the direct appreciation of oneself.

—*Arthur Schopenhauer*

Pride, like all emotions, has two faces: one healthy and one sick. It is our challenge to use the healthy side well. Sick pride fills us with ourselves, looks down on others, and has no room for generosity. Healthy pride is heavy with humility. If we can feel joyful when we succeed, and tell others about it honestly, we are not being boastful.

Sick pride often keeps us from doing things because we are too proud to ask for help when we need it, or too proud to risk failure, or too proud to do anything that might not turn out perfect.

Healthy pride about our greatest victories always comes with the awareness that we did not do it all by ourselves. We had the aid, advice, and encouragement of loved ones. In all things that really count, we never walk alone. Even those who claim pride is not a virtue admit that it is the parent of many virtues.

What makes me proud of myself today?

It is the weak who are cruel. Gentleness can only
be expected from the strong.

—Leo Rosten

When we think of strength, do we think of someone who shows no emotion and intimidates others with physical power? True strength is the freedom to show all kinds of feelings. Strong people aren't afraid of being vulnerable. A person who feels insecure may not feel free to show any kind of softness or be able to share gentle feelings. If we have true inner strength, we are not afraid to show what is a part of us, gentle feelings included.

It is wonderful to see a well-conditioned athlete cry tears of joy after a victory. In such an example we can see physical and emotional strength. In our lives together, we will be stronger if we do not try to hide our feelings out of fear. As our feelings flow, we will increase our self-understanding and build our true strength.

Am I strong enough to show how I really feel today?

When I look back on all these worries I remember the story of the old man who said on his deathbed that he had had a lot of trouble in his life, most of which never happened.
— Winston Churchill

A rolled-up ball of yarn does not take up much space—it sits, ready to be used when needed. It gets unrolled a little bit at a time—just as much as is needed and no more. But a ball of yarn that gets unravelled can be strewn across an entire room. It becomes a jumbled mass, entangled and confusing.

When we live our lives a day at a time, we are like that rolled-up ball of yarn. Our thoughts, feelings, and skills are ready to be used as they are needed. But when we worry, our spirit becomes a jumbled mass of yarn. We get ahead of and behind ourselves—our thoughts are scattered and often our feelings are confused. Worry adds clutter and confusion to life.

What is most helpful is to put the worry away—to roll up the ball of yarn and bring ourselves into the present moment. In this way, we stand ready for each new stitch—and we will never be given more than we are able to handle.

Do I have worries that are cluttering my life today?

Leave yourself alone.

—*Jenny Janacek*

Three women were talking. One blamed herself for an unkind remark someone had made to her. Another blamed herself for not getting work done. The other compared her looks to those of the movie stars and thought she was ugly.

The women each noticed how the other two had put themselves down without being aware of it, and they began to laugh. Then they vowed to be as kind to themselves as they were to each other. Each time they caught themselves being mean to themselves, they imagined they were their own best friend, and were as understanding to themselves as they were to one another.

When we are kind to ourselves, only then can we be truly kind to others, and make ourselves a gift to those around us.

How have I been kind to myself lately?

A bird does not sing because he has an answer.
He sings because he has a song.
                              —Joan Walsh Anglund

Each of us has a song to sing, just as birds do. Part of knowing who we are is appreciating our own songs. Are our songs gentle like the robin's, or are we brilliant leaders like the bluejay? Are we easy to be around like the sparrow, or do we radiate joy and laughter like the loon?

Each of these birds has something special to offer. So do we, with our own unique personalities and talents. What a waste it would be if the loon never dashed across the lake because he wanted to be a robin instead. It is important to learn who we are and to believe we are special in our own way. We give joy to the world around us when we sing our own songs.

Have I listened to my own song lately?

Life deals more rigorously with some than others.

—*Lewis F. Presnall*

How often we think about a friend, He sure is lucky! And probably just as often we say to ourselves, Why did that happen to me? It's not fair! The truth is, life isn't always fair. We don't all get the same experiences, the same lessons. But we each learn what we need to learn in order to fulfill our destiny.

We have to learn to trust. Maybe a bike gets stolen or a friend moves away. It's not easy to accept such things as these, but we must all learn to understand and accept losses in our lives.

Perhaps we fail a test. The lesson we learn from this may be to study harder or to consider a different course of study in school. There are always reasons for why things happen, but we don't have to know them.

Can I trust in the lessons of my failures today?

Oh, a trouble's a ton, or a trouble's an ounce,
Or a trouble is what you make it,
And it isn't the fact that you're hurt that counts,
But only how you take it.
—Edmund Vance Cooke

Once, a woman decided to throw a problem-exchange party. As guests arrived, they shed all their personal problems and tossed them onto a pile with everyone else's. After all had discussed their own problem for others to hear, the party ended with guests selecting from the problem pile those they wished to carry away. Each person left with the same troubles he or she had brought to the party.

We who worry a great deal about our problems are always sure no one else has troubles as bad as ours. Too often, we complain, "If you had my problems, you'd really hurt." Our problems are tailored to us, and geared to help us learn by solving them. No one else's would be quite right.

When we cope with problems, rather than wailing about them, we discover that our own are minor irritations compared to those we see in others.

What problems am I lucky to have?

"Shall I give you a kiss?" Peter asked, and jerking an acorn button off his coat, solemnly presented it to her.

—*James Barrie*

If kisses can be made of acorn buttons, they can be made of any good thing. Think of kisses made of candy. Therefore, there must be a thousand and one ways to give a kiss. We can give one made of wild flowers picked in the ditch, the melody in a music box, the few true words in a note, or the picture we ourselves draw to give to the one we love. Think of how we can hide them here and there under pillows, in corners, in pockets where they're sure to be seen and felt. Think of how hearts kiss when we hug or hold hands, how sleeping beauties suddenly wake up.

Can we find new ways to show our love?

Love cures people—both the ones who give it and the ones who receive it.
　　　　　　　　　　　　　—Karl Menninger

Receiving a loving hug from a parent or perhaps a smile from a friend or even a stranger gives us a special feeling inside. We know we are important to others when they show us their love through attention. And we sometimes forget that we matter to others. Family members and friends feel good in the same way when we show them our love. Everyone needs to be loved.

How can we show our love? Must it be through a hug? Doing a favor for someone is loving. Helping around the house or the yard is loving, particularly when we've volunteered our help. Giving an unexpected gift to a friend is a way of showing love. Showing others we care, even when they are angry, is perhaps the nicest of all expressions of love.

What new way can I show someone I care today?

It is always a mistake not to close one's eyes,
whether to forgive or to look better into oneself.
—Maurice Maeterlinck

It is easy to look outward and find faults with the world and people around us. We criticize family members or complain about our friends. We always notice disease in the trees around us.

But if we take time to be quiet, to sit alone in a tree or by a lake, we become more aware of how connected we are to the life around us. We are part of the beauty and the imperfection. When we notice our own tree is not perfect, it becomes easier to forgive the blights of those around us. It is also important to forgive ourselves our faults. Though all the trees are beautiful, they each have their scars. Being human means we are, like all humanity, both beautiful and imperfect.

Will I see through the flaws to another's beauty today?

Shame-filled people feel that something is wrong at their very core. It is a sense of being bad. . . .
—Susan Kwiecien

Nobody is rotten to the core. Whenever we start to believe we are bad all the way through, we can picture good things we have done, days when someone else was happy to be with us, and see for ourselves that we have many good points that outweigh the bad.

If we have done something wrong, we must apologize and make amends. Making a mistake is not the same as being worthless. Mistakes are a natural part of living, not something to be ashamed of. Our freedom to make mistakes is one of our greatest assets, for this is the way we learn humility, persistence, courage to take risks, and better ways of doing things. All of us are valuable and loveable. How could we be otherwise? Since mistakes are natural aspects of growth, we can salute them in ourselves and others as signs of life and celebrate our ability to learn and to forgive.

What mistakes have helped me grow?

There is glory
In a great mistake.

— Nathalia Crane

Once there was a big girl who liked to play with little kids and their toys. One day she rode one of their small bikes and her foot slipped off the little pedal and her leg got caught and dragged along the sidewalk.

She went home, limping and howling. Her mother put ice on the terrible scrape. The next day, the girl's mother told her she was too big for the little kids' toys. The girl looked up defiantly and said, "I can TOO ride that baby bike!"

The girl's mother didn't say anything else. She knew people must be free to make mistakes. We cannot protect another person from the experiences of the world. It would be harmful to both of us to try.

What mistakes have I made more than once before I learned my lesson?

United souls are not satisfied with embraces, but desire to be truly each other. . . .
— *Sir Thomas Browne*

If hugs could melt, if kisses were made of nothing but pure air, if talkers always agreed, and if hearts all beat to the same drum, would we desire any longer to be truly each other? No two leaves on a tree turn the same way in the wind; no two fish in a school tread the same water; and no two people can live the same life. Therefore, when we hug let's leave some space; when we kiss let's allow each other to breathe; when we talk let's permit each other to disagree; when we love let's honor each other's rhythm and way.

Is it our similarities or differences that make us want to know each other better?

I have often thought morality may perhaps consist solely in the courage of making a choice.
—Leon Blum

Sometimes, trying to do the right thing isn't easy because it isn't what we want to do. For instance, we may want to sneak a cookie to take to bed with us, or we may want to stay out late. But is that the right thing to do?

One way to tell is to think how we'll feel after we've done it. Will we be happy, or will we feel guilty because we know in our hearts it is wrong? On the other hand, how would we feel if we resisted the temptation? Perhaps we'd feel great because we'd know in our hearts we'd done the right thing. And don't we deserve to feel good about ourselves? Of course we do!

How wonderful it is that our feelings can help us do the right thing when we're in doubt.

Will I have the courage to follow my true feelings today?

Say what you like: say I'm ill,
Say I broke my leg on the stairs,
Say we've had a fire.

—*T. S. Eliot*

Think of the trouble of excuses and lies. They force us to make ourselves sick, live with a whole broken leg, start some sort of slow burn. When we tell someone we're not at home, we have to hide in that place. When we invent a long line of lies, we have to memorize each one. It's easiest just to come clean, use plain and simple words, and speak true. When accusers spear us with their stares, we can disarm them by looking them right in the eye.

Not only do lies deceive others, they keep us hidden from ourselves, and make our real reasons for the choices we've made seem unworthy, if we feel we can't express them. Better that we be truthful, even if a little pain results. Truth keeps communication lines open. Then, when someone really wants to know what's on our minds, we can simply open our hearts.

Is anything too terrible to tell to a friend?

We cannot do all things.

—*Virgil*

We are each limited in terms of time and energy. If we try to do too much, we do everything half-rate. How much better it is to clearly sort out what is really important to us, and then give ourselves to those things or people wholeheartedly.

Famous writers have written about the difficulty of having more than one or two really good friends. That number seems so unimpressive if we equate popularity with the number of friends we have. If we want quality, we must accept our limitations. In this way we avoid wasting energy on unimportant tasks, on friends who aren't true or close, on goals which aren't what we really want. We can only commit ourselves wholeheartedly to a limited number of tasks and a limited number of people.

Who are my truly good friends?

In spite of everything I still believe that people are really good at heart.

—Anne Frank

In the face of being hunted for extermination, Anne Frank could write this from her hiding place in an attic. Was she naive? No. She deeply believed in the goodness of creation and the goodness of all creatures, including those who persecuted and murdered her people.

Somehow, young as she was, Anne Frank knew a truth we sometimes lose: that it is not what people do that makes them good or evil. It is who they are. And for Anne Frank, all people are made in the image of God—and therefore, deep down at their core, must be good. She was able to see through the brutality and hatred to that true creation of God.

We are left in awe at such faith and love. But we can draw from it too, and when our brother or sister or parent or child does something to hurt us, we can remember Anne Frank's ability to see what is good. We can look beneath the hurtful actions and forgive.

Can I forgive someone who has hurt me today?

A person's best ally is someone who takes care of herself.

—Susan Clarke

Once there was a little girl who was learning to walk. The trouble was, her mother wouldn't let her fall down. Every time she was about to fall, her mother would rush over and catch her.

It was hard to learn how to walk if she couldn't fall down, but the girl was too little to be able to tell her mother. Her mother thought she was taking care of her when in fact she was keeping her from learning to take care of herself. Letting her fall would have shown trust in the child, trust that she could get up. It would have taught her that she wasn't so fragile that she couldn't recover if she hurt herself.

We are all like this mother once in a while, protecting one another from important lessons in life. This doesn't mean we have to let someone get seriously hurt, but that we allow each other the freedom to learn and grow in individual ways.

What will I be able to learn from my little stumbles today?

Thoughts—just mere thoughts—are as powerful
as electric batteries—as good for one as sunlight
is, or as bad for one as poison.
—Frances Hodgson Burnett

The truck was in mud to its axles. Three lumber-jacks sat in stony silence in the cab. There they were, stuck in the woods on their way to the cutting site. The first man slammed the steering wheel, cursed, and stormed out of the truck. The second thought the early morning woods inviting, and said he'd just crawl under a pine to nap until someone came along to pull them out. The third man, left alone, grabbed an axe and a saw and set about cutting wood to slide under the wheels. Within an hour he managed to pull the truck out of its muddy bath and they got on their way.

We can choose how we respond to an obstacle. As with the three men, our response may be to curse and give up, to sit back and wait for someone else to help us, or to set to work fearlessly to try to overcome it ourselves. The event itself isn't important; how we think about it is.

___

Is there an obstacle in my way today?

The most useless day of all is that in which we have not laughed.

—*Sebastian R. N. Champort*

We are told that laughter is sunshine filling a room. And where there is laughter, there also is life. They say that people who laugh a lot live longer than do the sour-faced. When we laugh together, gratitude comes more easily, companionship thrives, and all praise is sincere. Laughter brings us joy that cannot be bought. Such joy is with us throughout each day. To hoard joy, to hide it away deep within us away from others, will make us lonely misers. We cannot buy or trade for joy, but we can give or receive it as a gift.

Laughter's joy celebrates the moment we are living right now. It is a gift we must share, or it will wither and die. Shared, it grows and thrives, and always returns to us when we need it most.

What can I find to laugh about right now?

From harmony, from heavenly harmony,
This universal frame began. . . .
                                    —John Dryden

Our family is like a small orchestra. Each of us has an important part to play. To achieve harmony we tune in to how others are sounding. We recognize that every orchestra needs a conductor, a center for direction. We rely on our Higher Power for this support and guidance, and we realize that our family's music exists in time. It changes, it passes, and we begin a new song. Our music comes and goes. It is not carved in marble. It is a free expression of family love.

No one of us has to play alone, because we are an ensemble. The time for soloing comes later. Today we rejoice that we can play together.

How can my music add to the family's symphony today?

The great pleasure in life is doing what people say you cannot do.

—Walter Babehot

Everyone knew Jacob was a bitter old hermit who hated people. He lived by himself in a cabin in the woods. He never came to town, never talked to anyone, and never put up a mailbox or put in a phone. But he had one thing the townsfolk wanted— the very first Bible brought by a preacher when the town was first settled. They wanted it for their centennial celebration.

Little Tom listened as the townsfolk complained daily about how much they wanted the old book to put on display. One day, he walked on out to the little cabin and just asked the old man if he could borrow the book, just for a week. Imagine the surprise on the faces of the people when the boy wandered back to town with the old dusty book in hand.

Are we like the townspeople sometimes? Do we assume things won't work out without even trying? Sometimes help is there, just waiting to be asked. What have we got to lose?

What can I request today that I have been afraid to ask for?

Nothing that is worth doing can be done alone,
but has to be done with others.
                    —*Dr. Reinhold Niebuhr*

We who are blessed with a close-knit family, where thoughts and actions can be discussed and developed, are aware that what is given is not as important as what is shared. As we help one another, we learn that sharing can never exist unless we care first. This is the major ingredient of love.

Albert Schweitzer described human service toward a common goal as the greatest of deeds. Charles Dickens assured us that when we lighten the burdens of another, we can never consider ourselves useless. Those of us who are led today may show the way tomorrow. In giving, we receive, and in getting we cannot avoid being givers.

What do I receive by giving today?

Belief consists in accepting the affirmations of the soul; unbelief, in denying them.
—*Ralph Waldo Emerson*

What do we believe? Do we believe in ourselves? Do we believe we have enough time and energy to do what we need? Or do we believe that things will turn out badly for us? Someone said that fear is faith in the negative. We can choose to believe the worst will happen, or we can choose to believe we deserve good things. We can believe the right things will happen at the right time. What we believe becomes true for us because we behave as though it were true. For this reason, it is wise to choose our beliefs carefully. The more we choose the positive, the more aware we become that our choices are many.

This means telling ourselves that we're all right just as we are, and acting as though it were true without question.

How can I make my world better today?

The only thing that makes life possible is permanent, intolerable uncertainty: not knowing what comes next.

—Ursula LeGuin

The world around us changes constantly. Trees turn from green to beautiful shades of yellow, orange, and brown in the fall. Yet, even if we watched the trees carefully, every minute of the day, we could not actually see the colors change. Change requires time, preparation, and patience.

To make the changes we want, we need to let go of unhealthy but comfortable patterns that we're stuck in, the way the trees let their colors change and finally let go of their leaves altogether. We can't have total change right now, no matter how much we want it. It's important to accept both who we are now and who we are becoming. Just as the tree trusts without question that its leaves will grow and lets go of them when the time comes, we can believe in our own power to grow and let go of our accomplishments when the time is right.

When we do, we can be assured that our lives will blossom again, like trees in the spring coming to life after a cold winter.

Do I have any new blossoms today?

I was angry with my friend:
I told my wrath, my wrath did end.
I was angry with my foe:
I told it not, my wrath did grow.

—William Blake

We have a right to claim our own feelings. Sometimes we get angry, but hold it inside because we think it's wrong to feel it. If anger builds inside us, it expands like a balloon ready to burst. If not released, it can make us depressed, or even physically ill. When we give ourselves permission to feel anger, we are better able to get rid of it in a healthy way. Our inner voice can tell us how to let go of our anger. And once we've released it, we can easily get in touch with the feelings that caused it.

When we recognize our anger for what it is—one feeling among many others that makes us unique—it loses its significance, and we can prevent it from consuming us. Indira Ghandi said, "You cannot shake hands with a clenched fist." When we let go of our anger we can honestly embrace each other with open arms.

Am I carrying around anger that could be released today?

Nothing is troublesome that we do willingly.
—*Thomas Jefferson*

Some of the necessary things we do are tiring and annoying. Many of these things we must do regardless of how we feel about them. Doing dishes day after day can be a tiresome job, but no matter how much we hate it, it must be done sooner or later. We might discover, if we look hard enough, how chores like this can actually be enjoyable, if we do them right. Perhaps dish washing is a time for listening to music and singing along, or an opportunity for conversation between family members as we help one another.

Our willingness to look for the hidden treasure and opportunities in tasks we might otherwise consider dreary will never fail to reward us.

What opportunity can I see in my next chore?

I celebrate myself, and sing myself, and what I assume, you shall assume.

—Walt Whitman

Some of us may think Walt Whitman must have been terribly conceited to have written words like that. But he wasn't. He knew himself well, and accepted himself, even his darker side. He could laugh at himself and celebrate his humanness.

And because he loved and accepted himself just as he was, others could do the same. That's difficult to understand sometimes, but it's true: no one else is going to love and accept us until we come to love and accept ourselves.

We teach others how to treat us by the way we treat ourselves, so perhaps it makes sense to apply a variation of the Golden Rule: "Do unto ourselves as we would have others do unto us."

Can I allow my kindness to myself overflow to another person today?

The farmer may only be planting a seed, but if he opens his eyes he is feeding the whole world.
—Omaha Bee

A traveler journeying through a small village came upon some workers building an impressive structure. "What are you doing?" he asked. The first worker, a young, impatient man, replied in disgust, "I am making three dollars an hour and I'm getting very tired!" The visitor asked another man the same question. "I'm mixing concrete, as you can plainly see," came the sarcastic reply. Finally, a woman working nearby left her wheelbarrow full of bricks and approached the stranger. "We are building a hospital," she said with pride. "Now we will be able to care for all the region's people. Babies will be born here. Lives will be saved."

The stranger looked at the woman with admiration and spoke directly to her. "I know, for this is my hospital. Only you hold the vision of what it is you are creating." The wealthy benefactor then put the woman in charge of construction so his hospital would be built by one who truly understood.

Will I see the importance of even the small things I do today?

This Mouse must give up one of his Mouse ways
of seeing things in order that he may grow.
—Hyemeyohsts Storm

There is an American Indian tale of a mouse who heard a roaring in his ears and set out to discover what it was. He encountered many animals who helped him on his way. Finally, the mouse had a chance to offer help to another. He gave away his eyes to help two other animals.

Without his sight, defenseless, he waited for the end. Soon he heard the sound eagles make when they dive for their prey. The next thing the mouse knew, he was flying. He could see all the splendor around him. Then he heard a voice say, "You have a new name. You are Eagle."

Like the mouse, we also feel something inside us we'd like to explore. That secret, like all others, has its answer hidden deep within us, yet right under our very nose. Often, we merely have to give up our eyes and see in a different way. When we do this, we are rewarded with a new kind of vision, one that lets us discover our true potential.

How can I look at things differently today?

*He who distributes the milk of human kindness
cannot help but spill a little on himself.*
—James Barrie

We like ourselves best when we like those around
us. When we smile at them, they smile back; when we
ask them, they tell us about themselves. When we
scowl at people, they'll frown back; when we ignore
them, they'll walk away.

It's true that we get back what we put into things,
whether it's work, play, love, or gardening. We decide
by the extent of our commitment how valuable or enjoyable or depressing an experience can be for us.

Our actions toward others come right back to us.
When we smile at people, they smile back, and we feel
good. Sometimes feeling good about ourselves depends on feeling good about others. When we send
out that smile of ours, those who get it pass it on, and
we have added power to the happiness of this world.

What can I do to show my fondness for others today?

Laughter by definition is healthy.
—Doris Lessing

A hearty laugh can warm a cold room and make our spirits soar. But many of us are afraid to laugh, especially when we make mistakes. We think we're supposed to be perfect, and we don't allow ourselves to make mistakes. However, we're not a mold punched out by a machine. We're human beings, with all our wonderful flaws. It is those flaws that make our lives interesting and surprising. Who knows when we might accidentally bump into a chair or catch our sweater on a doorknob? We needn't feel self-conscious, it happens to many of us.

The ability to laugh at ourselves is a gift from God. All we need to do is grab it and use it. Then we will see how healthy and powerful laughter can be.

Can I find the humor in my mistakes today?

*There is no such thing as a long piece of work,
except one that you dare not start.*
—Charles Baudelaire

A big assignment can be scary to face. We may start
to think that how we do on the assignment will determine if we're good or bad people. The more we think
about it, the harder that task seems. The key to overcoming our negative feelings is to say to ourselves that
we are capable of finishing our projects. We must say
it over and over until we start believing it's true. Then
we can attack the assignment with vitality and positive
energy we didn't know we had.

We can make up our minds to do our best and accept that from ourselves. We say Edison was a genius,
but our lightbulbs still burn out regularly. Even Einstein was wrong once in a while, and he knew it, but
that didn't stop him from trying.

When we feel afraid to start something because it
seems too big a job, let's stop and think what the first
step would be, and do each small step in its own time.

What can I start that I've been putting off?

The older you get the more you realize that kindness is synonymous with happiness.
— Lionel Barrymore

Once in a while, we forget about the kind things people have done for us. Do we remember the next door neighbor who helped us get our kite out of a tree, or the brother who helped us finish a project for school? If we think about these kindnesses, we will remember how happy we were to receive them.

These people and others may need a kindness we can give. Our next-door neighbor may get sick and need us to go to the store, a brother or sister may need to borrow a radio, or the elderly person down the street may need the lawn mowed. Whenever we take the time to give a kindness, we will find that like the boomerang, it returns to us in the form of happiness.

Will I be alert to my chances to give kindness today?

Being a healthy parent means being firm but nurturing, giving children a decent sense of the boundaries along with lots of unconditional love.
—Karen Shaud

In a healthy family, life goes along and everybody pitches in to do the housework. Some people wonder why housework is such a big deal. It is because people need to contribute to a group in order to feel they belong to it. Housework makes us part of the same group—our house, our family. We make our house comfortable so we can feel comfortable and safe in it. We show love for ourselves by making our surroundings likeable. And when we do physical work, we can do our inner housekeeping, letting go of negative feelings that pile up during the day.

On days when life feels out of control, we feel good when we do one simple job: clean the messy desk, wash dirty dishes, shovel the snowy walk. In this way we regain control of our feelings as well as a perspective on those things within our control.

What simple work do I need to do to feel better today?

Gentleness is not a quality exclusive to women.
—Helen Reddy

Each of us has our soft side: maybe it's when we're petting a kitten, caring for a baby robin with an injured wing, or soothing a crying child who is afraid. Behaving in a gentle way toward others gives us warm feelings inside. It also encourages others to treat us gently, too.

We don't always feel like being gentle. If we're sad or worried about school or a friend, we might not even notice the people around us who need our gentleness. But when we remember gentleness, it lifts our spirits. Two people will always be happier when we're gentle—the person we've been gentle to and ourselves.

Who can I share my gentleness with today?

I never dreamed of so much happiness when I was the ugly duckling.
—Hans Christian Andersen

The ugly duckling was not really ugly at all, he was just different. The other ducks teased and pecked and even bit him until the ugly duckling flew away. He wandered around for a year, and was treated as an outcast everywhere. In the spring, he saw a group of swans on a lake, and wanted very much to join them. As he swam out toward them, he was astounded to notice his reflection in the water—he was a swan! The other swans welcomed him warmly, and found him to be beautiful.

Most of us go through times when we feel different from those around us. These are painful and lonely times, but it doesn't mean there is anything wrong with us. Like the ugly duckling, we will come into a time when we will be loved. All the pain and loneliness we have felt will help us fully appreciate the acceptance when we find it.

How can I treasure the ways I am different from others today?

Each man with a new idea is a crank until the idea succeeds.

—Mark Twain

What does it mean to be different? How does it feel? Is it okay to act or look or be different from everyone else at times? Sometimes, maybe even most of the time, it feels safer to blend into the crowd. We don't want to stick out like a sore thumb. But sometimes it's when we are different that we discover new things no one has ever thought of or done before.

We don't want to spend our whole lives doing only what others do. And there are times when we must take a stand if what others are doing is wrong. Perhaps it's good practice to try to do some little thing differently once in a while, to stand out from the crowd, just to get used to it. We might even like it. After all, if no one ever dares to be different, how would our world ever change for the better?

What little thing can I do to stand out from the crowd today?

The difficulty in life is the choice.
—George Moore

How we choose to spend our time says much about what is important to us. If we have no goals, we may try to kill time. If we have too many goals, there may not be enough time in the day to do all we set out to do. We must make some choices based on our values. We may need to take more time for some things, and let go of others. For example, this year will we try to learn to play the guitar? Perhaps we have finally decided to drop out of that club which seems to have little purpose. Will we give more time to work, or less time? With each of these choices, we shape our lives. We can do it with the touch of an artist if we pay attention to the choices we are making.

What is truly important to me today?

'Tis God gives skill, but not without men's hands.
He could not make Antonio Stradivarius violins
without Antonio.

—George Eliot

When she was four years old, she climbed onto the piano stool. To her parents' astonishment, a simple prelude she'd heard on the radio flew across the keys from her fingers. That very week they found her a teacher, and the house was filled with the music of her developing talent.

While other girls played, made the honor roll, starred on the basketball team, and dated boyfriends, she sat inside at her beloved piano and practiced. At seventeen, when she made her debut, the critics said, "She's a natural. A genius!"

We know she was no natural, but through hard work, she made her piano playing part of her nature. When we put love into our labor, our own dreams grow into being.

Am I willing to make some sacrifices today to do the things I really want to do?

Love is always open arms.

—Leo Buscaglia

There is a story about a boy who left home and dishonored his father by spending a large amount of money on fast and reckless living. When the boy's money ran out, he was faced with the prospect of returning home to face his father, knowing the father had every reason to be disappointed in him. Filled with fear and shame he approached his home, his mind racing with words of apology. Before the boy could say a word, his father rushed to him with open arms and hugged his lost son in joy and love.

Have we done this? Have we found it in our hearts to approve whatever a loved one does, even if we would have wanted something different?

Love like this is the highest kind of love. It finds joy in others no matter what, because it recognizes the freedom of those we love, and doesn't chain them to our own wants. It is the same kind of love God has for us.

Are my arms open today?

Tyger, Tyger, burning bright,
In the forests of the night;
What immortal hand or eye,
Could frame thy fearful symmetry?
Did He who made the Lamb make thee?
          —William Blake

Is there a lamb and a tiger inside us? Is there any commandment, written on the sky or a stone tablet, denying us our perfect right to be both tiger and lamb? The tiger, beast made of fire and night, shows its teeth when it blazes with love; the lamb, orphan wrapped in soft blanket of cloud, weeps to receive that same love. So we give and take, are strong and weak, guilty and innocent, wrong and right. So we are balanced, even when we seem to be in conflict.

When we learn to accept all the things we can be, we will be able to love all the ways the world outside us can be.

What conflict is helping me grow today?

Where is the yesterday that worried us so?
—Joan Walsh Anglund

In the fairy tale *The Last Dream of the Old Oak Tree*, the oak tree felt sorry for the day-fly. The day-fly only lives for one day, and the tree was already 365 years old. But the day-fly was so enjoying his one day that the tree's sympathy puzzled him. The day-fly said to the tree, "You may have thousands of my days, but I have thousands of moments to be pleased and happy in."

And so the day-fly continued to dance in the sun and smell the clover and honeysuckle. His day ended as happily as he spent it, and he settled down on a blade of grass.

If all of us could approach our day the way the day-fly does, as though this were our only day, we would spend less time worrying about yesterday and tomorrow.

How can I show my gratitude for the gift of this day?

I want, by understanding myself, to understand others.

—Katherine Mansfield

Growing up to be the best people we can be is a life-long process. As teenagers, we may have thought that twenty-one would be a magic year for us because then we would become adults. We'd be grown up and able to handle any problems that came along, if any did.

But the older we get, the more we realize that growing up is a process that never ends. We are always becoming the people we are capable of being. We're always learning new things about ourselves, and in that process, we're always coming to new understandings about other people and how we can get along with them.

How wonderful that life always offers us room to grow! It makes new discoveries possible all through our lives, and ensures us that we will always have something to offer.

What discovery have I made just today?

Humpty Dumpty sat on a wall,
Humpty Dumpty had a great fall.
                    —*Mother Goose*

Poor Humpty ended up such a scrambled egg. Maybe that's what comes from sitting too long in one place, choosing neither this way nor that, playing both sides against the middle. Maybe he played too much politics, got too much advice, had too much to think about. When the centipede was asked which leg he first moved when setting out on a stroll, he got those legs all tangled in his mind and couldn't walk at all. It is better to be simply moved by those around us, or by our Higher Power, with faith and love. When our thoughts fail, their hearts, hands, and eyes will show the way.

Do I sometimes decide my fate by refusing to decide?

Real men don't vacuum.

—*Anna Genich*

Once, not so long ago, there was a family who tried to divide up housework equally. The father signed up for vacuuming, but he never got around to doing it.

One morning he told everyone about his dream the night before. He was lined up in the dining room with an entire football team, and they all ran in a line through the house, pushing the clutter and dirt up against the walls and out of the way. They came to a finish at the picture window, where the father turned and raised his arms in victory. Then he saw his wife watching him, so he explained, "Heroes don't vacuum."

Perhaps each of us is a hero at one time or another. In that case, we might take turns at different chores, rewarding the day's hero with a day off from vacuuming or dishwashing. When we work together to get the chores done, we become a family of heroes, and can feel a healthy pride in our warm, loving, and clean home.

How can we share housework more equally?

It feels so good to cry. . . .

—Susan Cygnet

Some of us were taught that it's bad to express our feelings directly—crying, wailing, jumping up and down for joy—that it's good manners to talk softly, slowly, and politely and to sit still.

But what happens to our feelings when we sit still? If they don't get expressed, they must be caught inside our bodies. Trapped feelings are like birds in a cage, or a rabbit in a trap—they try to get out any way they can. They peck on our heads and give us headaches. They scratch at our stomachs and make us hurt.

We must let them out. We must laugh and cry. Then our bodies will be happy, and our feelings will curl up in our laps like happy puppies.

Am I ignoring the physical symptoms of trapped feelings?

*The things we hate about ourselves aren't more
real than things we like about ourselves.*
　　　　　　　　　　　　　　　—Ellen Goodman

It is so easy, and tempting, to get down on ourselves, to focus on an imperfect face, a dismal batting
average, our fear of math, or our big feet. The trouble
is, the more we feel sorry for ourselves, the more we
have to feel sorry about. And though it probably
doesn't hurt to indulge in a little self-pity once in a
while, how unfortunate—and limiting—it can be to
let those attitudes define us.

The things we hate about ourselves are no more real
than the things we like about ourselves. The trick is to
dwell on the things we like instead of those we don't.
Even on days when we are sure we are the least loveable creatures in the world, we can "act as if" we like
ourselves. What a surprise at the end of the day, to
find out that we actually do!

What can I like about myself today?

My most irrational fear is that I've forgotten how to cook.

—Pam Sherman

Once there was a teacher who was having nightmares about not doing a good job. In one dream, he couldn't find his classroom and he had to run from building to building. In another dream, he started teaching the lesson in the middle of the woods and didn't notice he was in the wrong place!

Then one Sunday morning, he read an article about a wonderful baker. She baked every day, started bakeries, and fixed food for her friends, yet when the reporter asked her about her fears, she said, "My most irrational fear is that I've forgotten how to cook."

Suddenly the man felt better. He realized someone else had the same kinds of fears. In a miraculous way, our fears become less powerful when we discover that we share them with other people.

What fear can I share with someone right now?

There is a proper balance between not asking enough of oneself and asking or expecting too much.

—May Sarton

The boy's mother baked pies that morning before he was up. She left them on the back porch to cool, their warm aroma curling up through his bedroom window. His mouth was full of the smell when he woke.

Before she left for work, she said, "You may do anything you want today, anything at all. Except for one thing—don't step in those pies."

All day the boy could not get the pies out of his mind; his feet itched just thinking about them.

Don't step in those pies. He heard her voice inside his head. By late afternoon he could control it no longer. One, two, three, four, five six—his foot fell squarely into the middle of each pie.

When we expect the worst from others, we often get just that. The same goes for our expectations of ourselves. And when we trust others, it too is returned.

Do I expect the best of others—and myself—today?

We like someone because, we love someone although.

—Henri de Montherlant

Families are like scissors. They are joined in the middle but often spread wide apart, moving away from each other. When we're not feeling close to other family members—when it's hard even to like them—it seems as though we'll never come together again.

But pity the scrap of paper that comes between our scissor blades! The scissors works together again and slices the trouble clean. When trouble threatens our family, we can slice it through if we move together in love and acceptance.

No matter our small differences, we are part of the same living organism, in a way. The family we live in has been together for many generations, and we are just the most recent members. When we look at one another, we see the products of centuries of love.

When I feel distant from my family, can I locate where we are still joined together?

I have a feeling I should paint what I am supposed to paint. So I sit. And there my hand moves and I made a picture.
　　　　　　　　　　　　—Norval Morrijeau

The writer sits, head in hands, amid a mound of crumpled paper wads. The deadline is tomorrow and not even the first paragraph is written. The writer has been working nonstop since the early morning hours. Frustration pushes the writer up from the chair and out on a long walk in the woods to the stream. After an hour of plunging through lush woods, a rest by the stream listening to the sounds of the rippling water is refreshing. Back at the typewriter, the fingers move, the words flow, the job is done.

Sometimes we need to quiet ourselves to let our inner resources flow through our outer noise. We are always doing what we are supposed to do. Even when things don't seem to come together just right, there is a purpose, even if only to let us know we need to do something else for a while.

How much simpler our lives can be if we only have the faith to accept what happens as a guidepost along a path that is naturally correct.

Am I frustrated with something I should step away from?

*Drag your thoughts away from your troubles
... by the ears, by the heels or any other way
you can manage it. It's the healthiest thing a
body can do.*

—Mark Twain

It requires very little effort—and no imagination
—to start feeling sorry for ourselves. Often, it is easy
to feel sorry for ourselves in our families. Instead of
being inspired by the sports talents of an older
brother, the popularity of a lovely sister, or the fame of
a parent or relative, we often take the easier attitude:
"I'm denied all that he or she has."

If we work hard at developing our own abilities so
that we can excel, we will find ourselves proud of, and
applauding, what others do. If a personal problem
brings us self-pity, we must remind ourselves that all
people have problems. We can cope as well as the best
of people if we learn from them and think positively.

Who among those close to me can I be proud of today?

Come stand by my side where I'm going,
Take my hand if I stumble and fall
It's the strength that you share when
* you're growing*
That gives me what I need most of all.
                              —Hoyt Axton

The bear cub was miserable. Her father, the leader of the pack, had left a month ago to find them winter shelter and had not yet returned. Everyone went on as if nothing had changed.

One evening the cub had a dream in which her father appeared and said, "Daughter, I know you grieve for me, but your burden is too heavy to carry alone. Share it with the others and let them comfort you. Sharing will only lighten your load, and if you can accept help now you will find it easier to give when others are in need."

The next morning the little cub woke with a much lighter heart. As it turns out, everyone in the pack shared the same dream. There was much hugging and crying and reaching out and healing.

We can easily lighten our loads by asking support from those who love us, knowing our turn to help will come.

What help can I ask for today?

Withdrawal is a preparation for emergence.
—Nor Hall

A man lost his family in a car accident and wanted to be alone for a while, but he worried whether he was doing the right thing. Then one day a friend told him that when pine cones fall off the lodge pole pine trees, they are sealed shut so the seeds inside can't get out. The pine cones lie on the forest floor—sometimes for decades—until a forest fire sweeps through. Heat from the fire melts the seal and the seeds fall out and finally grow, and that's why the lodge pole pine is called a "fire-origin species."

The man felt good about himself when he heard the story. "Fire-origin species" is a good name for people who've been burned by life and find new growth as a result.

How have I grown because of pain and difficulty?

Then Bacchus . . . gave him the choice of making
a wish come true. . . . So Midas said, "Make
everything I touch turn gold."

— *Ovid*

Poor King Midas, already rich as a king, was made
poorer by his poor wish. Everything he touched—
small shoots, wet clay, a ripe head of wheat, apples
from a tree—all suddenly went bad, turned into gold,
pure gold. And how could he eat when bread and
fruits, even fresh running water, suddenly shined at
him, yellow, hard, and cold? He could have wished for
a wiser, smaller success. He could have had all familiar
things turn kind at his touch, or loving and good.
Then imagine how he would have touched everyone
he came near.

If some wishes are too good to be true, are others too bad?

It is wealth to be content.

—Lao-tzu

On the evening of the first day of spring, a woman gave her husband a bright red geranium in a clay pot. To celebrate, he placed it on the window sill, and together they marvelled at the delicate petals.

In the harsher light of morning, though, the man frowned at the geranium and said to his wife, "How shabby it makes the sofa look." They spent the day at the furniture store and came home with a new couch, blue with red flowers, like the geranium. They placed the couch in front of the window sill and admired together its grace and line and fashionable upholstery.

But the next morning, the man frowned at the couch and said, "How shabby it makes the carpet look." Soon they had a lavish new carpet, which led to new curtains, lamps, and chairs. When the room was completely redone, they set the geranium back in the window and surveyed the finest room in the neighborhood. The man frowned. "The geranium," he said, "it's out of place. It will have to go."

Will I be able to appreciate life's simple pleasures today?

If there is anything we wish to change in the child, we should first examine it and see whether it is not something that could be better changed in ourselves.

—Carl Jung

Children are smart. Remember how we used to imitate our parents' behavior? We'd dress up like them, mimic their words, even copy their attitudes. We wanted to be just like them because we thought they were the most wonderful people in the world. We can see this happen all around us, younger ones imitating parents, older brothers and sisters, and older friends. It's very flattering.

The problem is that children imitate not just healthy behavior and attitudes, but also sometimes the not-so-healthy. We get very uncomfortable when we look at a younger person misbehaving and see ourselves in that person. Suddenly, we aren't flattered any more.

When we see things we don't like in others, we must first look at ourselves to see if we need changing. This is all we can do—change ourselves. Others may follow our example or they may not, but we can be sure that, when we watch our own behavior, most of what we see of ourselves in others will be flattering.

What change can I make in myself to set a good example today?

One day at a time—this is enough. Do not look back and grieve over the past, for it is gone.
—Ida Scott Taylor

It's not always easy to understand that the day stretching before us is all that counts. Daydreaming about the party last week, or getting upset all over again about a fight we had yesterday with a friend doesn't help us right now. When our minds are on the past, we miss out on the conversation or the activity that is going on around us.

Every moment of the day is special, and guaranteed to help us grow and understand life. All of us have been taught to pay attention in school, or to pay attention when others talk to us. But we should also pay attention to the birds, the sky, even the grass. And we can learn a lot by paying attention to the conversations going on around us, and to the small voice inside us that helps us know right from wrong.

What's going on today is enough to pay attention to.

Am I ready to pay attention to what is around me today?

I measure every Grief I meet
With narrow, probing, Eyes—
I wonder if it weighs like Mine—
Or has an easier size.

—Emily Dickinson

How can we measure all the grief we feel, and how can we put up with it? Doesn't the Grief of Death weigh a ton or more? Doesn't it stretch out to a month, a year, or longer still? Is the Grief of Failure lighter than the Grief of Despair, but maybe longer? Isn't the Grief of Emptiness the heaviest of all? Whether we try to ignore or make light of it, our grief, like a ton of feathers or a ton of rocks, is all the same to us. This much is sure: if we lock our grief in, it will weigh more on us and lengthen out; if we open our hearts with weeping and words, others will help carry it away.

What old sadness can I let go of by sharing it today?

In quarreling about the shadow, we often lose the substance.

—Aesop

There is a fable about a man and his camel who were hired by a wealthy man to get him across the desert. The journey was so hot that they stopped to rest one day, and the only shade to be found was in the shadow of the camel. The two of them began to argue about who had the rights to the camel's shadow—the owner or the renter. They were so involved in their argument that the camel ran away and they didn't notice until it was long gone.

Sometimes we get so caught up in being right that we become like these two, fighting over a shadow. Instead of paying attention to our journey and sharing what we have, we let ourselves get distracted. It is more important to notice what we have, to share it as best we can, and continue our journey.

What can I share with another today?

Take time every day to do something silly.
— *Philipa Walker*

Spring fever may bring out our longings and our sense of unfilled needs for attention, play, or laughter. We may be afraid to express these needs because they are not often taken seriously, but thought of as childish. We may even be afraid our needs are so enormous that they will never be satisfied, and so we keep them bottled up inside ourselves, and all we can express to others is frustration.

Spring is a reminder that we can find a way to satisfy our needs. We can give ourselves a break from work or study, laugh a little, and try to share our laughter with someone else. There are many ways to fulfill a need, and by giving what we have to offer, we may find ourselves getting back exactly what we really need, even though it may not be what we had hoped for.

In the act of giving we learn we are worth giving to also. We learn that we deserve to be loved, most of all by ourselves.

What do I think I need today?

Any time you sense you are getting overrun by outside influences and losing your feelings, put your attention inside your body. Relax... let your breath sink low...breathe in your abdomen....

—*Anne Kent Rush*

When we are feeling as though all our energy is scattered throughout our bodies, we need to practice centering, or focusing this energy into one place. Our center may change from day to day, and each of us feels it differently.

When we're walking, we may feel power coming from our hips and spreading through the body, heart, and mind. When we're in a meditative mood, we may feel warm energy at the back of the head. At other times, we might feel a real centering place in the middle of the chest, right where our heart and arms and breathing come together.

There is no one way to be at peace. Centering is a way for each of us to find and picture to ourselves our focused energy. When we can do this, we increase our power to bring about those things we want from life, those things we really do deserve.

Where is my energy right now?

There are persons who have some parts like me, but no one adds up exactly like me.
                                        —*Virginia Satir*

Most of us feel pretty ordinary. We probably wish we were taller or shorter. Some of us are fat rather than thin. Few of us have perfect skin or teeth. Often we look at others, compare ourselves, and wish we were different. At these times, it's important to remember that each of us is special. We differ from others because we're created for different purposes.

Some of us will make a contribution to the world of sports, some to the art of music. Teaching or medicine will attract others and yet, no two of us will give to the world in the same way. Our unique mixture of looks, attitudes, and abilities will be special and very necessary to the people sharing our lifetime.

How can I give my special gift to the world today?

But don't go into Mr. McGregor's garden.
— *Beatrix Potter*

Since we are members of a family, we are not free to do anything we like. We may not be able to go as far from home as we would like. We may have to get up earlier in the morning than we would like. We may have only limited use of the car. Families set up limits in order to maintain order and happiness. If each of us demanded something different for supper each night, the situation would be unmanageable.

Limits also keep us safe. When Peter Rabbit was told not to go into Mr. McGregor's garden, it was for his own good. Limits and restrictions are a form of love and protection, and we all have them. When we bump up against one of these limits, we can be assured they serve to point us in another direction, one with freedoms of its own which we may never have explored without being forced to.

What freedom can I discover in a limitation today?

Listen to your feelings. They tell you when you need to take care of yourself, like finding a friend if you feel lonely, crying if you feel sad, singing and smiling if you feel happy, and acting frisky if you feel good.

— *Pat Palmer*

When we get too much of anything—too much fun or too much work—we may feel really crummy when it's over.

One way to listen to our crummy feelings is to say, "Here comes the letdown after all that fun." We can imagine a spaceship falling to earth, floating on the ocean. Coming down to earth is as much a part of the adventure as the countdown and blastoff.

A letdown for us means we need to let our bodies and minds rest, just like the spaceship, bobbing around without any special direction. We need to take it easy, do nothing, put off making plans.

Then we can ask God to help us let go of the crummy feelings that come along with a letdown. We can ask the spirit within us to guide us through this time of change. Then we will let down and let go.

What are some things I can do to take it easy the next time I feel down?

I come into the peace of wild things who do not tax their lives with forethought of grief.
—Wendell Berry

Blessed are all birds and animals, the wildest beasts, and, yes, all serpents, too, for they live in nature, in a state of natural grace. They live beyond the rules of evil and good. Their instincts are obedient only to the laws of survival, growth, and health. And as their lives unfurl in obedience to these laws, they suffer no shame, regret, or sin. Nor do they curse their failures, or themselves.

We can learn much from them. They harbor no evil toward one another, and they trust their own inner sense of how to live, and that their Higher Power makes sure everything which befalls them is for the best. Yes, they are blessed, and so are we, the highest animal.

What guilt can I free myself from today, just by letting go?

Nobody can be in good health if he does not have
all the time fresh air, sunshine, and good water.
—Chief Flying Hawk

Before this part of the world was colonized by Europeans, native Americans thrived here, living in wigwams and teepees, spending their time in the fresh air and sun, and drinking pure, fresh water from springs, streams, and rivers. They lived long, healthy lives and almost never were sick—precisely because they knew how important the natural elements were.

When we feel depressed or nervous, nature is a good listener. We can take a walk in the sun, listen to the small birds, or twigs cracking under our feet, or simply the sound of our shoes on the pavement.

We don't need to live in teepees to follow the Indians' example today. But getting out in the sunshine and fresh air every day, even on really cold days, rejuvenates us. Sunlight is healing, fresh air cleanses our lungs and brings more oxygen to the blood and brain. When we think enough of ourselves to take a walk when we need it, even that small amount of self-consideration is also healing.

Have I given myself time to live outside today?

There the penitents took off their shoes
And walked barefoot the remaining mile.
—*Robert Lowell*

Some people have to have pain. If dirt doesn't fall on their heads from the sky, they sulk in corners and hope their flesh turns to dust. They do everything the hard way, even when they know better, and often complain and accuse others for their pain. For people like this, even the song of a bird is a bother. It's better to smile when people like that accuse. It's better to wear shoes when walking on stones, better to take the shortest way. There is weeping and wailing enough in the world, dumps full of worn-out guilt and remorse. When the bird sings, it's better to look up and see that it beats its wings not to punish itself, but to fly.

Do I pity myself when I could be flying?

If I have freedom in my life,
  And in my soul am free,
Angels alone that soar above
  Enjoy such liberty.

— *Richard Lovelace*

When a cow decides to stop nursing her calf, she isn't rejecting it. She knows it's time for the calf to be on its own. Although the calf might feel rejected and puzzled at first, it soon adapts to its new independence and freedom.

When we feel rejected, it's useful to remember that whatever has caused us to feel this way might have nothing to do with us. It might be a reflection of what's happening with someone else, or just the end of a natural stage in life, as with the calf.

When we understand that others' actions toward us come from their own feelings, and that we don't cause their feelings any more than they control ours, we can free ourselves from a little bit of fear and self-hate. We can see what seems to be rejection as an open door, with our freedom on the other side.

What rejections have set me free?

. . . there is as much dignity in tilling a field as in writing a poem.

—Booker T. Washington

It's not what we do for a job that counts, it's how we do it. It's not what our chores at home might be, it's how we do them. And it's not what grades we get in school, but rather how hard we try. Doing our best, whether it's making a bed, writing a report, or listening to a friend tell about an experience gives us a good feeling about ourselves.

Each of us is special to one another. And we are special to this very moment. Because what is past can't be repeated, let's remember to enjoy every moment as it comes. Let's pay close attention to each person, each activity that we encounter today. It's not what we do today, but how we do it that counts.

Can I do each thing well today, even the small things?

If your heart catches in your throat ask a bird how she sings.

—*Cooper Edens*

The idea of your heart getting caught in your throat and then asking a bird how she sings may seem silly. It is, but being silly is sometimes exactly what we need. Instead of always trying to figure out the lumps in our throats, we can learn how to sing with them.

Birds sing all day. Their songs are lighthearted and playful. And they bring us color along with their songs. We have all stopped to notice a special bird outside the window. A bird song can be a lullaby. It can be laughter. We need these things in our lives, too. By playing and laughing, we change the lumps in our throats to songs.

What sadness can I turn into song today?

Gifts are for giving.

—*Ian and Sylvia Tyson*

Many years ago, a young woman named Dorothy was very talented at china painting. She painted tiny scenes on china dishes, the way people today paint on wood and Easter eggs.

Then Dorothy fell in love, got married, and decided she had no time to paint. But as her children grew, they loved to stand at the china cabinet and stare at all her tiny pictures—each one seemed to hold its own special world.

Years passed, and Dorothy's grandchildren also loved to stand and stare at the paintings. Everybody loved her work. They wondered why she didn't take up painting again, but she wouldn't say. Her love of painting seemed to be locked away.

When we give up some talent of our own because we don't have time for it, we lock away part of ourselves. When we imprison our talents, we limit our possibilities. But when we make self-expression a natural part of our day, others can gather around and enjoy the results. There is always room for our talents because they create worlds of their own.

Am I locking something away because I don't have the time?

Inch by inch, row by row
Someone bless these seeds I sow. . .
'Til the rain comes tumblin' down.
                                        —David Mallett

We plant a garden with faith, never knowing exactly what the harvest will bring. We attend to those aspects of gardening which we have some control over, planting good seeds in rich soil, in straight rows, the right distance apart. We weed and fertilize, and we tie up our tomato plants.

We may pray for rain, but we never know if we'll get too much or too little. We can't control the wind or rabbits or bugs or the strongest strains of weeds. Yet most of us do not let these things keep us from planting.

With this same sort of faith we can tend to ourselves. Though we don't know what each day will bring, we can plant the seeds in ourselves to meet most anything. We can rise each morning determined to give what we have. We can't plant the seeds for others, and we can't keep the storms from coming. The beauty is, we don't have to.

What seeds of joy can I plant today?

Hurried and worried until we're buried
And there's no curtain call,
Life's a very funny proposition,
    after all.

—George M. Cohan

Often, when we involve ourselves in a whirlwind of activities, plans, and expectations, we push ourselves so hard that we don't derive any satisfaction from success. We need to face our limitations. We can't do everything we want. Even when we can do a great deal, if we overextend ourselves, take on too much, we will not enjoy ourselves, and there is no reason not to enjoy our work.

Our activities are part of what we are. If we choose to live in a frantic hurry, worrying about the next moment instead of this one, we'll miss life entirely. Part of self-knowledge is learning to pace ourselves to our own speed, learning to set goals we can attain for each day. When we do this, we can say, "Now that I've completed this, I don't have to do one more thing to feel worthwhile."

Am I trying to do too much too fast?

In grief, healing helps us make peace with the meaning of death, which cannot be understood except as an unknown part of life.
—Alla Bozarth-Campbell

It is a sad occasion when we must say good-bye to a loved one or pet who has died. But grief is the only way we can come to understand our losses, and sharing grief helps us experience it more fully.

Perhaps we wish to grieve for something else we've lost, like fading youth, a job, a possession, or a habit we had come to enjoy. It's natural to feel grief over things like this, too.

We can share stories and good memories with other grievers, and give free reign to our tears. Sometimes it seems the more we talk, the sadder we feel about our losses, but when we share these feelings with others, we turn our losses into gain. We heal ourselves, pay tribute to those we grieve for, and share an intimate sense of loss with someone else.

Do I have grief to share?

I meant to do my work today
But a brown bird sang in an apple tree,
And a butterfly flitted across the field
And all the leaves were calling me.
— Richard LeGallienne

The harried hen scurried about her house, trying to put it in order. Some friends she hadn't seen for years were due to arrive later that day, and she wanted everything perfect for them. In a flurry, she made the bed, put away the dishes, and scrubbed the floor. Oh dear, she thought in dismay, I meant to wash the sheets today. Frantically, she flew back to the bedroom and tore the sheets from the made bed.

Just then, a neighbor arrived and stood at hen's door, watching her anxiously rush about. "Dear hen," he said in a patient, loving tone, for he was quite fond of her, "You will never enjoy your visit if you continue to race about. Come. Sit and rest and tell me of these friends. Have you any snapshots?" The hen did as her neighbor had suggested, and soon her friends arrived to find her relaxed, refreshed, and warm with the memories of them.

What is my real work for the day?

Courage is resistance to fear, mastery of fear not absence of fear.

—Mark Twain

It is not unusual to feel afraid. It is unusual, however, to hear anyone admit to feeling afraid. Sometimes we think there are some people who are so cool and calm that they never feel afraid. This may make us think we're not as good because we know how often we feel afraid. This is why it is important to think about what courage really is. It is not the absence of fear. Courage is not letting fear stop us from doing what we need to do.

We might have to get up in front of a group to give a speech. We could give in to our fear and not give the speech, or we could admit our fear to those who love us, and then go ahead and do the best we can. To go ahead in the face of fear is courage.

What am I afraid of?

My life has been a tapestry of rich and
   royal hue,
An everlasting vision of the everchanging view,
A wondrous woven magic in bits of blue
   and gold,
A tapestry to feel and see, impossible to hold.
                                        —*Carole King*

Our lives are patchwork quilts of mismatched fabrics, all stitched together by an invisible seamstress. The tattered, blood-red scraps of quarrels, the beige of pastry crust baked on Saturdays in a grandmother's kitchen that always smelled sweet, the brilliant colors of our happy moments—picnics and sunsets and laughter—all these are necessary pieces of the tapestry of our lives, even our cold, white doubts and emptiness.

All the colors of life sewn together with the green thread of growth. We are a mixture of feelings and experiences. Often, we want to cut away a square of painful memory. But without it, our quilt would lose its beauty, for contrast would disappear. If a piece is removed, the rest is weakened and incomplete.

How well can I accept any pain I feel today as a part of my own beauty?

Unused capacities atrophy, cease to be.
—Tillie Olsen

Those of us who have suffered a broken bone and had to put up with a cast for several weeks know how hard it is to use muscles that have been inactive for so long. They have gotten weak from lack of use, and we have to begin to develop our strength all over again.

The same thing happens if we don't use our other capacities. If we don't constantly use our minds to think and learn, we become dull people, almost incapable of new thoughts and insights. If we don't use our hearts to love, we become uncaring and insensitive—much like Scrooge in *A Christmas Carol*. If we don't use our creative talents—to draw or write or sew, or whatever it is we're into—we lose the ability to do those things.

On the other hand, like our muscles, our other capacities can be strengthened and developed by daily use. We exercise our hearts by being kind and loving, our minds by thinking, our imaginations by being creative. In this way, we become spiritually powerful, a force for good in the world.

How can I exercise my assets today?

*"The horror of that moment," the King went on,
"I shall never forget."
"You will, though," the Queen said, "if you don't
make a memorandum of it."*

—Lewis Carroll

Crises come in many forms. When we are in the middle of any kind of crisis, we may feel like we have fallen into a deep hole. We may see no way out, and begin to feel hopeless and overwhelmed by the size and darkness of the hole.

Yet we are not alone. An animal caught in a hole would cry out until someone came along and helped it out. We, too, can call out for help—to our Higher Power and to the important people in our lives. We can learn to trust that, with the help of our friends and our Higher Power, we will be able to crawl out of our holes.

With trust, we will climb out of our crises and be healed with the passage of time. Such holes are a part of our landscape, yet every time we will be able to climb out and walk, leaving the darkness behind us.

What help can I ask for today?

Crying only a little bit is no use.
You must cry until your pillow is soaked.
Then you can get up and laugh. . . .
                                    —Galway Kinnell

Many of us were raised to deny our feelings; that is, we might have been allowed to describe them politely, but we were not allowed to express feelings on the spot by wailing, jumping for joy, or dancing. These outward expressions are often considered rude. In a proper home, we often hear, if people have feelings, they have them quietly. But many of us have suffered living this way.

We need a full and thorough expression of a feeling in order to know it, experience it, and move beyond it. This is the way we let go of sadness, for instance.

Feelings come and go. If we are not afraid to let them have their moment, we will not be afraid to express them.

What am I feeling right now?

I will not cut my conscience to fit this year's fashions.

—Lillian Hellman

Every fall there seems to be something new and different to get for school—a special folder, a new style of pants, or maybe a different haircut. These things change from year to year.

Sometimes we get carried away with the current trends. We start putting too much importance on such things. We may be tempted to join our friends in teasing someone who doesn't wear the "right" clothes, or avoid someone who doesn't say the "right" things. This is when we need God's help. Perhaps we can become the leaders for the next trend—looking beyond appearances of others to the beauty inside them.

Will I see the true value in those around me today?

If there is a God, there must also be a Goddess.
Neither is more important than the other, both
are in balance, together they create a Whole.
—Marion Weinstein

In the olden days, the Goddess was seen as a Trinity: the Maiden or Virgin, the Mother, and the Crone. The Virgin was one-in-herself, owned by no man. The Mother was the one in the fullness of her creative powers, whether creating children, works of art, or other work out in the world. The Crone was the wise old woman.

Both women and men connected with the Triple Goddess. To women, the Goddess was a symbol of their innermost selves and the beneficent, nurturing, liberating power within. The Crone, for example, showed them that all phases of life are sacred, that age is a blessing rather than a curse. To men, the Goddess represented their connection with their own hidden female selves.

We are all made up of aspects of both sexes. This is our balance. When we accept what we know to be truly ourselves, which is often much more than the old role models for men and women allow, we become complete men and women.

What male and female strengths do I have within me?

The soul would have no rainbow had the eyes no tears.

—John Vance Cheney

If there were no rain, fields would become parched and brittle, and many creatures would die. If we could not cry, all our emotions would eventually dry up, too, and soon we would not laugh either. Our tears cleanse us. Our tears heal. They make us whole.

Tears are as important to our growth as rain is to a flower. They help release the pressure of sadness so we can feel better. After a storm, when the sun shines again through the clouds, a brightly colored rainbow appears. After our tears, our inner sun shines, and rainbows are formed from our pain.

How well can I accept my tears as part of my happiness today?

Hold fast to dreams
For if dreams die,
Life is a broken-winged bird
That cannot fly.

—*Langston Hughes*

Watching birds spread their wings and soar can re-mind us of the best in ourselves. In joyful moments we all feel our own desire to fly, to reach toward what we dream of doing.

Our dreams give us a direction to fly. Birds fly to-ward the light for joy, toward green leaves for shelter, to water and berries for food. In the same way, our dreams direct us to the course of our own joy, shelter, and nourishment.

Sometimes as we fly, we bump into disappoint-ments. They may temporarily stun us or slow us down. But just like birds that are occasionally wounded, we can heal ourselves and fly again. We can choose to not let the hardships of life break our spir-ited wings. Rather, we can keep spreading our wings, soaring in the spirit of joy.

Am I flying today, or must I heal a wound first?

A bird came down the walk:
He did not know I saw;
He bit an angle-worm in halves
And·ate the fellow, raw.

— Emily Dickinson

We must look very different to the birds than we do to each other. Likewise, birds look different to us than they do to each other. Neither the way we see birds nor the way they see us is the "right" way. They are simply different ways of seeing.

If we could turn birds into people so they would see things the way we do, eat the way we do, and think the way we do, we would lose the idea of flying. The knowledge that flight is possible is a gift birds have given us.

We do well to remember this when we get upset at others for not doing things the way we would. Varieties of styles, appetites, and ideas are gifts that enrich the world and bring more possibilities into our lives.

When others disagree with me today, will I accept their gifts?

Everyone has talent. What is rare is the courage to follow the talent.

—Erica Jong

How easy it is to look at others with envy, certain that everyone we know is better in every way: school, sports, games, appearance. What we may not know is that each of us is exactly right the way we are. And what's more, no one of us is without talent. Perhaps we simply have not discovered it yet, or maybe we've been certain we knew what the talent should be, rather than letting the talent within us emerge.

It's reassuring to know that we are talented, that we are special just as we are, that no one else is able to bring to this life exactly the same ingredients that we're able to bring.

What special talent shall I exercise today?

A person can grow only as much as his horizon allows.

—*John Powell*

Should you be a doctor or perhaps an astronaut? Maybe being a writer or an athlete appeals to you. Dreaming of what to be can be useful. It helps us set our goals and learn our values. Also, using our imagination lets us "try on" a future role. We learn about our life's direction through our dreams of where to go and what to do.

Not all dreams are helpful, however. Sometimes we daydream about other things when we really do need to listen. Learning how to use our imagination to guide our plans for growing up takes practice.

Imagining ourselves happy and brave will help us feel both. Imagining ourselves as failures can be just as powerful. Let's respect the power of the imagination and use it to form good images of our future.

How can I build goodness and success into my future today?

I have spread my dreams under your feet;
Tread softly because you tread on my dreams.
  —William Butler Yeats

When we hold a piece of crystal to the light, it paints rainbows on the wall. When we tap it lightly with a spoon, it sings like a bell. But when we drop it, it shatters in colorless, silent pieces on the floor.

Human beings, sometimes to our amazement, can be as fragile as glass. It's especially easy to forget what makes people we live with or have known for a long time shine or sing. We take for granted the very qualities that made us love them in the first place.

When we forget how to see and hear the people we love, how to appreciate them, we grow careless. Too often, from sheer neglect, the relationship between us grows dull and silent, then slips, falls, and shatters. Paying attention to other people's needs and feelings can prevent this.

Whose presence can I appreciate today?

"Take it away at once," stormed the Princess, stamping her tiny foot in its embroidered slipper. *"I hate real flowers; their petals fall off and they die."*

—Hans Christian Andersen

If love is reserved for things that never die, love is doomed to die. If flowers fade in a minute or two, will not stones wear to sand in time? Even this earth, this garden of life, one day will be like the dust of stars. We must walk gratefully, carefully on it now. Now is the lifetime that passes here, now is the best of all days; now is the flower's eternity in the sun, our chance of a lifetime.

This is all we have, this moment. Within it, anything can be done, any dream fulfilled, if we only use it well. Why hold back? There is nothing to stop us.

What can I do to use this moment well?

*Our deeds will travel with us from afar, and
what we have been makes us what we are.*
— George Eliot

We grow within, the way a tree does. We've all seen
the rings representing the years of a tree's life. We
carry our histories with us, too. Our actions, our attitudes, our goals, and our dreams all gather together
inside us to make us what we are today. We're probably ashamed of some of our past, but our behavior
each day adds to our history, and we control it.

We can't escape our mistakes, but we don't have to
repeat them; and every day that is lived well gives us a
history to be proud of.

*How can I add goodness to my past — and my future — by
my actions today?*

Talking little, and
with the low, tender part
of our voices, as in nodding to one who already
knows what you mean.
— Tess Gallagher

Once there was a small child whose only word was *no*. When she wanted to indicate yes, she nodded her head emphatically. What she liked to do instead of talk was play. She liked to play outside in the meadow with the bugs and rocks and plants.

The mullein was her favorite plant. She rubbed the soft, furry leaves across her cheek. Her mother told her that in the old days, American Indians used these leaves as bandages. Several years later, Lucy picked a mullein leaf and took it in the house to her mother. "Look, Mama. Indian owee."

We, too, can remember some surprising things from the dim past, before we could talk or understand all that went on around us. Communication does not always depend on words alone but on the tenderness with which they are spoken. Walking through the world in a tender, loving way is a form of communication that goes beyond words to our deepest feelings.

What are some of the ways we show our love without words?

Planning is deciding what to change today so tomorrow will be different from yesterday.
—Ichak Adizes

A house is like a lump of clay that can be molded and changed. It can be fixed and shaped, torn down and added to, painted, papered, carpeted, and panelled. We can think about how to change it, find pictures in books, and order plans. We can stock up on supplies, take fix-it classes, and get advice from others. But the house will remain unchanged until we pick up a brush, grab a bucket of paint, and get to work. Only then will we see tomorrow the results of what we did today.

Our plans help us construct a vision of how we'd like the future to be, but only actions will bring these things about. With confidence in the rightness of our desires, we can be assured that God never gives us a dream we can't reach.

What action can I take today to make tomorrow's changes?

To apologize: to lay the foundation for a future offense.

—Ambrose Bierce

"I'm sorry," said the blind man as he whipped the mare. "I'm sorry," said the mare, as she kicked the blind man in return.

"We're sorry," they assured themselves, as they pushed each other around again and again. Often, we push our troubles with other people around, creeping along in the old rough way, refusing to change because we're too involved to see another choice.

There's little sorrow in being sorry all the time. A true apology doesn't try to explain. Sometimes a true apology just breaks down and cries. Then maybe we're ready to go on—take someone by the hand, tell the whole sad truth, and work to find a better way.

Are my apologies excuses, or requests to be forgiven?

I'm delighted that the future is unsure.
That's the way it should be.
                              —*William Sloane Coffin*

Some of life's richest moments are the most unexpected: the old friend met by chance, or the new one discovered when neither of us was really looking; the toy at the bottom of the toy box, rediscovered and loved anew; the book, the flower, the shaft of light we were in the right place at the right time to notice and embrace.

It is important to dream and plan, to work toward goals, to mark the milestones we pass on life's journey. No less important, though, is to open ourselves to the unexpected joys awaiting us every day.

Am I ready, today, to expect the unexpected?

I would be honest, for there are those who trust me.

—Howard Arnold Walter

Some of those around us seem to see only the good in us. They trust and respect us, even when we ourselves may not feel we deserve it.

A young girl once talked about her grandfather. She said, "He was the only person in my life who saw the good in me." She mentioned that she sought to please her grandfather and not disappoint the trust which he placed in her. He brought out the best in her because of the way that he looked at her. Each of us can be like this grandfather by focusing on the good in other people. We can use our spiritual eyes to see love, honesty, trustworthiness, and unselfishness in the heart of another. As we look for the good, we are doing our part to help create it.

Do I see the good in those around me right now?

Talent—I don't know what that is. It's will. You dream a dream and then you build it.
—Philippe Petit

Even the most accomplished pianists begin at some point by playing simple scales and exercises. With daily practice, their hands learn to find the correct notes and become limber enough to play well. They learn each new piece of music very slowly at first, until, with study and practice, they can play almost without effort.

In the beginning, the pianist only dreams of being an accomplished musician. This dream helps the artist through many hours of practice and study.

Talent is really the combination of a dream and the time spent building it. We develop our ability by devoting time to the skills that interest us. Like the musician, we become talented through daily practice— the daily building of a dream. By developing our talents, we develop who we are.

Who am I becoming today?

Every tomorrow has two handles. We can take hold of it with the handle of anxiety or the handle of faith.

—Henry Ward Beecher

Once there was a boy who always looked on the bright side and always expected the best. He expected to like brussels sprouts before he had ever tasted them, for instance, and to like his teacher on the first day of school. Because he had such a sunny outlook on things, he was rarely disappointed.

One Christmas morning the boy and his brother awoke to find many presents. All except one small one were for the boy's brother. The brother opened his gifts with glee—a train set, a toy robot, a cowboy outfit, even his own TV.

Through all this, the boy smiled expectantly, confident the contents of his small box would equal the splendor of his brother's gifts. When it was his turn he ripped the box open to find only a pile of hay.

The boy clapped his hands with joy and ran immediately to the backyard. "Yippee!" he cried "I got a pony."

If I expect the best, just for today, what wondrous things might happen?

What is moral is what you feel good after.
—Ernest Hemingway

Each of us has a little voice inside us that tells us what is good and what is bad. For instance, if our friends are making fun of someone who is different than we are, how do we feel if we join in the laughter? Do we feel more comfortable if we refuse to join in, or if we tell them their jokes are not funny?

As we grow, we learn more and more to trust the inner voice. Sometimes, in times of dark confusion, we have to listen very hard, but it is there to guide us. It is a beacon showing us the way out of the darkness of uncertainty. It is our guide to goodness.

Will I have the courage to listen to my inner voice today?

More majestic than a cardinal, as shining as a pyx.

—*Gustave Flaubert*

What in the world is a pyx? If we don't have an expert nearby, we'll have to look in a book. There we'll find it defined, explained, fixed. Now what in the world is love? It doesn't live in a tree or a book, so where in the world do we look? Can we find love in the house, maybe swept under the rug? Can we know the feel of it in our hands, see it written on the lines of faces we know? Does it make a sound—maybe laugh and cry? Does it know how to speak, form words carefully, write letters? Is it only written on the heart?

We find love inside us, and our love seeks itself out in others. We find it in the familiar footfall of a brother or sister, the sound of a parent's voice in the next room, and yet, too often we don't express it directly. When we do, our love thrives in all we do together.

What does love have to do with the ordinary facts of life?

Growth is the only evidence of life.
　　　　　　　　—John, Cardinal Newman

We should be thankful we can never reach complete serenity. If we could, we would never have the need to improve ourselves. We would stop growing, because there would be no reason to learn any more than we already know, and we would become bored. Even the things which seem so serene in nature usually contain a struggle within. A lake, with a swan gliding slowly across it, seems a perfect picture of serenity. But, unseen below the surface, fish, turtles, and frogs struggle each day for survival.

The important thing is to accept the struggles as a part of the beauty of life, not as blemishes on it.

What struggles shall help me grow better today?

He that cannot forgive others breaks the bridge
over which he must pass himself; for every man
has need to be forgiven.
—Thomas Fuller

We have all seen adventure movies in which the heroes or villains are caught on a bridge that collapses. As they fall to whatever lies below, they are perhaps able to climb to one side or the other. But for the time being, their ability to cross between the two sides is gone.

When we have been hurt by people in our lives, or when we have hurt others, mutual forgiveness is needed in order to rebuild the trust between us. It is very much like rebuilding a bridge—one piece at a time. We take cautious steps at first—testing the safety and strength of our bridge.

When two people have become separated by loss or anger, it is forgiveness that can rebuild the bridge between them. Forgiveness needs time and so does the rebuilding of trust.

Can I begin to rebuild a friendship today?

As we learn we always change, and so our perception. This changed perception then becomes a new Teacher inside each of us.
—Hyemeyohsts Storm

Hyemeyohsts Storm's book, *Seven Arrows*, tells the stories of one of the Indian tribes in this country that believed change was important for growth. Change is sometimes frightening. We usually prefer the familiar, no matter how uncomfortable, over taking a chance on the unknown.

When fear gets in the way of making healthy changes, we talk to fear, inviting it along with us on our course of action. Getting to know fear allows us to ask it for a gift: the courage to walk with fear by our side and learn from it as we go. It allows us to learn which fear is blocking our progress and which fear is healthy—cautioning us against actions that might be harmful.

What fear might I make a friend of today?

For nothing can be sole or whole that has not been rent.

—W. B. Yeats

The maple out front is young and healthy, but it grows in the shape of a Y. Neighborhood tree experts have warned that as it grows, it will split in half as the weight of the two main branches pull down against each other. One of these two beautiful branches, already lush with new leaves, must be cut. But once pruned, the remaining branch will straighten as it reaches for the sun. It will grow faster, and the whole tree will live many years longer—all by cutting it back today.

Sometimes we are like this tree. We go in too many directions, and can't seem to do any one thing well. When this happens, we need to give something up, to choose which direction we want and stick with it. The results will be well worth the price.

What is holding me back from growth?

Who will tell whether one happy moment of love or the joy of breathing or walking on a bright morning and smelling the fresh air, is not worth all the suffering and effort which life implies. . . .
—Erich Fromm

A robin comes alive by breaking out of its shell. The small bird struggles to break out of the safety of the blue egg. Once out, it struggles to grow, slowly learning how to eat, walk, and fly.

We, too, struggle as we grow. There is brokenness in all of our lives—broken hearts and broken dreams. Yet these experiences open our way to a world of growing. We find comfort in the presence of a Power greater than ourselves, in the same way a baby bird finds warmth near the body of its mother. We, too, can grow stronger every day, learning to take in nourishment and trying out our new wings.

What struggles have made me as strong as I am today?

If it's sanity you're after, there's no recipe like laughter.
— Henry Rutherford Elliot

A smile is the earliest form of communication. A human infant smiles in the first few weeks of life. As the child grows, it learns how to turn the smile into a laugh—a joyous response reflecting pleasure.

A sense of humor, a feeling of fun, and an ability to laugh are all signs of emotional maturity. Healthy laughter frees us; it is the sunshine that makes life's shadows interesting. When we develop the ability to see the humor in a situation, we gain the ability to handle it.

We were born with smiles. They are as much a part of us as our teeth and hair. Polished and cared for, our smiles can grow into a sense of humor that will help us through the painful times.

How can I turn troubles into smiles today?

The prayer of the chicken hawk does not get him the chicken.

—Swahili proverb

Imagine flying high over the grassy plains searching with piercing eyes for dinner down below. The sun is warm on our backs as we catch the heated updrafts and rest, always watching, always praying, that dinner will be provided for the little ones back in the nest.

Dinner will be provided, of that the hawk is sure. It has faith. But the faith and the prayer will not put the chicken in its talons. It is going to have to keep looking, and, when it spots the prey, its wings will fold back, and its sleek body will plummet out of the sky. It will brake quickly with broad wings and clasp the unsuspecting supper on the fly.

Like the hawk, once we have prayed, we must get to work. Our goal isn't going to be done for us. We can pray for the strength and wisdom we will need to get it done, and that prayer will be answered. But, as the hawk knows, it's up to us to do the work.

What is my goal today, and my first step toward it?

*Spring does not ask an audience, but shapes
each blossom perfectly, indifferent to applause.*
—Joan Walsh Anglund

In the spring each blossom brings its own shape,
color, and fragrance. The lilacs come early to spread
their lavender splash. Apple trees burst into white,
cherry blossoms into pink, and each weaves its
unique and pleasant perfume.

They don't bloom because someone told them to,
or because they will receive anything in return. They
bloom for the pure joy of blooming. They bloom because that is what they are here to do.

Each one of us blooms in our own time, with our
own color and fragrance. Every one of us is a special
and important blossom, and we are all part of the tree
of life.

How will my day today help me grow?

Do we really know anybody? Who does not wear one face to hide another?

—Francis Marion

A woman in her fifties watched her mother in her eighties struggle against the wrinkles in her face and neck, trying to hide them, pretending they weren't there. She wanted her mother to accept that she was getting older but found her unwilling to listen.

Haven't we all run into this situation? We can learn so much just by remembering that what is right for one person may not be right for another, and others are entitled to decide how they want to behave. Often, we are just worried about ourselves, concerned, for instance, with our own ability to age gracefully. We don't need someone else to do it for us. We can take care of ourselves.

What do I worry about in another that I can take care of in myself?

An oak and a reed were arguing about their strength. When a strong wind came up, the reed avoided being uprooted by bending and leaning with the gusts of wind. But the oak stood firm and was torn up by the roots.

—*Aesop*

Within each of us, as in the reed and the oak, is a single characteristic which is both our strongest and weakest trait. The bending which keeps the reed alive makes it weak, we might think. Some of us see both sides of every argument and are good team players, fair judges, and compassionate friends. But like the reed—always bending to the needs of others—we may never know what we want or who we are.

Some of us believe we are like the oak: strong and tough and successful in the face of most difficulty. But we may never learn to accept flaws in ourselves.

We are wise to remember that no trait is strong or weak, but we make it so by how we use it. We can use our strength to stand straight in the face of hardship, and we can use our strength to bend.

What is my strongest and weakest trait?

If your life is ever going to get better, you'll have to take risks. There is simply no way you can grow without taking chances.

—David Viscott

One sunny day a caterpillar who was afraid of the dark came to a tunnel which lay squarely in its path. It had a choice of going back where it started, or summoning the courage to crawl into the darkness. "What shall I do?" wondered the caterpillar. "If I go back home, I won't get where I want to go, but I'm so afraid!"

Just then, a voice called out from the tunnel. "I can hear you, Mr. Caterpillar. I am Mr. Beetle. I am here in the tunnel and I can see the other end. If you come through, you won't lose your fear of the dark, but you will get where you want to go."

We are all like the caterpillar once in a while. But if we let our fear stop us from doing things which are necessary to our growth, we will never realize what courage we really have.

Is my fear a necessary part of new experiences?

Though we travel the world over to find the beautiful, we must carry it with us or we find it not.

—Ralph Waldo Emerson

The little rabbit stood alone, watching her family and friends hop and skip about her in the forest, playing her favorite rabbit game. Try as she might, each time she attempted to join in, she tripped about awkwardly. When this happened, the other rabbits laughed uproariously at her and called her "Grace." Soon even she forgot her real name. But in the moments when Grace was alone, she danced around the trees with ease. She was as smooth and graceful as any ballerina. An old owl sat high above her one night, watching her intently. The moonlight streamed through the treetops like a soft spotlight and he sat and watched as little Grace moved in and out of the moonbeams. Finally he said, "Grace, you are more graceful than any creature I've ever seen." Grace was startled that someone had been watching her, but listened carefully to the wise owl's words as he continued. "You have carried this beauty within you all the time, but locked it inside when you tried too hard." If we remember to relax and trust in ourselves, we, too, will discover that we are able.

What hidden ability can I set loose today?

The only people who never fail are those who never try.

—Ilka Chase

A boy once asked his grandfather how he had become so happy and successful in his life. "Right decisions," replied his grandfather. The boy thought for a while and then asked a second question, "But how do you learn to make right decisions?" The grandfather answered quickly with a twinkle in his eye, "Wrong decisions!"

We, too, will learn from our "wrong decisions," our mistakes. Whenever we try anything, there is always the possibility of failure. We must learn to not let this keep us from trying. When we are willing to try, we have already conquered our fear. We can grow no matter what the outcome is.

What failure have I turned into success?

The cut worm forgives the plow.
—William Blake

Would anyone believe that rain abuses grass, or accuse roots, hungry for a better hold on life, of digging too far into earth's flesh? And if the earth should have to quake, would anyone blame it for cracking here and there? Look closely at the small world of busy life overturned in the garden each spring. No ant there curses another bug, and no worm curses itself. Though they can neither speak nor think, even small creatures know enough to accept their pain as a natural part of life.

Why, then, should we waste time blaming others, or ourselves, for the natural sensations of life?

In the process of new growth, can we expect no pain?

It is only with the heart that one can see rightly;
what is essential is invisible to the eye.
—Antoine de St. Exupery

A tuning fork is a small tool that is used to tune musical instruments. It is tapped softly and then set down. As it vibrates, it gives off a musical tone. When its vibrations perfectly match the vibrations of the note played on the instrument, the instrument is in tune. When the note matches the tuning fork, this can be both felt and heard.

Our hearts work like a tuning fork. When the heart feels completely in tune with a decision or thought or action in our lives, then we know it is the right one for us. We can actually feel the harmony inside our bodies.

Sometimes what we know deep in our hearts gets clouded over by doubts and questions and other people's opinions and judgments. We need to clear away such clouds and listen to our hearts, for our hearts carry the wisdom of God.

Am I in tune with my heart today?

Everything has its wonders, even darkness and silence, and I learn whatever state I may be in, therein to be content.

—Helen Keller

Close observation of small children playing, ants moving across a dirt mound, a bird building a nest, a plane flying overhead, tomatoes ripening in a garden are quiet reminders of the many miracles surrounding us at any moment. Often we may wonder just how a carrot grows from a small seed. What enables a robin to fly south in the winter without getting lost? And then we remember the power of the Creator, and the presence of that power everywhere.

Just as the squirrel knows to collect nuts for winter, each of us knows we're always being watched over by God. When we remember that, we feel safe and happy wherever we are, at school, a new friend's house, home alone in the evening. Every moment is full of wonder, and God is always present.

What small things will I share with God today?

Thoughts, rest your wings. Here is a hollow of silence, a nest of stillness, in which to hatch your dreams.

—Joan Walsh Anglund

There is silence in the nest before an egg is hatched. The mother robin must sit quietly and warm them enough to be hatched. During this time, the mother concentrates only on her eggs. She does not let herself be distracted.

There is a time of silence before anything creative is born. And there is silence in the mind before an idea is discovered. A nest is a safe place birds can always return to and be at home. We all need such a nest of silence—a place where we can be quiet and safe, where we can let ourselves be held, and rest.

Often, our best ideas come out of these quiet moments. Times of silence are good for our souls. Just like the robin eggs hatching, so will dreams and solutions grow out of our own nest of stillness.

How well will I use my quiet time today?

Men will find that they can prepare with mutual aid far more easily what they need and avoid far more easily the perils which beset them on all sides, by united forces.

—*Baruch Spinoza*

Three travelers stopped in a small town on their way to the city. They had tents to sleep in, but no food or money. They knocked on doors asking for a little food, but the people were poor, with little to eat and nothing to spare.

Cheerfully, they returned to their camp and built a fire. "What are you doing?" asked a bystander, "Building a fire with nothing to cook?"

"But we do have something to cook!" they said. "Our favorite dish, stone soup. We only need a pot."

"I think I can find one," said one of the bystanders, and she ran home to fetch it.

When she returned, the travelers filled the pot with water and placed two large stones in it. "This will be the finest soup we've ever made!" said the first traveler. "I agree," said the second, "but don't you think it would taste better with a cabbage in it?"

"I think I can find one," said another bystander.

And so it went the whole afternoon until, by evening, the travelers had a hearty, fragrant feast, which they shared with the hungry townspeople.

What can I do with help today, that I couldn't do alone?

"Oh, 'tis love, 'tis love, that makes the world go round! Somebody said," Alice whispered, *"that it's done by everybody minding their own business. Ah well! It means much the same thing."*

—Lewis Carroll

No one helps a caterpillar become a butterfly. First it must crawl through the leaves as a many-legged creature, and then it weaves its own cocoon. Nature does its slow, daily work inside the cocoon and one day a butterfly emerges—and each butterfly is a different shape and color. No other creature can step in and speed up this process without hurting the butterfly.

Sometimes we humans confuse love with playing the part of God. We think we can speed up the natural growth of people around us. We interfere by telling them to do what we think best.

Sometimes the greatest love we can offer is to accept our loved ones the way they are. We need to remember that each caterpillar weaves a cocoon in its own time and becomes a butterfly in its own way. The wisdom of the universe is greater than our own.

How will I show my acceptance of others today?

*To render ourselves insensible to pain we must
forfeit also the possibilities of happiness.*
—Sir John Lubbock

A caterpillar knows instinctively that it must spin a
cocoon. When finished it will use the protection it has
made to turn itself into a beautiful butterfly. When the
time is right, the butterfly will break through the cocoon and stretch its wings to meet the world.

We sometimes protect ourselves by withdrawing
into a cocoon of our own. We stop talking to others
and find ourselves growing lonely and longing for our
friends. Perhaps it was some pain that made us retreat,
but the pain of loneliness is greater. When we have the
courage to break out of our cocoon, knowing and
accepting the fact that we will experience both pain
and happiness, we will change. We will become, for
that moment, something new and beautiful like the
butterfly.

What fearful thing do I have the courage to face today?

A good anger acted upon is beautiful as lightning and swift with power. A good anger swallowed clots the blood like slime.

—Marge Piercy

How does it feel when someone tells us we should play basketball when we don't want to? Often, it angers us that someone else is telling us what to do. After we have been told we should do something many times, we begin to believe it and forget how we really feel. Even though we have forgotten what we wanted to do, we feel angry, often without realizing it. Such hidden anger can leave us feeling bad without knowing why.

It is important to know when we are angry, and to say so. There are healthy ways of expressing anger without blaming others. Saying we are angry, and thereby claiming it as our own feeling and not something others force on us, is a way to express it which also affirms our right to be angry.

If there is anger in me today, can I express it correctly?

The human brain forgets ninety percent of what goes on.

—Jan Milner

There were two women who shared a house and raised their daughters, two toddlers, together. Then one of the women got transferred to another city and moved with her daughter.

Ten years later, they had a reunion. The mothers asked their kids what they remembered about living together. Did they remember all the books? No. Did they remember a mom in the kitchen every morning, fixing eggs and toast? No.

What they remembered was playing in the pink bathtub for hours, pulling the pink shower curtain shut for privacy. And the morning the mothers sneaked in, turned off the lights, threw plastic cups and spoons over the curtain and cried, "It's raining spoons!" They laughed and laughed.

We are lucky in this life—our minds think laughter is what's worth remembering.

What laughter from yesterday can I remember today?

Caring is everything; nothing matters but caring.
—Baron Friedrich Von Hugel

The caring we receive from someone we love when we're sick can heal us just as much as the medicine we take. For children, Mom is usually the one who makes sure we get enough rest by having us stay in bed. By bringing us juice and aspirins she helps us keep our fevers down. She also lifts our spirits when she tells us a funny story.

Perhaps the next time a loved one is sick we can do the special and caring things. We can bring a favorite magazine or a cold glass of water, tell a joke, or just sit and be there for a while. Whether the sick person is a parent or a brother or sister, when we help care for another, we complete a circle of caring begun by a parent so long ago.

Does someone need my care today?

We never know how high we are
'Til we are called to rise;
And then, if we are true to plan,
Our statures touch the skies.
—Emily Dickinson

We are all capable of far more than we think we are. It's in the tough times, however, that we discover the depths of our strength, and it's then that we know that some power has enabled us to do what we thought we could not. Whatever we call that power, it is there for us when we need it.

To do what seems impossible, all we need to do is ask for the help we think we need. And we can look within, too, and summon our whole selves to the task at hand. With all that going for us, how can we fail? And when the tough work is over, we'll look back and know we've grown from the experience. And yes, our statures will have touched the skies.

When I am faced with a tough task, how do I respond?

Whoever I am or whatever I am doing, some kind of excellence is within my reach.
—John W. Gardner

It's easy to forget how important we each are—to our parents, to other family members, to our friends. We are in this world, even in our particular family, because we are important and necessary in the lives of others. It's easy to feel not so important though, especially when we think we're not good enough at anything we try. School or work comes easy for some. Maybe not us. Athletics come easy to others. Maybe it's helping around the house that's easiest. Each of us is very good at some things. And it's okay to not be good at everything.

How can I show my talent today?

Worry never robs tomorrow of its sorrow, but only saps today of its strength.

—A. J. Cronin

There is always something to worry about. What if it rains tomorrow on the family picnic? What if the baby gets sick and we can't go? What if we can't find a shady spot for our lunch table? Will the water be too cold for swimming? Will the boat motor conk out in the middle of the lake? What if we forget the charcoal? Or the lighter fluid?

Today, while preparing the potato salad for tomorrow's picnic, all we need to know is whether the potatoes are cool enough to peel and slice.

Our worries about tomorrow change nothing but ourselves, and they have nothing to do with what we are doing right now. Tomorrow will become today soon enough, and today is the day we have.

Which of my worries belong only to tomorrow, and should be left alone until then?

The more a diamond is cut the more it sparkles.
—Anonymous

There is something of value to be found even in the worst of things. Consider the oyster. When a grain of sand penetrates an oyster's shell, it irritates the oyster, making it uncomfortable. The oyster relieves the pain by coating the sand with a soothing liquid. When this liquid hardens, a pearl is formed. The very process that healed the oyster created a precious jewel for others to cherish and admire.

The way in which we deal with our own frustrations—painful though they may be—can make a difference. Pearls can be formed from our experiences, making us wiser and stronger, or grains of sand—anger, bitterness, resentment—can remain imbedded inside us. The choice is ours.

How can I turn my irritations into pearls today?

Let the gentle bush dig its root deep and spread upward to split one boulder.

—*Carl Sandburg*

There is a fable about the sun and wind having a contest to see who can get the old man to take his coat off first. The wind blows fiercely, but the old man just pulls his coat tighter around him. Finally, the wind gives up and the sun comes out. The sun shines a steady warm light down on the old man, who soon takes his coat off.

More and better things are accomplished in this world by kindness and gentleness than by force. When we find ourselves most frustrated, it is often because we are trying to force certain things to happen. Our own patient and steady desire to grow, fed by the love and kindness of others, will not be stopped by anything or anyone. Our own gentleness is a powerful force in our lives. It is like the gentle bush that grows through granite.

What can I gain by gentleness today?

Fear not that life shall come to an end, but rather fear that it shall never have a beginning.
—J. H. Newman

Our fears lock us up if we let them. They can prevent us from tasting adventure, from experiencing new wonders. We are often terrified of unknowns and fret about what might happen if we try something new. We worry if new people will like us—if we'll fit in.

It is natural to be cautious about the unknown, and anything new is just that. But we can keep our caution from becoming fear by taking action, with the faith that we never encounter anything we can't handle in some way.

Unknowns are merely joys we haven't met. We hold the keys to our own cages and can free ourselves when we use our courage and inner strength to overcome our fears.

What new joy can I discover beneath my fear today?

Bad moments, like good ones, tend to be grouped together.
—Edna O'Brien

Once in a while, we have days when we think the whole world is against us. A parent has reprimanded us, a brother broke our new game, or the teacher at school disciplined the whole class. We sometimes let our thoughts center on a cluster of bad moments and forget the good moments of the day.

We shouldn't forget about the two ducks we fed part of our sandwich to, the friend who made us laugh, or the gym teacher who praised the whole class. Deciding to think about these good moments can allow our spirits to rise and make the bad moments fade away.

After all, if life were all good moments, we would take them for granted. Let us accept the bad ones gratefully, then, as opportunities to appreciate the good.

What good moments can I remember right now?

Being alive is being creative. You need do nothing but affirm your aliveness.

—Gay Bonner

What does it mean to be alive? Does it mean merely breathing, eating, and moving around, or is there more to it? Being alive can mean different things to different people. To some, it's sewing a baby quilt for a new life about to be born. To others, it's singing, or walking, or running. Still others find it in the exhilaration of skiing, or the tropical splendor they find when scuba diving.

Each of us has our own favorite activity that lets us feel our creativity and vitality, that lets us feel a part of the larger world. Two gifts these activities leave us with are joy and energy. Joy is one of the most creative forces we can call on, and energy gives us the power to do an activity well.

What will my creative activity be today?

You will jump to it someday. Then you'll fly. You'll really fly. After that you'll quite simply, quite calmly make your own stones, your own floor plan, your own sound.

—Anne Sexton

A young man sat beside a whispering creek all day for years, never moving. The townsfolk who watched him wondered whether he heard the gurgling creek sounds, or felt the sting of insects, or saw the raccoons when they came at night to sip from the cool, dark waters.

One day the young man rose and dashed up the hill above the creek. There, using all the healing strength of the stream which he had quietly absorbed over the years, he gathered stones. He arranged them layer by layer to fit the plan he had thought out by the creek, and feverishly he built his home. When done, he let out a brassy, booming holler of joy. Imagine the townsfolks' surprise when they turned their eyes to that lonely spot by the creek and saw a huge castle of stone above the place where the young man once rested.

What plans can I make during my idle hours today?

Let your conscience be your guide.
—*Jiminy Cricket*

Crickets sing on summer nights because it's their nature to do so. They don't think about whistling or trumpeting or sleeping or changing the world. They've figured out their role on earth, and they do it.

We are a bit more complex than crickets, and most of the time that's lucky. In most of our affairs it's our conscience more than sheer instinct that helps us choose those thoughts and acts and feelings that are right for us.

Each of us has that little voice inside, relentless as a chirping cricket, telling us what to do. Even in the middle of our toughest decisions, we always have within us the solution that is right for us. All we have to do is listen—and trust.

What does my inner voice say about today's decisions?

Jealousy is cruel as the grave.
                                —*Song of Solomon*

Most bushes and small trees need trimming every year. They have branches that hang out over the sidewalk and get in people's way. Sometimes the branches grow so long and low to the ground that the tree looks weighted down.

Jealousy is like an overgrown branch—it weighs us down. It is one of those feelings all of us deal with. We may be jealous of someone's looks or talent, or maybe even their good luck. Like the overgrown branches, jealousy sticks out all over and gets in other people's way as well as our own. It is a part of us we need to keep cutting back.

If we are good gardeners, we will get out the clippers. Seeing and talking about our jealousy is the best way to start using those clippers. If we do this, our own leaves will be healthier, and our blossoms will grow.

Is there someone I am jealous of? Can I use my clippers today?

The most valuable thing we can do for the psyche, occasionally, is to let it rest, wander, live in the changing light of a room, not to try to do or be anything whatsoever.

—May Sarton

A whole world can be seen through even the smallest window. Knowing this can help us slow down and enjoy everyday events. We can listen to the regular rhythms of letter carriers and school children, dogs and delivery trucks, city buses and song birds playing out a piece of their daily lives outside the window.

We can greet the letter carrier who comes up the walk, feed the robin who lands on the sill, wave to the kids who've found a shortcut through our backyards on their way home from school.

It is not necessary, today, for us to fill our lives with important meetings, gala parties, expensive treats, toys, or outings to be happy. There is a whole world to be discovered just outside the nearest window.

What worlds lie on the other side of my window today?

To be able to invite pain to join in my experience and not have to control my life to avoid pain is such a freedom!

—Christina Baldwin

If we really stopped to think about it, we would be astounded to discover how much of our time is spent trying to avoid pain. We are afraid to say what we think or tell others our needs because we fear rejection. We are afraid to face the pain of our own anger. We are afraid of telling others who we are. When we are afraid of opening up to others for fear they will hurt us, we are not free, we are prisoners of our own fears.

Pain is a natural part of life, and we are gifted with the ability to feel it. Pain teaches us, makes us work harder sometimes, and it helps us appreciate pleasure.

When we accept pain, and stop exhausting ourselves trying to avoid it, we will be free to live life more fully and without so much worry.

How has my own fear limited my freedom?

When fate hands us a lemon, let's try to make lemonade.

—*Dale Carnegie*

Good fortune is built on misfortune. By losing a race we learn what mistakes to avoid next time we run. A burglar may make us install the lock that will keep out a murderer. Each time a toddler falls is a lesson in how to walk.

We can never assume that, because things are not going the way we want, they are not following a better plan. God is a better manager than we can hope to be. If things aren't shaping up the way we like, let's wait with curiosity to see that better things are in store for us. Let's look for lights in the darkness and follow them to the bright day that always will follow. We will remember our lessons of misfortune with gratitude.

What can I learn from delay today?

Real friends are those who, when you've made a fool of yourself, don't feel that you've done a permanent job.

—Erwin T. Randall

What kind of friends do we have? Are they people who complain a lot? Are they people who laugh at us or put others down?

The kind of people we want to be will decide what kind of friends we have. If we want to feel sorry for ourselves, we will choose friends who will tell us how rotten their lives are. If we want to think we're better than others, we will hang around people who laugh at others' mistakes.

But if we want to be the best we can be, we will pick friends who see the good in life, people who will encourage us to be ourselves and who will help us try harder at things that are difficult for us.

How can I be a better friend today?

Self-image sets the boundaries of individual accomplishment.

—*Maxwell Maltz*

The way we think about ourselves determines how we behave and who we become. If Eileen believes she is good at baseball, she will swing the bat more confidently and catch fly balls more easily. And her extra effort will generally pay off. At math, Steve thinks he's a whiz and it makes him proud. He studies so he'll continue to be a whiz.

The image we have of ourselves is like the blueprint the contractor follows when building a house. When we see ourselves sad or angry, our behavior and personality will match it. When we see ourselves withdrawn and afraid, we seem to avoid activities that involve others. How wonderful that we can change our behavior and thus ourselves by changing the picture we carry in our minds.

Do I have a good picture of myself today?

It is good to have an end to journey towards, but it is the journey that matters, in the end.
—Ursula K. LeGuin

Billy and his dad were excited about fan appreciation night. They wanted to get one of the souvenir baseballs thrown into the stands. As they hurried toward their seats, they saw a man drop a ten-dollar bill. Billy picked up the money.

"Hey, Mister," he said loudly. The man in front of him turned around. "You dropped this." Billy handed him the money.

"Thank you," said the man. Billy returned to his dad. Just as they reached their row, a ball came sailing towards their empty seats. Someone from the row behind caught it. Billy swallowed hard.

"I know," said his dad, looking at Billy, "But you did the right thing."

For his effort, Billy will bring home a souvenir far more lasting and valuable than a baseball or a ten-dollar bill. He will know the bittersweet feeling of making a sacrifice to do what is right.

What sacrifice have I made to do what is right?

One cricket said to another—
come, let us be ridiculous, and say love!
                                    —Conrad Aiken

Let's all sit in a circle and take turns being ridiculous about what our love is like. Let's play tag with it, and pass it on. Let's say that our love is like diamonds sprinkled on a clear moonless sky, and let's pass it on. Let's say it's like one rose petal too tender to touch, and let's pass it on. Let's say it's like rainbows filling a city sky, and pass it on. Let's say it's small and hard, like an agate or shell, and let's keep passing it on.

We can find images for love all around us, and when we express it to others this way, it grows.

What is my love like today?

When one door of happiness closes, another opens; but often we look so long at the closed door that we do not see the one which has been opened for us.

—Helen Keller

In the game of musical chairs, everyone walks around a circle of chairs. When the music stops, they scramble for the nearest open chair. If we were playing this game and found the nearest chairs taken, wouldn't we quickly look around for the next open one? To remain immobilized, angry that the chair we wanted was taken, would undoubtedly lose our place in the game.

Sometimes in life, we set our sights on a particular chair. Perhaps there is an award we want to win, or we want to be the high scorer on our team. Perhaps there is a promotion or a job we would like to get. When we do not get what we want, it is easy to keep looking at what we didn't get instead of seeing all we have.

It is important to be grateful for what we have—for the open doors and empty chairs waiting and inviting our attention. Loss and disappointment are a part of life—but the music will play again and our lives can move on.

What is available to me today?

It's the deepest channel that runs most true.
—Kate Wolf

The greatest rivers spread themselves out wide and lazy over the earth. They roll over on themselves like great lizards turning in the warm sun. A river flows, drawn to the oceans, carving ever-deepening channels, nestling snug in the earth's welcoming lap. The current is strongest in the deepest channel. Boat navigators know that finding that channel means finding the swiftest current and the safest voyage home.

When we look at a river, or at another person, we see only the surface. What keeps our attention is usually some movement or activity on the surface. But there is more than meets the eye, especially to people. When we overlook someone because that person is quiet or simple, we may be robbing ourselves of an eye-opening discovery.

Which deeper things can I look for in my day?

Let us open our natures, throw wide the doors of our hearts and let in the sunshine of good will and kindness.

—*O. S. Marden*

Kindness is among the gifts we can most easily spread among others. The more we give of kind words and deeds, the more we discover that kindness is like a burning candle which lights many other candles without losing a trace of its own brightness. Our kindnesses are assets which return unexpected dividends when we invest them in the happiness of others. Kindness is the very basis of love. It softens the most severe anger and gladdens the hardest hearts.

No kindness is too small to win and hold the affection of others because it is made up of gentleness, love, generosity, unselfishness, and caring.

What kindness do I have to offer today?

Cultivate your garden. Let it take root in you until your thousand eyes open like violets to morning light.

—Nancy Paddock

In our imaginations we can mix images and ideas from all over the world—imagine the thousand eyes of a peacock growing among the purple violets, or babies that grow on trees! In our imaginations we can also nurture feelings of love, affection, self-esteem.

All of us—not just writers—can learn to see the images in our own minds. We can do this by breathing slowly, relaxing, and looking at the movie in our minds. We may see a field of wildflowers, or find ourselves wading across a stream in the mountains. We might see happiness as wildflowers and grass coming up through the sidewalk, breaking the concrete into chunks and sand, growing so slowly yet with such great power. It may help us appreciate our growth today to look at it this way.

Can I visualize my happiness right now? What does it look like?

Those who contemplate the beauty of the earth find reserves of strength that will endure as long as life lasts.

—Rachel Carson

Beauty is everywhere. It is in the daisies, in the lavender wildflowers, in the new green grass of spring. As we walk through life, noticing such beauty strengthens us. It reminds us of the spiritual creative force alive in this world. On better days, we can feel our own creativity gaining power from such beauty. On harder days, nature's sunset can help us step out of our suffering for a moment to be comforted and inspired by its splendor.

Even storms, in their wild and angry way, show us a power greater than ourselves. Such awesome beauty is beyond our understanding, and yet it is part of the earth we live on.

What lessons will nature teach me today?

Now my soul hath elbow room.
> —William Shakespeare

If we spend too much time together we are bound to grow weary of one another. This would happen regardless of who the other person was. In a family, we need some time apart to pursue other interests and friendships. We may be able to meet many needs for each other, but there will be some we cannot meet. If we press too hard upon one another we will cramp our life together.

Our needs for space aren't just physical. Freedom to think and feel what seems appropriate for us, to be alone if we want, is a large part of our lives together. Only with this kind of freedom is love possible. Love requires freedom. We need to value each other, and at the same time realize that no one person or family can fill us with all life has to offer.

What are my own freedoms at home?

You are here for a purpose. There is not a duplicate of you in the whole wide world; there never has been, there never will be. You were brought here now to fill a certain need. Take time to think that over.

—Lou Austin

No other person is exactly like you or me. No one can do exactly what we can, or touch another person in exactly the way we can. Out of all the people who could have been created, we were chosen to be a part of this time and place.

We are needed to fulfill a plan, in our families as well as in our relationships. Knowing we have unique abilities, we will spend less time feeling jealous of what others can do.

Through our dreams and yearnings, God shows us who we can be. It is up to us to have the courage to follow that dream with action.

What unique gift can I offer the world today?

In Micronesian, there's a word, kukaro, *which has no corresponding word in English. When people say they are going to* kukaro, *they mean they are going to relax, sit around, hang out. They are being, not doing.*

—Eli and Beth Halpern

As children, our best times are often trips to an amusement park, fishing at the lake, camping, or just sitting idly under a tree. These make the best memories, and times sitting around a campfire roasting marshmallows or having a root beer after a family outing seem to bring out the love we share.

We don't seem to be accomplishing anything at these times. No chores are getting done around the house, no schoolwork, no repairs, no moneymaking.

But these times of peace, relaxation, and a sense of endless time of being, not doing, may be essential to our ability to get other things done later. Certainly we are most receptive to our feelings, new ideas, and unplanned adventures at these moments. Maybe we should add *kukaro* to our vocabulary.

What timeless thing can I do today?

In uplifting, get underneath.

—*George Ade*

A sandpile in the summer is deceiving. The topmost sand burns hot on our feet. But as we push down toward the center, we come to a damp, cool place that soothes and oozes between our toes.

The nature of most things is not revealed at the surface. Like the sandpile, many people and situations we encounter are, on the surface, downright uncomfortable. The reward is in digging deeper—to the essential goodness, the core or meaning, the true friend. It takes time, a little knowledge, and abundant trust that we will not be burned.

What have I discovered by digging a little lately?

Forgiveness is all-powerful. Forgiveness heals all ills.

— *Catherine Ponder*

Getting mad at someone, a friend perhaps, is normal. Everybody gets mad sometimes. But when we stay mad for very long, it ruins all the fun we'd planned on having throughout the day. Staying mad multiplies. Sometimes it seems we are mad at the dog, our mom, another friend, even the TV.

Forgiving the people we're mad at works like magic. We don't even have to forgive them out loud. We can forgive them in our own minds. The result is the same. Pretty soon the whole day looks bright again. When we're mad, we are the ones who suffer most.

Who can I forgive today, and make my day a better one?

I found words to every thought I ever had, but one. . . .

—Emily Dickinson

What kinds of thoughts can't be put into words? We feel lost in space, mind-boggled by how small and big the stars are. We are sure and unsure about death, its blank and steady stare. Or we have done something that makes us feel both good and bad. Sometimes we hate someone we love, but we aren't sure what hate is, or love. We are scared of crowds and afraid of being abandoned, always alone. Sometimes we just want to laugh and cry, and when words fail we expect someone to know what our silences mean.

What are some ways I try to express my feelings without using words?

Hurry, hurry has no blessing.
                              —*Swahili proverb*

In a busy family there is a lot of activity. We sometimes feel imprisoned by all the work, school, extracurricular activities, housework, meetings, and special events. In the press to do it all, we may lose our peace because of the hurry. We rush to eat; we rush to work; we rush to get there on time. Much of this cannot be helped. But hurry has no blessing, as the proverb goes. We can create quick tempers and a lot of frustration if we try to hurry too much.

When we allow enough time to slow things down, we give ourselves a chance to enjoy what we're doing, and to develop along spiritual lines. Inner peace depends on our keeping a balance in all the things we do. Only then can we feel the joy that comes from having enough time to do things quietly and smoothly, and value the inner peace that comes when we do not hurry.

How can I take my time today and enjoy myself?

A mother is not a person to lean on, but a person to make leaning unnecessary.
                              —*Dorothy Canfield Fisher*

A strong, healthy tree is one which is free to grow straight and tall. A weak tree often must lean against another for support. It is not that different with people. We are not healthy and strong when we must always lean on another to support us.

This doesn't mean it isn't healthy to accept help. But the best help we can get or give is that which enables us to do things without it. Sometimes we think we lose a relationship when others don't need our help, or when we don't need theirs all the time. The reverse is true. Only when we are each strong enough to stand on our own can we really share the kind of help which allows both helped and helper to be independent.

Have I been giving the right kind of help?

What a man thinks of himself, that is which determines, or rather indicates, his fate.
—Henry David Thoreau

Let us think of ourselves as made of dust, and allow us to be as proud of it as if it were true. For dust is everywhere. We see it in solemn rooms streaked by sun, dancing like fine angels in a cathedral light. It is the stuff of life. And it drifts down on fancy tables where the richest people eat. It cannot be denied a place. And it returns time and time again like the seasons. It is one of the wonders of the world. And when no one sees or cares, it finds a secret corner in which to keep a solitary peace. It intends no harm. We find it at home on old leather books, the ones that preserve our noblest thoughts.

And from where we stand, it seems that even the stars are made of it. When we feel low, unworthy, or useless, let's remember that these feelings are only a small but important part of us, that even great things are made of small parts, and that we, as whole beings, are always greater than the sum of these parts.

What feelings am I made of today?

Always think of what you have to do as easy and it will become so.

—Emile Corie

How we think about the activities before us is very important. If we think cleaning the garage is hard, dirty, and no chance for fun, that's just how it will feel. We'll be tired before we even begin. However, if we approach it like a treasure hunt, expecting to rediscover some long-forgotten treasures, we'll enjoy the task. In fact, it will feel like a game.

The thoughts we carry in our minds determine whether our tasks are fun or not. What good fortune it is that we can control those thoughts. If we approach an assignment for school or a job believing that we're able to do it, that it's not too hard for us, we'll finish with ease. Our thoughts determine our successes. In this way, our lives are in our own hands.

How much better can I make my life today?

We love the things we love for what they are.
—*Robert Frost*

Once there was a little girl who had a stuffed frog named Jeremy. Jeremy went everywhere with the girl—to imaginary picnics with her other dolls, to school, on trips, and, once, even into the bathtub! Every night, Jeremy slept cradled in her arms.

Over time, Jeremy grew old and tattered. He had lost an eye, and he limped because the girl used to use one of his legs as a handle, and it had gotten crushed. His nose was a little mangled too from being dragged on the ground.

But the girl loved that frog, no matter how bedraggled he looked. And he never did anything. He was just always there. He was just Jeremy, and she loved him for that.

Today, that girl is a young woman and has outgrown childish things. But in her bedroom, you'll still find Jeremy, tattered and repaired, asleep on her bed. She still loves him dearly, for what he is.

Who do I love, and why?

When you have to make a choice and don't make it, that is in itself a choice.

—William James

There are times when it's hard to make a decision. When we go to the fair, for instance, we may want to do more things than we have time for, so we don't know what plans to make. Waiting to decide until we see what the fair has to offer is one choice. Not deciding because we're afraid of what may happen is also a choice. We may find ourselves thinking so much about what could happen that we miss all the exciting things going on around us.

It's necessary to keep in mind that any course of action is a decision, but no decision is irreversible. We are free to do what we decide, and are freed by the awareness that whatever we do is based on our own decision and no one else's.

What important decisions shall I make without fear today?

Happiness is not a matter of events; it depends upon the tides of the mind.

—Alice Meyvell

It's thought that Abe Lincoln once said we're as happy as we make up our minds to be. In other words, we decide to be happy. Bad weather, lost toys, broken plans, even angry friends, don't have to ruin our own happiness unless we let them. We're always in control of our own thoughts and feelings, and happiness is a feeling we can choose even when others around us have chosen to be angry or sad. Even when the day is gloomy and none of our plans are working out, we can still be cheerful if we decide to be. How lucky we are that someone else can't decide for us how to feel. We'd be nothing more than robots if that were true.

Am I ready to make this day a happy one?

I was forced to live far beyond my years when just a child. Now I have reversed the order and I intend to remain young indefinitely.
—Mary Pickford

We can all learn to change our lives so the child within each of us can live in balance with the people we have become. We can learn to give the child a voice, let the child play, let the child express needs and fears and pleasures.

We might look at our old baby pictures for a valuable lesson. We will see pictures of ourselves on rocking horses, grinning and waving; pictures of ourselves with our most precious toy—a crude metal car, perhaps; pictures of ourselves rolling in the grass. The lesson we learn is that it doesn't take much to make this child happy—even today.

We keep our own happiness safe inside us to call on whenever we need it, as long as we keep a healthy relationship with the child within. When we nourish the child, we can be assured the child will also nourish us.

What simple thing will make me happy today?

Let a joy keep you. Reach out your hands and take it when it runs by.

—*Carl Sandburg*

There is a song that says joy is like the rain. It comes across our window pane and then goes away again. When joy comes knocking at our window we can reach out and let it in. Joy comes to us in many ways—through deep laughter, through games played together in a spirit of fun and sharing. Singing together, skating, and being around a campfire are all ways we share joy. Yet joy can also be felt alone.

Each moment of joy we reach for strengthens our spirits. Joyful memories can sustain us through days of long hard work. Like rain, joy comes and goes, yet its nourishment keeps our spirits alive.

How can I share my joy today?

When you feel rejected, start accepting yourself,
and then go out and accept someone.
—*Sondra Ray*

There was once a mother who felt rejected when her children grew up and needed to separate from her. She felt hurt when they pushed her away and no longer wanted all the love and caring that she wanted to give them. She thought, What's wrong with me?

Encouraged by her friends, she began to ask herself another question: What's right with me? The more answers she found to that question, the better she liked herself. The better she liked herself, the more she was able to see her children's need to separate from her as their own natural and healthy urge for independence, and not the result of her shortcomings.

Our good points may seem undesirable to others, but that's not our fault. Sometimes, too much of a good thing can be inappropriate, but that doesn't make it bad.

What's right with me today?

The great end of life is not knowledge but action.
—Thomas Huxley

Sometimes we have good ideas about how to make things better. We might know we need to spend more quality time with others. We might know it would be better if mealtime were not so hectic and really became a time for sharing the day's events. Knowing what needs to happen is part of the process of change. But we have to put that knowledge into action.

All our good intentions, no matter what they may be, do not really mean anything until we move into action. A hug is better than a thought of love; a story read together is better than a wonderful vacation that did not get past the planning stage, just as a finished house is something we can live in, while the blueprint is soon forgotten. When we act on our ideas, we put ourselves into the world as a force for change.

What change can I set loose in the world today?

Trust takes time. If you don't invest it, then you don't get it.

—Anonymous

Trusting other human beings is like planting a garden. First we must choose where to plant—is the soil healthy, is it open to sunlight? We would not plant seeds on rocks that are hard and ungiving. In the same way, we need to choose friends who are trustworthy, who are like rich soil open to planting and sunlight.

Then we need to plant the seeds of time and care. If we share some of our feelings and are welcomed, we will know it is safe to share more. We can share ourselves in our own time—even a garden grows slowly, and can take only so much sun and rain in one day.

Having trust in someone feeds the spirit. Trust also gives us the courage to be beautiful, like the flowers of our gardens.

Am I brave enough to trust others, and to be worthy of their trust?

It is terribly amusing how many different climates of feeling one can go through in a day.
—Anne Morrow Lindbergh

When we travel by canoe down a river we can notice the changes that take place. In one spot the river is wide and the water moves slowly. Around the next bend the river narrows and the current speeds up. Ahead of us we see rapids waiting to test our skill.

Our feelings can also change as quickly as the river. We may have times in our day when we feel good about ourselves. Then, all of a sudden, someone may tease us about something. We begin to feel like the scared canoeist shooting the rapids for the first time. How wonderful it is to know that we are never given a test we can't handle, that everything that happens in our lives is for the sake of our growth, and that we are watched over at all times by God.

How can I use today's obstacles for my own growth?

Dependency (on another human being) is the inability to experience wholeness or to function adequately without the certainty that one is being actively cared for by another.
—*M. Scott Peck*

No matter what we may think, overdependence on another can be very unloving because it drains others of any chance for personal growth. Those of us who have been dependent on other people are so busy acquiring love that we ourselves have no energy left to truly give love. It's as if we're starving, and scrambling for every little bit of love we can find, with no thought to offering it to others. No wonder they often quickly get tired of us.

We can't force or expect others to do things with us, talk to us, or love us. The way to be surely loved is to be worthy of it. We can work at being worthy by exercising our freedom to feel and do things without others' permission, and to allow them the same opportunity.

What can I do on my own today?

A good laugh heals a lot of hurts.
—Madeleine L'Engle

The ability to laugh at ourselves has always been important. In the past, fools and jesters held an important place in the royal courts. Today we have clowns who make us laugh.

If we look closely at a clown's face, we will often notice a bit of sadness around the eyes. Clowns are able to move easily from sad expressions to ones full of delight very easily. For all of us, laughter and tears come from the same deep well inside. And often, after a good cry, we find ourselves ready to laugh, easily and joyfully.

Laughter is a gift waiting for us on the other side of our sadness.

Can I begin to laugh by smiling now?

There is no reality except the one contained within us.

—Herman Hesse

Claude Gellee painted lovely pictures of the English countryside. Europeans loved his landscapes, with their blue hues and mild distortions. But when the people went for the carriage rides in the country, they were disappointed because it didn't look the way Gellee had painted it. Then someone discovered that if you held blue glass up to your eyes and looked through it, the trees and hills and sky looked just like a Gellee painting! Soon everyone was looking through "Claude glasses" when they traveled.

We often let others do our seeing for us. We get lazy and rely on the images of television and movies, instead of really seeing with our own eyes. Our world becomes distorted and we lose sight of the natural beauty that surrounds us.

Each of us carries reality inside ourselves, and as we grow stronger within, we discover that we can see clearest when we trust our own eyes. There is a glorious world, full and rich, just waiting for us to glimpse it.

Will I see the world through my own eyes today?

I had crossed the line. I was free: but there was no one to welcome me to the land of freedom. I was a stranger in a strange land.
—Harriet Tubman

Harriet Tubman was a Black woman who devoted her life to helping slaves escape their bondage. In her youth, she had been hit on the head, so she suffered dizzy spells for the rest of her life. In spite of this, and at great risk to her own life, she guided many slaves on the Underground Railroad to freedom.

Freedom from slavery is different today but just as necessary. It may mean freedom from being a slave to what others think of us, freedom from eating more than is healthy for us, freedom from jealousy, freedom from trying to force others to do what we want them to do.

We are free to be the very best people we can be. Our own freedom can be even more fulfilling when we welcome others enthusiastically into that land of freedom by allowing them the room to be themselves without fear of judgment. In this way, by freeing ourselves, we free one another.

How can I free myself today?

*He wanted to hold onto his fury, to guard it like
a treasure. He would not let it be stolen from
him. . . . But already, he felt it slipping, softened
by Ben's compassionate touch.*
    —Joe Johnston and Nilo Rodis-Jamero

The glassblower is an artist who takes broken glass
and melts it in a very hot furnace. Then the glassblower blows through a long tube and creates objects
such as cups and plates and pieces of art.

The sharp edges of our anger are like pieces of broken glass. We all have things in our lives that anger
us—it is only human to bump into our sharp edges.
One edge might be crabby, another silent and withdrawn, and still another yelling and screaming.

The heat of love and compassion can melt our anger. This may take the form of sympathy for ourselves,
or for the people we love. More often, it is the compassion of those around us that helps melt our anger.
Sometimes saying I'm sorry is a good way to melt anger and find the love underneath it.

What beauty can I create with my anger today?

Isn't it great life is open-ended!
　　　　　　　　　　　　　—Brigitte Frase

Elizabeth Lawton, known as "Grandma Lawton," is an American artist who never drew a picture until she was sixty-eight years old. She spent all the years before that time trying to cope with depression. She had gone through therapy, medications, and shock treatment and continued to be severely depressed. But then she signed up for an art class and the act of drawing cured her depression. She continues to make fabulous pictures.

What does she think about the critical acclaim her artwork has received? She says she wants others to know about her art so it may give hope to those who have also "suffered from feelings."

Many of us have suffered from feelings. We must remember that we can each turn to our creativity—at any age—as a source for our well-being. All we need to do is have faith in the potential goodness within ourselves and those we love.

What creative activity can I look to for comfort today?

In summer I am very glad
We children are so small,
For we can see a thousand things
That men can't see at all.
—Laurence Alma-Tadema

Out behind the house a little boy is turning over stepping stones which form the sidewalk. Underneath these stones he has discovered many different kinds of worms and bugs. They wiggle this way and that when their cover is removed. He is only four, but he is the only one in the family who has made this discovery.

In a child's eyes there are many wonderful things which escape the attention of the adult world. In order to see them, we must often take the time to let those younger than we are show the way. Even though we may have lost our own childlike view of the world, others can guide us and thereby enrich our lives. We have much to teach and share with each other, regardless of our ages.

What can I learn from one younger than me today?

One law for lion and ox is oppression.
—William Blake

What would the forest be like if deer, squirrel, and owl alike were required to sleep only at noon? Or the sky, if all birds were forced by law to fly in lines? Or the sea, if all fish had to stay forever in schools? We all know a lion and an ox, and we've all acted like a chicken, jackass, goat, or fox. Now and then we're slow or fast, bright or dull, willing or not.

So when others go the way we know we must go, we will follow the same law. But we don't have to be as others are, just to avoid being thought "strange." How truly strange life would be if everyone were the same. We have our own way, our own good time, and own free laws to discover and obey.

Will I need to obey someone else's rules if I govern myself well?

A good marriage is that in which each appoints the other guardian of his solitude.
—Rainer Maria Rilke

Solitude is vital to our well-being, but in a family it's hard sometimes to find the space and time to be alone. The house is often crowded with laughter, voices, the radio, and the TV. There are often many things going on at the same time.

It's true that our family is a team, and that we work together, whether we intend to or not, to create the environment we live in. If it's noisy, that's the way we live. Noise is life to some. The fact that others need our help or company is wonderful proof of our value. But if we can be guardians of each other's solitude, out of love for one another, we will each come back renewed, strengthened, and recreated. We can bring new life into our days when we are alone with ourselves and God.

How can I help someone find rest and renewal today?

The hopeful man sees success where others see failure, sunshine where others see shadows and storm.

—O. S. Marden

When wise men say, "Hope springs eternal," they are reminding us that no matter how great the obstacles, the hope of winning out in the long run still exists. Hope is our friend when all else has failed. When we have strength of character and an energetic mind, hope always flourishes.

We discover that at the very brink of despair, we will find courage to keep trying as long as there is hope for success. After all, what have we got to lose? Without hope, we have no chance anyway. Our chance for glory comes when we keep trying even though all seems lost. Our hearts remain strong and brave when hope reminds us that challenges last until a game is over.

What light of hope can I keep burning within me today?

Sometimes it's worse to win a fight than to lose.
—Billie Holiday

We all see things differently. It is part of the wonderful variety of the world that we all have different points of view. We've all seen baseball players arguing with an umpire over a close call, but in order to play the game, they must accept the umpire's judgment.

When we stubbornly refuse to let friends or family members speak their ideas simply because we disagree with them, we risk the loss of a friend or the understanding of a family member. It is when we allow others to disagree that we take a step forward—a step that opens our ears and our hearts to all sorts of people and ideas.

How well can I accept others' opinions today?

Flying is largely a matter of having the right attitude—plus, of course, good wing feathers.
—E. B. White

The swan flies with majesty, confidence, and grace. It is made to fly, of course, but it learns as much about flying from its parents as it knows by instinct. It is not born with the ability to fly, but with the potential.

Each of us is born with the potential to fly in many skies. We may sing or dance or write or run, fix machines, teach children, speak, listen, sympathize. And we can do all things well, as only humans can. It is not the *ability* to do these things that makes us human, it's what we *do* with that ability.

Knowing how to prepare ourselves before we spread our wings is part of discovering what we can do. When we learn to ride a bike, we *know* we can do it; our parent's hand on the seat helps us know it.

Wanting to soar is the first part of the flight; it is studying, practicing, and asking for help that allows us to get off the ground.

What steps can I take today toward reaching my potential?

Happiness is a mental habit, a mental attitude, and if it is not learned and practiced in the present it is never experienced.
—Maxwell Maltz

If only I had a new bike, then I'd be happy. If only my family were more understanding, then I'd be happy. If only my hair were styled better. If only I had more friends. If only ... Sometimes we begin to sound like a broken record when things go wrong, so certain that if the events and conditions of our lives were different, we'd be happy.

It's an old and unfortunate habit that we look around outside ourselves for happiness. We can never be sure of it if we count on certain conditions to guarantee it. However, we can always be sure of happiness if we carry it with us wherever we go. The happiness habit can be developed, with practice, just as surely as good piano playing or accurate pitching. We can control our own thoughts. The decision to make them happy ones is ours to make.

Am I carrying my happiness within me right now?

Creativity is so delicate a flower that praise tends to make it bloom, while discouragement often nips it in the bud.

—Alex Osborn

A garden of flowers blooming is a beautiful sight to see. Through the green leaves surrounding a tulip we see hints of yellow or pink or red. Each day the flowers greet us with their radiant color. Yet, a sudden frost would wilt and fade the flowers.

Each time we create something new with our talents we are like a young flower opening. Whether we draw or write or sew or play a musical instrument, all creativity has this in common. Appreciation from those around us is like sunshine for the flowers. Harsh criticism, however, is like the cold air—it wilts and deadens our desire to create.

We all need warm encouragement for our endeavors, and we can give as well as receive it. In this way, creativity can bloom in our homes and our friendships, bringing a garden full of color and delight into our lives.

What encouragement can I offer to someone near me?

Do I love you because you're beautiful
Or are you beautiful because I love you?
　　　　　　　　　　—Oscar Hammerstein

Once, a powerful king agreed to help a small lost boy find his mother. Since the boy described his mother as the most beautiful woman in the world, the king commanded all the beautiful women in the kingdom to come to the castle.

From miles around they came—women with complexions of porcelain and hair of spun gold, with cheeks the color of apricots and eyes as dark as the raven's. But none of them was the boy's mother. When the last of the women had paraded before them, and the king and the boy had begun to despair, they heard a timid knock on the door. "Come in," the king said wearily. In shuffled an old washer woman, her grey hair tied up in a kerchief, her hands rough and red, her dress coarse and patched.

"Mother!" the boy cried when he saw her, and he leapt from his chair and raced into the woman's arms. The king stared in amazement.

Will I be able to see the real beauty in others today?

There is surely a piece of divinity in us,
something that was before the elements. . . .
                              —Sir Thomas Browne

One definition of *divinity* in the dictionary is "supreme excellence." It also means "god-like character" and "divine nature."

Doesn't that describe someone we love? When we are in love with someone, we see only the best of that person—it's impossible to see anything else. That person is "divine," we say, perfect for us, because he or she loves us and is loveable.

Each one of us has a part that is divine. We see it occasionally in others, and they see it in us when they love us. We can draw on that divine part of every person for strength and hope and courage and faith and love. There is wonderful, mysterious beauty in all of us, even when we behave badly.

What divinity do I see in those around me right now?

What matters?. . . Only the flicker of light within
the darkness, the feeling of warmth within the
cold, the knowledge of love within the void.
                              —Joan Walsh Anglund

If we were lost at sea, surrounded by darkness
pierced only by one distant blinking light, we would
follow that light. As we followed it, it would become
clearer and brighter until it brought us safely to land.

Sometimes when we're depressed, we feel as though
we're lost on a dark sea. But there is always a flicker of
light for us. It may be prayer, or the love of a special
friend. When we see that light, we need to move toward it. Whatever brings us hope is like that flicker of
light. The more we seek it, the clearer and brighter the
light will become.

When we are cold and our bodies begin to numb,
we must keep moving. Movement will keep us alive.
When our emotions are numb, we need people or
things or places that will warm our hearts. When no
one else is around, hot baths or a favorite treat can
bring the warmth of our own self-love into our lives
when we need it the most.

How can I brighten my inner light today?

Love consists in this, that two solitudes protect and touch and greet each other.
—*Rainer Maria Rilke*

For a relationship to be healthy and fulfilling, each of us must respect the other. "Two solitudes" is exactly what we are, and we will never be one, no matter how close we become. It may feel like that at times, but we always remain separate persons with our own thoughts, feelings, dreams, and interests.

When we love one another, we allow each other to be who we are, to have our own lives, for it is out of those separate lives that we bring strength and energy and life into our relationships.

We are meant to honor the differences between us. Often these differences lead to squabbles, but when we recognize that each of us is necessary to the union we have created, we create a better one, far superior to the sum of its parts.

What differences between us make our lives together better?

The important thing is not to conquer but to have fought at all.

—*Olympic motto*

People come from all over the world to participate in the Olympics, and they come with a wide range of talent. A lot of them know they will not win a medal, yet they have trained hard for their event. They meet people from all corners of the earth who love the same activity.

There is a contagious joy and excitement the athletes share in their time together. It is a sense that the sharing of worldwide joy and peace is indeed possible.

Whether we succeed or fail in what we do is not the essential thing. What is important is the heart with which we live our lives.

If I could share something with the world, what would it be?

What is without periods of rest will not endure.
—*Ovid*

When we are tired, we need to stop and give ourselves time to rest. Sometimes we think we can't spare the time. But without rest, all our activity soon becomes a burden and there is no joy in it. Animals know it is necessary to take time to rest. This is part of the rhythm of life: activity and rest, effort and relaxation.

Our bad moods are often our body's way of telling us we need rest. When we were little, we needed naps. Somehow, we forget to allow ourselves this right when we are older. We are wise to remember we never outgrow this need for rest to make the day go better.

When we return to our day refreshed, we have given ourselves and all those around us the gift of ourselves at our best.

What can I do better when I am rested?

It may be those who do most dream most.
— *Stephen Leacock*

Where would we be without the dreamers of the world—the ones who took the time to balance on the edge of wonder? Amazing connections, powerful images, and creative ideas come to us in daydreams. They creep in when we least expect them, like sleek cats, then make their presence known to us with a gentle pounce.

When we give ourselves permission to daydream—to sit for a while and do nothing but be quiet with our thoughts, we give ourselves a precious gift. And who knows, we just might be giving the world a priceless gift, too! Out of the seeds of some of our dreams, great ideas will blossom.

What first step can I take today to make a dream come true?

Friends are people who help you be more
yourself, more the person you are intended to be.
                                        —*Merle Shain*

Sometimes a teacher, sometimes a neighbor, almost always our moms and dads, encourage us to try new activities or to improve our schoolwork, sports, drawing, or gardening. Because they are our friends, they want us to be the best we can be.

Not everyone knows how to be a friend. Some people only criticize, and never praise. People who never encourage or praise us are usually unhappy with their own achievements. They don't mean us harm. Perhaps they just need a friend, too. Not only do we each need friends to help us grow, we need to be friends to others. To encourage and praise those who need it will help us in return.

Whose friend can I be today?

*I don't think of all the misery, but of the beauty
that still remains.*

—Anne Frank

We don't find the rewards of today by searching
through our misfortunes. Pausing to seek out something good for everything we find bad is a step in the
right direction. We may find the good outweighs the
bad.

But how much more chance we will have of living a
happy day if we skip over our setbacks and concentrate as much as we can on what is going well. It is
smarter to look for diamonds in a diamond mine than
in a garbage dump.

Let us discard our failures, using only what we have
learned from them to achieve success. Looking back at
missed opportunities will make it impossible for us to
recognize new chances to enjoy life to the fullest.
Looking only for beauty is a beautiful thing in itself.

What beauty can I see around me right now?

Many of our fears are tissue-paper-thin, and a single courageous step would carry us clear through them.

—Brendan Francis

There was a huge slide at the park and Jason was afraid to go on it. There were so many steps to climb to reach the top. All of his friends were climbing up the steps and yelling as they came down the long rolling slide.

"Come on," said his friend Steve. "It's lots of fun!"

"Isn't it scary?" asked Jason.

"A little bit," answered Steve, "but you get used to it." He ran off to go again.

Jason walked to the steps of the slide, his heart pounding in his chest. Slowly he placed his foot on the first step and lifted himself up. Courageously he climbed the ladder. When he reached the high platform he felt as if he were standing on top of the world.

We can learn from Jason that by taking that first step we can experience many exciting and wonderful things. We have all done it before—on the slide, on a bicycle, in school. Why not again?

What fear can I walk through today?

The moment an individual can accept and forgive himself, even a little, is the moment in which he becomes to some degree lovable.
— Eugene Kennedy

If we owe a bill and pay it in full, do we return to pay that same bill over and over again? If we did, someone would surely question what was wrong with us. Yet, how often do we ask forgiveness for the same thing over and over again?

How wonderful to know that we do not have to condemn ourselves, even for not living up to a goal we have set for ourselves. Once we say we are sorry, we need to be willing to forgive ourselves. After all, how else do we learn and grow except by mistakes?

When we have forgiven ourselves, we become free to take risks again without fear of unforgivable failure, and who knows what new successes we might attain?

Is there something I can forgive myself for today?

Roots nourish, give us life and bind us safely to earth. Plant them well.

—*Anonymous*

All trees have different root systems. The pine grows quickly, with shallow roots that spread in every direction. A maple is a slow-growing tree, whose roots run deeper, seeking out moisture far into the earth. Both root systems give life, but when the weather turns stormy and the wind howls through the branches, the maple, with its deeper roots, will hold fast. Though the pine grows faster and needs only surface moisture, it cannot withstand the storm as well.

We often want things immediately. We want to play the piano, but only if we can learn it fast. We want others to love us right away, or we'll give up on them. If something we're doing doesn't go just so right from the start, we give up.

But the permanent things in life take time to develop. If we want our relationships, our skills, our accomplishments, to resist the storms we all encounter, we must allow time for them to grow and deepen within us, and marvel, in the meantime, at how much we can learn from the world around us.

What deep roots am I setting down right now?

I'll be the sun upon your head,
The wind about your face,
My love upon the path you tread,
And upon your wanderings, peace.
—Gordon Bok

Today I will feel. I will feel wind and water, earth and sun. I will feel rain, the taste of it, the soft sting of its coolness. I will feel the familiar touch of my shirt against my skin, my hair across my face in the wind.

Today I will feel love like a candle on a birthday cake that never goes out no matter how much you blow on it. I will feel compassion like a toothache, a dull pain that lets me go about my business but never goes away. I will feel joy and sorrow, pain and pleasure. Today I will feel. I will feel like a human being, unique as a snowflake, common as grass.

How many different ways do I feel today?

The word image *is nothing more than the French word for* picture.

—Roseann Lloyd

A positive image of our family can help us imagine healthy relationships. It can help us appreciate our family when it is working in a healthy way.

One woman took up looking at the pictures in her mind. At last she found one for her family, after considering ordinary pictures like a garden, a team, and a zoo. When her family is happy and thriving, she sees it as a mud pot in Yellowstone Park. Each person is energetic and relaxed. Each is free to bubble up ideas and feelings and projects, free to spout off, gurgle, and pop! Yet the family is together, sharing one old mud hole, warm and cozy, surrounded by beautiful pine trees.

Can I think of an image for my family?

Large streams from little fountains flow.
                              —David Everett

Somewhere nearby, no matter where we are, runs a creek. We've seen plenty of them, narrow and rocky. In summer it's hardly a creek at all, but in the spring, it feeds a mighty river.

Each of us is like that creek, a trickle contributing to some greater plan. Sometimes we feel dried up, contributing nothing. Often we feel small, rocky, not up to the task—when we can understand what the task is.

Sometimes the task seems too simple—get up each morning, love and work and live the day as honestly as we can. What kind of contribution is that? Sometimes it seems too complicated. How much more we could contribute if we could see the whole river—where it begins and ends—if we knew what would happen tomorrow.

So we ebb and flow. And in our moments of contentment, we know we are doing the best we can each day.

What contribution, however small, can I offer the world today?

A tree grown in a cave does not bear fruit.
—Kahlil Gibran

A tree planted in a cave would soon be stopped short in its growth. There would be no room for it to grow tall or blossom. It would only grow so far and then would grow no bigger.

Fear can be like a cave. We sometimes become fearful for the same reason we might enter a cave, looking for protection. But fear protects us from the new ideas and behavior we need in order to grow. Fear can keep us huddling inside it, watching life's opportunities pass by. When fear threatens to enclose us, we can take a deep breath and begin to do what we are afraid of doing. The cave will fade away as we step out into the sun, fresh air, and storms that are a part of growing.

What fear can I overcome today?

Life can only be understood backwards, but it must be lived forward.
                                    —Søren Kierkegaard

Once, in a small village, there was a huge fire. The blaze spread and several homes and businesses were burned to the ground. After a long while, the fire was brought under control and put out. Villagers banded together to rebuild their town, but one quite persistent young man insisted on searching the rubble for the cause of the fire. Impatient townspeople scolded him, saying, "Why waste time searching for causes? Knowing them won't put out the blaze or repair the damage." "I know," replied the young man, "but knowing why might prevent other fires."

Sometimes we have to look at painful past experiences in order to prevent their recurrence. When we understand ourselves better, we can move beyond the past and walk toward the future with surer, safer steps.

How well can I use my past today?

*Thunder is good, thunder is impressive; but it is
the lightning that does the work.*
—Mark Twain

Thunder demands our attention. From the ear-
splitting boom overhead to the faint rumble in the distance, it is an impressive part of nature. Yet, it is the
lightning that discharges electricity from one cloud to
another, or to the earth.

We are sometimes like thunder. We may shout our
intentions to family members, or quietly tell our
dreams to friends. No matter how we say it, it is the
ability to follow through that is most important.
When we've completed what we've set out to do, we
will feel a sense of satisfaction and energy. With this
energy, and the knowledge we can finish what we set
out to do, we will make our dreams come true.

What is left incomplete that I can finish today?

. . . sparrow, your message is clear: it is not too late for my singing.

—Tess Gallagher

There was once a mother who loved to hang the laundry out on the clothesline in the backyard. Her baby crawled through the sheets and towels that almost touched the grass. The baby didn't talk yet, so nobody knew what she was thinking.

Ten years later, the baby, twelve years old, told her that her happiest memory of childhood was playing in her "playhouse" of laundry on the line. She remembered thinking that her mother hung the sheets out there just so she could play in the grass and wind and sun!

How wonderful to be living in a world where we can accidentally make people happy! This knowledge is a miraculous gift, and can give us reason to do every task well and with love, because it may be remembered for a lifetime by someone near to us.

What happy memory do I have of childhood?

Whenever you fall, pick something up.
—Oswald Avery

There was once a very active boy who fell and broke his leg. He could run again in the spring, the doctors said, but only if he stayed in bed for an entire month and kept his leg still. At first the boy fought the rule, but he found that the more he thought about things he couldn't do, the more tired and angry he felt.

His parents put in a phone by his bed and friends called every day. He'd never much liked talking on the phone, but he felt better when they called. He wrote letters and got replies, and was surprised at what fun it was. Usually, he didn't have time to write letters.

He learned to play chess and began to enjoy reading. His days were slower and quieter than he'd been used to, but he learned a month really isn't a very long time. When spring came, he was running again, a little more joyfully than before.

When we can learn to accept our troubles, we find, like the boy, that they are just packages in which new growth and discoveries are wrapped.

If something unexpected slows me down today, what joys might I find at the slower pace?

To those of us who knew the pain
of valentines that never came
and those whose names were never called
when choosing sides for basketball.

—Janis Ian

Each of us at some time has known the feeling of not belonging, the painful emptiness of feeling left out. We've stood on the sidelines, longing to be invited into what we think is some sort of magical circle. If only they would ask us in, we think, we'd be transformed—we'd be somebody then.

But look around. The circle is composed of people just like us: insecure at times, frightened, unsure. They have felt anxiety and feared rejection just as we have.

The pain will pass, and if we use these times to get to know and understand ourselves a bit better, we'll be better able to understand others when they're feeling left out and lonely. And when it's our turn to choose a team or send a valentine, we'll remember.

Who can I remember today?

. . . self-love is an unequivocal acceptance of the validity of getting what one wants—of respecting one's needs.

—Marion Weinstein

Once there was a woman who loved her husband and children so much that she did everything for them and nothing for herself. She thought taking care of herself was selfish. She never considered taking a vacation when she needed it. She stayed to take care of her family no matter what it cost her personally. Then she realized how much she resented them because she wasn't taking care of herself. So she began to ask for what she needed. At first, her family didn't like it. Little by little they began to notice that when she was relaxed, their lives were more serene, too. It wasn't always easy for her to love herself enough to ask for what she needed, but she learned that when she said no to demands she couldn't meet, she felt calm and centered. Best of all, she no longer resented them for asking. When she said yes, she did what they asked with real pleasure.

Do I sometimes resent doing things I could have chosen not to do?

. . . I cannot see
The love you offer.

—*Emily Dickinson*

How can we make love visible; how can we give it eyes? We can make love a present, wrap it carefully as if it were a beautiful thing. We can make love a favor nobody foresaw; we can fill a cup, prepare a meal, run an errand with our love. We can make love out of real words—in a letter, a note, a simple unrhymed poem. And we can make our love visible with our eyes by making our eyes meet those of the people we love.

When we turn a feeling like love into an act, we share it with those around us, and they are encouraged to return the favor. In this way, the world's storehouse of love increases.

How can I show the love I feel today?

*If you have butterflies in your stomach ask them
into your heart.*

—*Cooper Edens*

We've all had butterflies in our stomach. It happens
on the first day of school or the first day on a new job.
It happens almost anytime we try something new or
risky. These butterflies are nervous and fluttery, and
sometimes we wish we could just go back to bed.

But the best thing we can do, and sometimes the
only thing, is to go right ahead and walk into that new
situation with head held high. We will probably feel
awkward at first, but that is natural and will pass.

Our nervousness can change into excitement and
joy for what we are doing. We can begin to feel proud
when we walk through our fear. It is a true accomplishment when we don't let our fear stop us—when,
instead, we let the butterflies in our heart unfold.

---

*When I have the butterflies today, will I enjoy their
beauty?*

The route you take depends a good deal upon where you want to go.

—Lewis Carroll

Day after day, the father drove to work along the same dreary highway to the same dreary job. Sometimes his daughter went to his office with him. On one of these occasions she noticed a winding road running parallel to the highway. "Oh, Daddy, let's take that road today," she suggested. After some grumbling and mumbling, the father agreed and turned off to take the side road.

To their delight, the road was lined with full trees and a rainbow of flowers. They came upon a quaint little village in which where was an office with a sign in the window that said, "Clerk Wanted. Inquire Within." The job seemed perfect and the man accepted it with excitement he hadn't felt in many years.

Sometimes we have to risk taking a different path in order to arrive at a different place. How else can we change things in our lives that need to be changed? And how easy to do it, once we're willing to risk something out of the ordinary.

What can I do that's out of the ordinary today?

When you meet a man, you judge him by his clothes; when you leave, you judge him by his heart.

—Russian proverb

The woman on the park bench was gnarled and dirty. Her hair was an uncombed mess, her clothes torn and old. She clutched a paper bag, which seemed to contain her belongings. She sat in the sun, humming to herself. Occasionally she threw a bit of popcorn to ducks who waited at her feet. A little boy and his mother sat by the lake, not wanting to share the bench with this wild-eyed old woman. But when the old woman beckoned to the little boy to share her popcorn with him, he ran to the bench and let out squeals of laughter as they fed the hungry ducks.

Our world is full of variety and surprises. Would we have it any other way? When we shun people because of the way they look, we cut ourselves off from part of life. But when we are ready for anything—accepting and trusting—we are a wonder to everyone.

How shall I judge people today?

If I cry tears let them wash away your fears—
make a rainbow of love for you.
                                    —*Thom Klika*

It takes both sun and rain to make a rainbow in the sky. The rainbow is a rare and beautiful thing—each color brilliant beside the other. Rain falls to earth like the tears we all shed sometimes. Sunlight shines like the happiness we find inside when we feel peaceful.

The colors of the rainbow are like all the different feelings we have. Let's say red is anger and green is fear and orange is joy and violet is contentment. All these feelings create a whole person, in the same way that all these colors make the whole rainbow. We become more colorful people as we learn to express all our emotions.

A person who is learning to share feelings radiates the same kind of beauty as a rainbow in the sky.

Who can I share a feeling with today?

I'm a trader at heart. . . except that I don't like trades that come out equally—that's too much like borrowing. I'd rather trade a strong hand for a patient ear or a story for a meal: anything that keeps things turning over.

—*Gordon Bok*

There is an old saying that there are just two kinds of people in the world: givers and takers. Those of us who are givers delight in it. We have a buck to lend when someone is broke, a kind word when someone's down, a helping hand when someone needs it. But sometimes we givers are uncomfortable when we're on the receiving end. We brush off thanks and gifts and help, even when they're needed or deserved.

Those of us who are takers, on the other hand, know how to receive graciously what others have to give; we know how to ask for what we need. Often, however, we don't know how to give. We may be afraid our gifts will be wrong or rejected or laughed at.

We can all strive to become traders, people who have learned how to both give and receive. We each have the capacity to give what we have freely and to ask, gratefully, for what we don't have. That is the greatest gift of all.

What can I give and take today?

Faith is the bird that feels the light when the dawn is still dark.
                                        —*Sir Rabindranath Tagore*

In the darkness of early morning, the bird outside the window begins to sing. Soon the eastern sky turns pink. The bird continues singing until the first yellow rays warm its soft wings. Then it flies away, not returning to the window until the next morning.

We can learn from the small bird how to have faith. We don't need to wait for something we want before having faith we'll get it. We can begin to show our faith by celebrating the things we usually take for granted. After all, when we take something for granted, isn't that a selfish form of faith? We can start by singing a song to celebrate the new day, a day that will warm our hearts and shed light on our actions. Like the bird's faith in the sunrise, we need only have faith that God meant each day to enrich our lives.

What faith can I celebrate right now?

The answer, my friend, is blowin' in the wind,
the answer is blowin' in the wind.
—Bob Dylan

A family is like a windchime: each member hangs in delicate balance with the others. When a problem develops for one family member, the rest of us often take on roles to try to deal with the situation. But what happens to our windchime when we're all pulling and pushing in different directions? Our balance is lost and we either all clash together or none of our chimes connect at all and there is only painful silence.

If we let go and trust in that spiritual force beyond ourselves, we discover that it is like the wind. It moves our windchime gently with a soothing breeze that allows us to relax in our places or move together as the force directs us. It brings out the beautiful harmonious notes we weren't able to produce ourselves.

How can I help us make better music together today?

Into each life some rain must fall. Some days must be dark and dreary.
                            —Henry Wadsworth Longfellow

Coping with problems and weathering troubled times are part of life. Those of us who have survived painful experiences have a duty to help younger ones prepare to face bad times by sharing the solutions we found.

When stormy weather comes, we need to feel we are like other people. It's not that misery loves company, but that we don't want to feel we're in this alone.

We will never have perfect living conditions. The only place where every day is a sunny one is in the desert. When pain comes, we can walk through our problems and settle things quickly, rather than prolonging the hurt by battling our way around the obstacles in an effort to avoid them.

What problem can I confront and eliminate today?

Most folks are about as happy as they make up their minds to be.

—*Abraham Lincoln*

Our negative thoughts can be like pebbles rolling down the mountainside. One pebble bumps into another one. The second begins rolling and slams into a third. On and on it goes until thousands of pebbles, rocks, even giant boulders, are hurtling down the mountain.

When we find ourselves stuck in a rut thinking a negative thought, we can decide to stop and replace it with a positive thought. At first our single positive thought may not dislodge another one. We may have to think of several and start them rolling down the mountainside. If we practice, we will find it becomes easier for that first good thought to shake loose others. We will see our lives change when we begin to look at the positive side of things.

How can I begin to shape my outlook today?

Take care of yourself my darling
And I'll take care of me
Live your loneliness knowing
That we can both be free.
                                    —Mary Lee George

Loneliness is something inside us. It's not caused by other people's behavior, though what others do may let us know we are feeling lonely. We have all experienced being alone and really enjoying it—walking by the river or singing a song we like. Feeling lonely is when we feel as if nobody cares about us or wants to be with us.

Sometimes we need to give ourselves permission to feel lonely and know that we are okay no matter what we are feeling. Other times it may be wise to check with others if our feelings are true. We can ask our mother if she cares about us or ask a friend if he wants to play, and be open to the answer. When we feel lonely, we often ignore what others do or say if it doesn't agree with what we believe to be true. The important thing to remember is that we are okay no matter what choice we make.

When I feel lonely, what can I do about it?

I never lose sight of the fact that just being is fun.
—*Katharine Hepburn*

The first good news each day is that we wake up. We are breathing. Our hearts are beating, our minds working. The adventure of living begins. What does the day hold in store? We have no way of knowing what surprises lie in wait for us today.

We may look forward, not just to the expected, but to the unexpected. Whom shall we meet? What will we see? What will we learn? How will we be entertained? What chances to help others will come our way? What chances to love and be loved?

Now that our eyes are opened to today's beauty, let us remain alert for new sights. Let us cry when sad, smile when touched, and laugh at what is funny in a whole new lifetime before us.

What can I be thankful for today?

The sun's the lifegiver ... I talk to it like you would to a god.

—*Peter Firth*

Having a Power greater than ourselves to believe in is like knowing the sun is in the sky. There are days when the sun shines with a brilliance that lights up everything around us—tree branches, snowflakes, the faces of our friends. When a seed is planted, it is the sun's warmth that invites it out of the ground to grow into a fruit or flower. The sun is the center the earth rotates around. The sun gives warmth and light to the earth, sometimes in ways we don't always notice.

There are days we do not see the sun—it is obscured by thick clouds. Yet even on these days, we know the sun's rays still reach the earth and nourish it.

God nourishes and warms our lives the same way the sun does the earth. Some days we easily see the presence of such a power in our lives, and other days we cannot see past the clouds. But God gives our lives a light-filled center and nourishes us even on quiet cloudy days.

How is God present in my life right now?

One must lose one's life in order to find it.
—Anne Morrow Lindbergh

We are often so busy trying to control the outcome of the happenings in our daily lives, so intent on projecting our tomorrows, that we let life slip by. Life is today. This is all we have for sure—the moments in our lives we cannot hold. Sometimes it feels as if those moments were beyond time and place, gifts from God to receive and give up at the same time, like a dragonfly that lights on our hand and will either be crushed or will fly away if we try to close our fingers over it.

Life is a series of things to let go of—our friends and loved ones, our children as they grow, our dreams, or our youth. Only we ourselves, our inner selves, are a constant to be found and learned about every day, in the present moment.

How well can I enjoy each moment today?

A terrace nine stories high begins with a pile of earth.

—Lao-tzu

Imagine yourself with a pile of dirt in front of you and building plans for a one-story structure. It would be easy to think, "Oh, this is impossible—it will never get done."

But the architect hires people to help. A foundation is built, and then the frame. From there, step by step, the rest is filled in. We have all watched a building take shape and become a finished product.

Building plans are like the goals we all have. We want to be a better person or friend, a better artist or athlete. Reaching a goal is like putting up a building. Once we have a goal, we need a strong foundation to support us. All of us need the help of others to reach our goals.

What small step can I take toward a goal today?

Give to the world the best you have and the best will come back to you.

—*Madeline Bridges*

Sometimes we feel lazy or bored, and then we don't do our best work. Maybe our writing becomes hard to read, or we miss a porch when delivering newspapers. Perhaps we are daydreaming instead of listening closely to what a friend is trying to tell us. When we are not really paying attention to our activities or the people around us, we'll likely miss out on something important, because we do receive in equal measure what we give. And this truth works in every aspect of our lives.

When we treat our friends, our families, even people we don't know well with kindness, we'll experience kindness in return. Our own actions and attitudes toward others are what we can expect from others as well.

How can I increase the kindness in the world today?

Good friendships are fragile things and require as much care as any other fragile and precious things.

—Randolph Bourne

A good friendship is like a flower garden. It needs attention and care. We start by preparing the soil and then planting our tiny seeds. Our friendships have foundations like the soil, and in them we plant seeds of trust and understanding.

Like a garden, friendships need care and love in order to thrive. We nourish friendships with visits, thoughtful favors, and trust. When we are feeling down or in need of help, a friendship can offer us more than just beauty.

When we work at our friendships, they are not seasonal but bloom in any weather, and they surround us with comfort and the knowledge that we have, and deserve, love.

How can I nurture a friendship today?

No yesterdays are ever wasted for those who give themselves today.

— Brendan Francis

We often find ourselves yearning for tomorrow. We get carried away thinking about the next day's big game or camping trip. We find ourselves daydreaming about how much fun we'll have with friends or what animals we'll see in the park.

The next day comes and perhaps the excitement about the game diminishes because our friends can't make it or the camping trip is cancelled because of bad weather. We feel cheated and begin regretting the missed opportunities of yesterday.

When we find ourselves concentrating only on tomorrow, we need to stop and look around. We'll begin to notice the joke a friend is telling, or the bird flying overhead. We will begin appreciating the joys of the moment.

When we live in the moment, we have no expectations about the next moment, and without expectations, we can't be disappointed, only surprised.

What is delightful about this moment right now?

Love, a thousand, thousand voices,
From night to dawn,
from dawn to night,
Have cried the passion
  of their choices
To orb your name and keep it bright.
  —William Rose Benet

We are each in the midst of unique lives, and our choices are based on our own experiences, so it's only natural that they all be different. One of us may choose to go to jail for protesting nuclear weapons; another may choose to pray for peace. Both are working for the same goal.

It is a sign of our love to respect others' right to choose for themselves, even to make choices we may not agree with. Perhaps a brother or sister likes music we hate, or a son or daughter wants to wear an unusual style of clothing. How often do we, in the name of love, try to force our choices on others? When we give the gift of letting loved ones choose what is right for them, it strengthens our ability to choose what is right for us.

Whose choices can I honor today, even if I disagree?

Something can't happen every day. You get up, go to work, come back, eat again, enjoy some leisure, go back to bed. Now that's plenty for most folks.

—Ntozake Shange

When we were all little kids, before we started school, the days felt so long it seemed as if we had time for everything.

But when we started school, we had to start living by the clock, and in this way, we became very grown up. Sometimes we feel angry about living by the clock, all of us who are first grade and older! But there are things we can do to help us live with these limits.

First, we can learn to set a goal for each day, and once we have reached that goal—whether it's doing spelling homework, mopping the floor, or writing three business letters—we can announce to whoever happens to be around, "Now that I've completed that, I don't have to worry about one more thing to feel worthwhile."

Second, we can believe what we said! We can relax, do something fun, enjoy the pleasures that the day offers.

What is my goal for today?

He felt frightened at being different from his brothers and sisters. It scared him to be different.

—E. B. White

How ugly and wrong it makes us feel to be different: to be tall when others are short, slow when others are fast, black when others are white.

The miracle, and paradox, is that everyone is different—and that is what makes us all the same.

When we think honestly about the people we admire—friends, sports heroes, actors, musicians, parents, teachers, employers—we know that all of them, as human beings, not heroes, have felt out of place in their lives, probably many times.

Believing we are alone or different cuts us off from others. Climbing over that protective wall of "differentness" is scary, but it is guaranteed to set us free.

How can I let go of my "differentness" today?

The sign must come like dawn. You cannot see its arrival, but know when it is there.
                                        —*Diane Wakoski*

Let us take a break, sit by the river, and watch the current quietly flow. Let's just think, for a moment, about where the current is going, the shores it will brush on its way, the clouds reflected on its surface, the animals that come to drink from it, the bobbers it gently nudges downstream.

Our lives sometimes seem like the river, wandering to the west, the south, back toward the east, seemingly without direction at all. Yet we can take comfort in this thought, for, like the river, we are always headed in the direction we are meant to go. Without trying, without knowing, we are part of the larger pattern of things, and we nourish many others just by passing through their lives.

What shores will my life touch today?

Hope is the thing with feathers
that perches in the soul
And sings the tune without the words
And never stops at all.

—*Emily Dickinson*

We often hum and sing to ourselves because it makes us feel content. It is the melody itself that makes us feel good—words and thoughts do not matter.

Having hope for ourselves and for our universe is like having a melody always moving inside us. The melody may be calm or exciting, but most of all it brings with it beauty and a sense of peace. Hope can overcome the need for words and thoughts and promises. Hope is the melody that keeps us going, the hum that continues even when there are no words to the song. Hope is not a melody we think about—it just comes when we believe in the goodness of our world. If we have faith in a power greater than ourselves, we will be able to find the melody of hope inside us at all times.

What is my hope for today?

I will, I will accept myself
With hope and fear and wonder
And what I have joined together
Let no man put asunder.

—Dory Preven

There is a wonderful freedom in acceptance. When we accept ourselves, with all our imperfections, we can then begin to accept others just as they are. This is especially exciting when we apply this discovery to our own families. A family is like a bouquet of flowers arranged in a common vase. Each flower is different. One might be blue, one white, one a rose, one a chrysanthemum. But each adds to the beauty of the whole bouquet and enhances the vase that holds it.

It isn't important that we know why one flower is blue and one white. We don't have to understand how a rose becomes a rose to appreciate the arrangement. We just accept it for what it is. Acceptance of others does not mean agreement or approval. How boring if we only accepted those who reflected our own ideas and opinions! How dull to look upon a bouquet of exactly the same flowers.

Today, will I accept the differences between us as part of our beauty together?

Young man, the secret of my success is that at an early age I discovered I was not God.
—*Oliver Wendell Holmes*

Sometimes, in our families, we try to get parents or brothers or sisters to treat us the way we want them to, to do things we want them to. When they're upset or angry with us, we try to get them to stop, rather than allowing them to be angry.

But our feelings are ours alone, and only we are responsible for how we feel. Those around us are not the cause of our feelings. We are.

This knowledge is a big responsibility, because we know we cannot blame others for our bad moods. But it is a fact. And this fact is also a wonderful freedom for us, for it means that we also have the power to make ourselves happy, no matter what goes on around us.

How can I make myself happy today?

Education should be the process of helping everyone to discover his uniqueness.
—Leo Buscaglia

We are each special, which means there is not another person just like ourselves. Nobody looks just like us. Nobody's voice sounds quite like our own. And nobody thinks through a story just as we do.

Each of us has been created for a special purpose. Maybe it's for what we'll teach a friend, or the way we'll help a sister or a brother. Every day will give us chances to offer our special talents to others. Our being alive is God's way of proving that we're important to the family, the neighborhood, the world.

What important task lies before me today?

Silently one by one
in the infinite meadows of heaven
Blossomed the lovely stars,
the forget-me-nots of angels.
—Henry Wadsworth Longfellow

Tales told about the stars reflect a lot about the people who tell them. The constellation now called Orion was once called Hippolyta. Hippolyta was one of the Amazon queens. The Amazons were women warriors who had four leaders instead of one: two older women and two younger women. Everyone could benefit from the experience and wisdom of the older and the strength and vigor of the younger.

After Hippolyta died, they named this constellation for her to honor her and remind themselves of her wisdom and bravery.

We can draw a good lesson from the value the Amazons placed on the contribution each one could make, no matter how young or old. When we remain alert to the possibility of learning from people we hadn't seriously considered as teachers, we are reminded of our often-forgotten value to others.

What can I offer in wisdom or strength to others today?

Kindness and intelligence don't always deliver us from the pitfalls and traps.
—*Barbara Grizzuti Harrison*

Being human means we'll have hard times along with pleasant ones. Whether with friends, at school, or at home, we'll find reasons for sadness or anger as easily as for laughter. In every part of our lives, we're offered just what we need for growth.

Being the best we know how to be doesn't mean we'll escape confusion or pain. Through the troubling times we learn to trust in a Higher Power; we learn patience; we learn to let go and let God decide outcomes. The troubling times offer us growth and serenity, our keys to happiness.

What hidden gifts will I find in today's troubles?

When we do the best we can, we never know what miracle is wrought in our life, or the life of another.

—*Helen Keller*

It is a great loss when we underestimate the importance of our efforts in the life of another. One man who had to spend some time in a hospital waited day after day to receive a card or a telephone call from those who cared. Some people whom he expected to call or write did not. Others whom the man had not felt close to and whom he did not expect to hear from surprised him with their concern. He came to place greater value on those who had cared enough to call or send a card.

A little act, the best we have at that moment, makes a big difference to the person on the other end. Knowing this helps us make sure that all our acts, even the smallest, are as good as we can make them, because they all make a difference.

What small acts of those around me have made a difference to me?

Notice the difference between what happens when a man says to himself, I have failed three times, and what happens when he says, I'm a failure.

—*S. I. Hayakawa*

What happens to us when we call ourselves names like "failure" or "dummy"? We feel we're no good and never will be. We want to stop trying because we think we'll flub up again.

But what if we begin to use different words to describe the same results? It won't change the results, but it will change us. And it will change the way we see ourselves and our actions.

Just by changing the words we use we can feel better about ourselves. Saying "I've failed three times" means we'll try again and again and again until we succeed. It means we know God doesn't make any failures or dummies. It means God is always with us, loving us and helping us, even when trying seems difficult.

What can I change my thinking about today?

Things don't turn up in this world until somebody turns them up.
　　　　　　　　　—James A. Garfield

We could learn from the bears in the woods how to turn up opportunities. To nourish themselves, they turn over logs and stumps to get insects. When they smell honey they will climb a tree after it, and when they see berries they will move branches aside to get at them.

Like the bears, we need to turn up things for ourselves. Perhaps we can enter a drawing or writing contest. Maybe we can try out for a team sport or the orchestra. By doing this, we take risks that foster our growth and build confidence, and we turn our lives into fulfilling adventures.

Why wait for opportunity to knock when we can knock at opportunity's door? Whatever our interests, finding ways to enjoy them can make the most out of the opportunities around us.

What opportunities are available to me today?

There is no hope of joy except in human relations.

—*Antoine de Saint Exupery*

It is hard to imagine being really joyful and excited without our family and friends. We can imagine a birthday party with no one but us attending. Even if we got many gifts, we would feel empty if there were no one around to share our excitement with.

Our joy comes from each other. Even the hard times furnish us with wonderful memories for later in life. We share the good and the bad, and the rewards of both. When our lives together seem too difficult, when it's too hard to share, too crowded to think, when there are too many disagreements, we can find comfort by looking at one another once again and seeing all the ways we are truly alike, and what we share every moment that we sometimes take for granted— our food, our thoughts, the very air we breathe.

What are the things we share right now?

Let me fly, says little birdie,
Mother, let me fly away.
        —*Alfred, Lord Tennyson*

Don't we all want to fly away? Isn't there a better place out there away from home? The boy can't fly, but he can climb a tree and ride the wind. The girl, high on imaginary wings, flies to her own land of dreams. Even mothers and fathers, together and alone, need to fly—away from work, house, and the everyday same old things. But we all need to return as well. We need to know that home is the one safe place to land, that there we can rest, recover our strength, tell our tales to family and friends.

Our home is safe and comfortable, but if we never leave, even for a short while, we will never take the action necessary to bring our dreams to life.

What small comfort might I give up for today in order to make a dream come true?

One is happy as a result of one's own efforts, tastes, a certain degree of courage, self-denial to a point, love of work, and, above all, a clear conscience. Happiness is no vague dream, of that I now feel certain.

—George Sand

"We always go get a hot fudge sundae after the school choir concert," the girl said. Her parents laughed because their daughter said *always,* and they had gone to a school choir concert only once. Then the parents realized that the girl really had a great idea.

"Yes," the mother said, "we always get a sundae because we like to make up new traditions. We'll have to be sure and do it tonight so we don't let the tradition fall apart before it even gets started!"

They all laughed together and started debating which restaurant had the best hot fudge sundae.

We all need to have special traditions with our families. We need celebrations that have nothing to do with official holidays. Family holidays can mean so much more to us sometimes because they celebrate our shared experiences in life and become the source of happy memories for a lifetime.

What tradition can I start today?

When people envy me I think, Oh God, don't envy me, I have my own pains.
—Barbra Streisand

A forest is full of many different kinds of trees—they are all sizes and shapes and shades of color. It is hard to imagine a pine tree wishing it were an oak. Or a fir tree envying the birch its white bark. Instead, each tree catches raindrops and reflects the sunshine in its own way.

We often find ourselves envying others. We think they have more money or more friends. We see them as better looking or luckier in some way than we are.

It is so easy to overlook our own gifts when we do this. We get fooled by what looks good and forget that all human beings have some weaknesses and pain, just as we do. Like the trees in the forest, we each have our own unique beauty and talents to offer. If we believe in ourselves, rather than envy those around us, we will grow green and tall in our own way.

What qualities do I have that someone might envy?

*The house, the stars, the desert—what gives
them their beauty is something that is invisible.*
—Antoine de Saint Exupery

What makes our home special? Is it the shape of it,
or whether or not we have carpeting? Probably not.

More likely, what makes us love a place is how we
feel when we are there. Home is the familiarity of
pleasant smells, activities, and special people.

And when we are caught by the beauty of the stars,
isn't it something that happens inside us—the breath-
taking feeling of joy that is so hard to describe? The
beauty of a day or a special person in our lives cannot
be captured, but it can fill and warm our hearts.

Can I measure beauty today by what I feel inside?

Perhaps nature is our best assurance of immortality.

—*Eleanor Roosevelt*

Everything in nature contributes to something else—like the hundred-year-old tree that stood tall until a wind storm. The protection it gave to thousands of birds and squirrels it now gives to insects and fungi. As it slowly decays, it nourishes the ground, and from the enriched soil grow several other trees. We human beings are part of this eternal cycle, our ideas and actions enriching those around us and influencing generations yet to come. Being part of this vast plan gives us comfort, and faith that everything that happens is meant to be. Our hearts fill with joy with the knowledge that we are needed, just as every tree is needed.

How do I fit into nature's plan today?

Stars have always helped me to get things into perspective ... I tried to let the starlight heal something deep in me that hurt.
—Madeleine L'Engle

For a long time, people have used stars to find their way in the dark. Many a lost soul has been guided by the North Star or the Big Dipper.

If we watch the sky at night, we can see thousands of twinkling stars. They are our friends. They remind us how small we are. They remind us of the vastness of the universe, of the power and beauty that surround us.

Starlight in the sky, or reflected on a lake, can comfort us when we hurt. With safe and open arms, nature accepts our sorrow, no matter how we express it. Starlight, like all of nature, reflects a light that comes from way beyond us. It is that light that heals us in a deep and quiet way.

How has nature comforted me when I am troubled?

How easy the breath that kills a flame
How hard to kindle that light again.
Cold words kill and kind words kindle,
By words withheld a dream may dwindle.
                              —Joan Walsh Anglund

How we treat the people we live with affects the happiness of our family. Just as a breath can blow out a flame, a mean remark can cast a shadow across a brother or sister's heart. People of all ages have left dreams behind because no one encouraged them. They are like candles snuffed out.

On the other hand, if we see friends or family members feeling good about something they have done, we can learn to be happy for them. If we notice their excitement and encourage them with kind and sincere words, it will help their candle burn brighter. Sharing the happiness of others will make our own candles burn brighter, and it always feels good when we receive kind words ourselves.

In what ways can I bring light and warmth with my words today?

The reason why birds can fly and we can't is simply that they have perfect faith, for to have faith is to have wings.

—James M. Barrie

As children, we are taught to act and think with confidence. If we have faith that something wonderful can happen, it will bring us joy. Confidence gives us the will to succeed. Without faith, we invite despair. Faith lets us win by teaming us with love and hope. When things are going well, faith encourages growth. During hard times, faith falls upon trust for added strength and inspiration. It takes such a small amount of material things to have faith. Once, a four-year-old girl found a penny and showed it proudly to a stranger. The man scoffed, "What do you expect to buy with a penny?" The child with faith replied, "I can buy a wonderful wish at a wishing well with it."

What can I have faith in today?

*I think of the trees and how simply they let go,
let fall the riches of a season, how without grief
(it seems) they can let go and go deep into their
roots for renewal and sleep.*

—May Sarton

"How can I do what you say," asked the child, "and still be me?"

"Look at me," said the tree. "I bend in the wind, droop in the rain. Yet I always remain myself, a tree."

"Look at me," said the man. "I can't change."

"Look at me," said the tree. "I change every season from green to brown to green again, from bud to flower to fallen leaf. Yet I always remain myself, a tree."

"I can't love anymore," said the woman. "With my love, I have given away all that I am."

"Look at me," said the tree. "There are robins in my branches, owls in my trunk, moss and ladybugs living on my bark. They may take what I have, but not what I am."

Whether we know it or not, we are like the tree. Only our pride hangs on to a false sense of self, wanting to keep everything, refusing to follow advice or orders. What we do doesn't matter; how we do it is what counts.

What changes have I gone through without losing my real self?

What we do upon some great occasion will probably depend on what we already are: and what we already are will be the result of previous years of self-discipline.

—*H. P. Viddon*

In the ninth inning of the baseball game with a tie score and the bases loaded, the batter hit a home run. The fans and the team cheered wildly, and the batter was jubilant.

What many fans did not know was that he had been playing on baseball teams for fifteen years. Many times he struggled without being noticed. He wondered if he was any good or not, and there were days he had to make himself go out and practice. He made many mistakes, but his love and dedication for the game had always won out.

It is the years of discipline that prepare us for our big moments in life. Daily practice and love give our lives a direction, even through times of doubt and despair. By doing our best each day and learning from our mistakes, we prepare ourselves for the big moments—the home runs—in our lives.

How are my mistakes and pains today a part of my future success?

There are two kinds of slaves, the prisoners of addiction, and the prisoners of envy.
—Ivan Ilich

No emotion brings us more personal pain or wastes more of our time than envy. When we envy, we are never free from stress, because envy takes no holidays. Shakespeare called envy the green sickness. Envy magnifies molehills into mountains.

Just how foolish envy truly is becomes clear when we think of it as a row of hooks on which to hang grudges. When we envy others, especially our family members, we blind ourselves to the good we could see in all people. We are ignoring life's flowers to gather bouquets of weeds.

When we envy the accomplishments or possessions of another, we will be better off if we look to our own prized possessions, to those things in ourselves that no one else has in exactly the same way.

What riches do I have within and around me?

Learn what you are and be such.

—*Pindar*

The most precious gift we can give those closest to us is honesty. Yet we often hide our true selves from friends, fearing we won't be accepted or loved if we let them see the real us. Often, we show parts of ourselves that hide who we really are. We have often heard ourselves or others say, "My parents would just die if . . . ," or, "Don't argue in front of the children."

If we hide too much behind false images, we run the risk of losing track of what is real and what is false. We become actors instead of real people, trying to please Aunt Jane, our grandparents, our big brother, or our children.

When we conquer our fear of letting others in, we are able to see ourselves honestly. When we discover that others accept us as we are, we can accept and love ourselves. To know oneself is to know a person of value.

What part of me have I been hiding?

. . . but time and chance happeneth to them all.
—*Ecclesiastes*

Life, director of the comedy, always lets things get a little out of hand. We all know what would be normal and right, but the right horse sometimes finishes last in the race, and the jerk has all the money. The wise people, like us, are ignored by all, and the good woman gets in trouble with the law. The rich man cheats on his income tax, but he never gets caught the way the needy ones like us do, and the worst sinners get saved in the nick of time, while the fittest sometimes just drop dead.

If all the best-laid plans go wrong, maybe we are meant to learn that such important things aren't so important, after all.

If the skies are custard pies waiting to plop down on our hopeful faces, maybe it is best to accept the gift, count it a blessing, and lick our chops.

How have my failures been successes in disguise?

Look, the wind vane fluttering in the
*   autumn breeze*
Takes hold of certain things that
*   cannot be held.*

—Feng Chih

When we think we are losing our grip, we have good reason to look up. Consider the moon suspended in the sky, how it continues to come and go, follows its natural law, and never really loses face. Consider the sun, the stars, the seasons, how they refuse to abandon us, to let go of their hold on our lives. And come closer to home. We can marvel at the magic of small efficient things—the toaster and stove, the light in the room, the words in a good book that are permanent, faithful, and clear. We can consider how music, without saying a word, still speaks to us, and how a few friends, maybe miles away, continue to hang on to the strength of our small and faithful words.

We can keep in mind that we are part of a complex and loving system, and our grip can never be lost.

How do I see my unity with my surroundings today?

A musician must make music, an artist must paint, a poet must write, if he is to be at peace with himself. What a man can be, he must be.
—Abraham Maslow

The same is true of a seamstress, carpenter, homemaker, lawyer, or mechanic. The question is, Who and what am I? What must I do to be at peace with myself? What can I be? (For that is what I must be.)

A lucky few of us find the answers to these questions fairly early in life, and we work to develop into the people we can be and must be. We do that by looking at our deepest desires, and ask what would bring fulfillment for us. We ask what we would enjoy doing most, what we believe we have the ability to be really good at. What is it that sometimes burns within us to be expressed or done? The answers to what we can be, what we must be, come from within, through asking ourselves these questions.

What kind of a person am I capable of being?

We can secure other people's approval, if we do right and try hard; but our own is worth a hundred of it. . . .

—*Mark Twain*

There was once a young girl who thought that if only she tried a little harder, she could please her parents; if only she were prettier, her friends would like her better. She tried constantly to gain their approval. Sometimes they said they liked her, and sometimes they didn't.

Then one night a fairy came to her in a dream and told her, "You are fine just the way you are. You don't have to change. I want you to start noticing your own beauty and loving yourself exactly the way you are."

Doing what the fairy suggested—giving love and approval to herself—wasn't easy, but she found that when she did it she felt a peace that was not dependent on what others thought. She thanked her fairy for caring enough to come and give her such wise advice.

What are some things I like about myself?

. . . [the king] can deprive them of the benefit of
sun and rain, . . . and they are at the same time
pelted from above with great stones, . . . while
the roofs of their houses are beaten to pieces.
—Jonathan Swift

How do we punish those momentarily gone wrong?
Do we try hurting with words—jab them in the heart
with some spear-shaped phrases, slap them in the face
with an insult or two? Maybe we like to poison them
with a strong dose of silence. Have we tried to make
them feel bad by making them feel sorry for us? Do we
remind them daily that what went wrong with our
lives is really all their fault?

We must remember that we are the rulers of our
own lives only, and this knowledge gives us the power
to punish only ourselves. It also gives us control over
our lives, so that others' actions need not wrong us,
and we need not punish.

Have I been punishing someone?

If you're never scared or embarrassed or hurt, it means you never take any chances.

—Julia Soul

Do we avoid making new friends because we're scared they won't like us? Do we get embarrassed when we make a mistake and avoid trying again? When we get our feelings hurt, do we think we're bad, or that something is wrong with us?

Being scared or shy or hurt are all part of being alive. When we try to stay away from painful feelings, we keep ourselves from having many wonderful adventures. If we're afraid to meet new people, we may never have any close friends. If we stop trying when we're embarrassed, we may never learn a better way of doing things. And if we don't share our hurt feelings, we may never find out that everyone else has the same feelings we have.

What can I try again today that I failed at yesterday?

. . . ere it vanishes
Over the margin
After it, follow it,
Follow The Gleam.

—Alfred, Lord Tennyson

It is difficult to find words for the "Gleam" we pursue. What it is, we are never too sure. We see it best in our daily dreams, while we're staring out a window at nothing at all. Sometimes it appears between the words in a book; it is always sure to be there when we sit alone to write down our own thoughts. We see it in the autumn woods, feel its heavy breathing in ocean waves. It is suddenly a skylark in flight, a falling leaf, a flower we have reluctantly picked. It makes us feel sad but good. It is always luring us on, always beautiful.

Is it love? Success? Peace? It may be any or all of these things, and we may find it through another person, or some talent we have, or a thing of beauty we stumble upon. And it is there within us, always, waiting to be found.

In what ways can I follow the Gleam I see in my life today?

Therefore do not be anxious about tomorrow, for tomorrow will be anxious for itself.
—Matthew 6:34

To worry about something ahead of time is a waste of time and energy that could be better spent on living a full life today.

For instance, if we spend hours today worrying about an important test at school tomorrow, we can't very well concentrate on studying. And if we lie awake tonight agonizing over what we don't know or haven't studied, we're going to be exhausted tomorrow when we take the test.

Wouldn't it be much better to focus on doing all we can today to prepare for the test, and then, knowing we've done our best, let go of it tonight and get a good night's sleep? In fact, if we do that every day of the year, when a big test comes along, we'll know we're as ready as we can be, and won't have a thing to worry about. What a relief it is to know we've done our best today and every day.

What can I do well today so I won't worry about it tomorrow?

Fear makes strangers of people who should be friends.

—*Shirley MacLaine*

No one is brave every moment; each of us feels awkward, shy, perhaps even ugly or dumb part of the time. If we could understand that about each other, it would make it easier for us to be friendly and willing, to talk to someone new. Instead, we often sit back, waiting to be noticed; waiting for someone to invite us to join in an activity.

We are all so much alike, yet we are so certain we're different. Being self-conscious is normal. Even those who are the most popular suffer the same fears as the rest of us. The better we understand the ways we are the same, the easier it will be to make friends with someone new. And it's through friends that we grow and are strengthened for whatever lies ahead.

What new person can I offer friendship to today?

One will rarely err if extreme actions be ascribed to vanity, ordinary actions to habit, and mean actions to fear.

—Friedrich Nietzsche

Sometimes we begin to believe someone close to us is being mean deliberately. This may happen when a good friend suddenly stops inviting us to her house. She may be scared to have others over because her parents are having problems, or for some other reason that has nothing to do with us.

But we often fear that it is because of something we said or did. We find ourselves becoming scared and pulling away. If we ask for God's help in turning our fear around, we can overcome it and ask our friend why she stopped inviting us over. Most times we will find that our friend had no idea her actions affected us the way they did. We can then laugh at ourselves for our fears and applaud ourselves for overcoming them.

What treasure might I find beneath my fear today?

All power is a trust. We are accountable for its exercise. From people and for people all power springs, and all must exist.
—*Benjamin Disraeli*

The sun is power. It warms, it burns, it feeds the plants, without which we could not live. Yet, for all its power, the sun cannot make so much as a rainbow by itself. For that, it needs the rain, at just the right time and angle.

No matter how strong we are—or smart or talented or attractive—we realize our full power only by filtering it through others. Our most meaningful achievements are born of combined efforts. Even when we do something that feels like ours alone—paint a painting, win an award, hit a home run—there is always a constellation of friends and family and teachers, even enemies, who've been a part of our success.

Like the rain's part in the rainbow, the contributions of others do not detract from our achievements, but enhance them and bring them to their fullest light.

How are others enhancing my growth today?

The bough which has been downward thrust by force of strength to bend its top to earth, so soon as the pressing hand is gone, looks up again straight to the sky above.

—Boethius

When we are down, low, depressed, why can't we ignore the desire to rise up again? Because we're like plants that need pure air, water, and sun. Because no matter how bent and old, we just keep wanting to grow up. Because there is a natural spring in us like that which makes flowers leap from the earth in May. Because we have hidden wings. And if we listen, we can feel the difference between wrong and right: we know the difference even with our eyes closed. Therefore we should not try putting ourselves down, for we will spring up again, sure as Spring.

What is the main way I try to put myself down?

Great events make me quiet and calm; it is only trifles that irritate my nerves.
—Queen Victoria

Isn't that always the way? We cope with major events, like births and weddings, fairly well. It is the little things—so inconsequential in the long run—that upset us. If the kids don't pick up their rooms, or dinner is late, or we can't go to the movies because we haven't done our homework, we become irritated and annoyed. Minor things like these upset us much more than they should.

Are they really so important? A messy room is not a terminal illness. A late dinner won't affect our health unless we get so upset about it we make ourselves sick. We'll survive.

If we think back to the last time we were angry or upset, does it seem important now? We probably can't even remember why we reacted that way. How much better life is when we let go of the little irritations.

What irritation can I let go of today?

Sometimes it takes a rainy day just to let you know, everything's gonna be alright.
—Cris Williamson

Rainy days let us slow down. We are busy people, driving ourselves to go places and get things done. But rain seems to slow life down, even in our hearts. And slowing down can show us the peace in our lives, the peace of knowing we have all we need right inside us. The pressures of the world can drop away for a time while we reflect.

As the rain soaks into the ground, its serenity enters our hearts. Leaves on trees begin to look more green. Plants and flowers are no longer thirsty. When we slow down, we can be comforted by what we have in our hearts, knowing everything is going to be all right.

What comfort can I find within myself right now?

I never saw a wild thing sorry for itself.
—D. H. Lawrence

Sometimes when we feel sorry for ourselves we will sit alone in our bedroom. We may even feel so down in the dumps that we decide to stay there, indulging in self-pity, thinking about how the world is against us.

However, if we use our imagination to step outside our own point of view for a moment, we might think differently. If we were deer in the forest, we would be thinking about keeping safe from the wolves, and where our next meal would be coming from.

The animals have no time to feel sorry for themselves. They are too busy doing what has to be done to survive, and each thing that happens presents a new survival problem to be solved.

When we feel blue, it helps to keep this in mind. If we have the time to feel down, and can get physically comfortable while doing it, how bad can the problem really be?

In what ways is my life comfortable, easy, and full of love?

Before he closed his eyes, he let them wander round his old room ... familiar and friendly things ... which were so glad to see him again and could always be counted on for the same simple welcome.

—Kenneth Grahame

When they moved into the house, the room at the top of the stairs was just a junk room. As the years passed, they slowly transformed the room into a guest room.

When they decided they needed another voice in the house, they transformed the room again: out went the fold-out couch, in came a crib and rocking chair; off went the art gallery prints from the walls, up went Winnie the Pooh. It was no longer a guest room, but a place for the baby, a new—and permanent—member of the family.

We always have room for more in our lives. When we are ready for it, what we need for growth will emerge.

What do the rooms inside our homes and ourselves have to tell us about the way we live our lives?

I love him and I cannot seem to find him.
                                    —*Ovid*

Where can we find the ones we love? Do they always live in our world, or do we have to go out of our way? They often are not at home; we can find them at their work. Their play is different from ours; we could try having their kind of fun.

Too often, we look only for friends who are much like ourselves, and we tend to avoid those who are not. This kind of narrow-mindedness isn't fair to ourselves or others. We are each unique, like the pieces of a puzzle. We are each necessary to the whole picture.

When we go out of our way to know someone else better, we stretch our own boundaries, we give ourselves new space in which to grow.

What part of my life can I discover in someone new today?

Whoever is happy will make others happy, too.
—*Anne Frank*

Anne Frank had good reason to be unhappy, full of fear, and deeply discouraged. Years of her life were spent in a small apartment hiding from the Nazis who wanted to destroy her and her family. Yet even in this little hiding place she had happiness. It was something she had inside which did not depend on what happened around her. She had riches of the heart. She had faith that kept her going. She had love and concern for her family and others which made even a restricted life very rich with feelings. It is tempting to believe that we will be happy when we have something outside ourselves which will make us happy. But happiness is not something we have to find outside; the seeds are in our hearts already.

What happiness can I find in my latest setback?

Walk. Don't walk.

—*traffic light*

Signs direct us on our way in life. Traffic lights tell us to walk (or not), Golden Arches point us to dinner, geese flying south herald the coming winter, flashing neon tells us what to buy. We know how to read these signs of worlds and weather; they help to guide us on our journey.

We can learn to read the signs of human beings, too, to be detectives of the human spirit. Laugh lines around eyes and mouth, the texture of hands, tension in jaws and shoulders can tell much about a person, if we stop to look. All around us are signs that tell us others feel the pain and joy we feel, others need us as we need them, we are understood, and we are not alone.

The marvelous bonus in learning to read these signs in others is that we can begin to let ourselves be read, also.

Will I make good reading for others today?

I feel no need for any other faith than my faith in human beings.

—Pearl S. Buck

We owe each other respect. We cannot expect to be respected if we don't respect others around us. When we respect others, we respect their property and personal belongings as well as their self-esteem and their right to voice an opinion. Respect is a way of cooperating with each other.

We can imagine a submarine where crew members did not respect each other's personal belongings or their ability to do the job. The ship would soon stop functioning because of the chaos. In a family we live in close quarters, like a submarine crew. Respect for each other is one of the things that keeps chaos from breaking out. When we grow in respect for each other's property, abilities, and self-esteem, we soon see how valuable each member of our crew really is.

How can I show respect to those around me today?

There is nothing so moving—not even acts of love or hate—as the discovery that one is not alone.

—Robert Ardrey

Our fears are normal. Some of us fear going to a new school and making new friends. Taking an important test causes jitters in the bravest looking person. Maybe staying alone in the house for the first time has you looking under beds and in closets every time you hear a strange noise. Our fears are merely reminders that we've forgotten to let God help us out.

So often we think we're alone, but we never are. We each have a Higher Power just waiting to be relied on. Nothing is too difficult or fearful for us to handle with the help of our Higher Power. When we develop the habit of letting God ease our way, our fears are gone.

Today, which fear can I replace with trust in my Higher Power?

You have three choices: keep on fighting, ignore each other, or make up and be friends.
—John Knoblauch

Once there were four sixth-graders—two boys and two girls—who started to fight even though they'd been friends for years. One morning at the bus stop, the boys started playing keep-away with the girls' shoes and wouldn't give them back. One of the mothers called the school.

Later that day, the counselor called them in and asked them what the fight was all about. They said they didn't really know.

"Well," said the counselor, "it doesn't really matter why you started fighting. Right now, you've got three choices: keep on fighting, ignore each other, or make up."

The group chose to ignore each other, after discussing it among themselves. They were happy to be able to stop fighting. About the time of winter vacation, they decided to be friends again.

What conflicts can I resolve by letting them be?

The only sense that is common in the long run is the sense of change—and we all instinctively avoid it.

—*E. B. White*

Nature reveals to us a world that is always changing. No two sunsets are alike. Winter brings invigorating days while spring brings new buds and blossoms every day. Summer brings lazy warmth and star-filled evenings while fall brings crisp afternoons and a sense of nostalgia.

Even though nature shows us a constantly changing world, we often resist the changes in our own lives. Changes can be both hard and sad, yet they are a part of life. Perhaps we are moving on to a new school or a new neighborhood, or perhaps we are feeling the changes that come with a divorce in the family.

With every change we say a sad good-bye to something old, something familiar—in the same way we feel sadness for summer's end when the first leaves begin to fall. Yet every change also offers us the excitement and potential of a new season—with its own opportunity for new smells, special gifts, and invigorating days.

How have I changed today?

Oh, this is the creature that doesn't exist . . . . In fact, it never was. But since they loved it, a pure beast came to be.

—*Rainer Maria Rilke*

The unicorn, serene and white, is a strong and graceful animal with the body of a horse. A single white horn grows from its brow, making it unique among all animals. It is gentle, shy, and good, and though stories have been told about it for centuries, many people say it never existed. We call it a myth, yet in telling its story, we make it real.

Friendship is like the unicorn: created from faith. Before we speak, reach out, believe in the possibility of relations with another, friendship does not exist. But when we share a meal, a joke, or a walk—a piece of ourselves—we open up to two friends . . . one in the other person, the other within ourselves.

How does sharing myself with another create a friend within me?

For no actual process happens twice; only we meet the same sort of occasion again.
—Suzanne K. Langer

Today is not going to be like yesterday. Nor will it resemble tomorrow. Each day is special and promises us many new ideas—perhaps the chance to make a friend, or to learn something interesting from a teacher or a book. Some activities today will be familiar, just like playing a game for the second, third, or tenth time is familiar. And yet, the way each player moves the pieces around the board will be different. The excitement about today is that it is full of surprises. Every thing we do, every conversation we have, will not be repeated in just the same way again, and this reminds us how special each of us is.

What new discovery will I make today?

Here's Sulky Sue
What shall we do?
Turn her face to the wall . . . .

—*Mother Goose*

When she put her Sulky Sue up against the wall, was this mother a wise or silly goose? If Sue was confused, could she talk sense with a wall? If she was angry, would the wall ever know why? If she was sad, would the wall wipe her tears away? If she was lonely, would the wall take her by the hand? Some walls are built for support, others to keep people away. To sulk is to look for support, someone strong to hold us up, not a silly goose who will turn us away.

Sulking is not the best way to look for help, and when we sulk, we are likely to end up isolating ourselves in some corner of our own making. And on the other hand, when we see another sulking, how much better it is to offer support instead of isolation!

Do I build walls of isolation or walls of support?

Being entirely honest with oneself is a good exercise.

—Sigmund Freud

The truth is our friend. It is a rough and humble kind of friend—but a friend nonetheless. Each of us will need to learn to spend time with this friend because it is one that is not easy to escape. It is always turning up when we least expect it. The truth about ourselves is hard to avoid. It seems to knock at our door until we let it in.

Perhaps we have played the game of hide-and-seek sometime in our lives. Sometimes we tell little lies about ourselves to impress others, or we act in ways that, deep down, we know are not really the way we want to be. We can never be comfortable this way. We know what it is like to hide and try to keep from being found. The truth about us is an expert player. It seeks us out until we put our arms around it and welcome it.

Is there something I am hiding from today?

Nature, the Gentlest Mother, is
Impatient of no Child . . . .

—*Emily Dickinson*

When a girl sits on the seashore, the waves do not try to slap her around. When a boy wanders alone in a field, the sky does not accuse him of talking back. When a man is alone in the woods, does the earth nag him for failing once more? And when a woman is alone in the park, does the wind whisper behind her back? Nature never blames or condemns; she gives us freedom of thought and plenty of space. Nature's ways are proven and true; she lets us grow at our own rate. Nature brings us sleep, dawn, new days; she is full of new life.

We are a part of nature, and everything we do is part of it. We can find comfort in this knowledge, if we take the time to remember it when we are feeling bad. Nature is always willing to share its serenity.

When we escape to nature, what feelings do we have that we want to take back home with us?

Work is love made visible.

—*Kahlil Gibran*

Family members show love and concern for others through their work. Parents might build a bookcase or prepare the meals. Children might help by emptying the wastebaskets. All are showing love through what they do. In our lives together, our work is an important way of saying I love you. We will still want to give them lots of hugs and kisses. But our work shows how much we care, and who is important to us. Our work around the house is an investment. It makes a home for all of us, constructed of visible love.

How can I make our home a better one today?

I never found the companion that was so companionable as solitude.
—Henry David Thoreau

One of the greatest gifts of our lives is the ability to enjoy solitude. Many of us are unable to enjoy this gift. We are too busy—busy with work, with friends, with entertainment.

When we slow down, we find out we can feel peaceful when we are alone. For most of us, solitude is ordinary—we each find our private place and take up our favorite activities: fishing, sewing, writing, building models, making pictures. These simple activities are so much fun it's hard to figure out why it took us so long to calm down and enjoy them.

Our dreams may be quite ordinary. We can learn how to find them.

What ordinary activities have I been putting off because I think I'm too busy?

All acts performed in the world begin in the imagination.
—*Barbara Grizzuti Harrison*

We use our imaginations to plan how we're going to build a model car or plane, rearrange the furniture in our rooms, even dress for a special party. The imagination is like a big piece of drawing paper on which we sketch the way we want something to look.

When we don't know just how to begin a task, the imagination gets us started. It's like having the directions for playing a new game. Dreams about the future, where we want to go, the jobs we want to have, are made more real when we "draw" them in our minds. The imagination gives us courage, too.

Do I have the courage today to imagine a better me?

Love is something if you give away, you end up having more.

—*Malvina Reynolds*

The other side of giving is taking. Many of us were brought up to believe that it's not okay to take, so we diminish admiration that people give us. "Oh, this old rag, I got it at a garage sale for next to nothing." This response to a compliment can take away the joy of giving it from the person who admired the way we looked.

Giving needs taking to complete it. We can keep the cycle of generosity going by taking gracefully. A world without those who take would be unbalanced. When someone gives us love, appreciation, or a gift, we can show our real pleasure with a simple thank you, and stop thinking we don't deserve it.

Can I accept what's given to me today in the spirit it's offered?

He who has courage and faith will never perish in misery!
—Anne Frank

Someone once said happiness is like a butterfly: if we chase it, we'll never find it. But if we sit quietly, it will come and land on us. Faith and courage are the same. All we have to do is sit quietly and ask for these gifts from God. In time, and with patience, they will be ours, and so will the happiness we can then pass on to others.

Anne Frank wrote the above words facing a concentration camp and certain death. If she could find happiness and faith and courage within herself under those circumstances, then certainly we can too. These gifts are ours, already within us, if we but look for them.

What can I ask for today?

We shall not cease from exploration,
And the end of all our exploring
Will be to arrive from where we started
And know the place for the first time.
—*T. S. Eliot*

We spend much of our lives looking forward to milestones we hope will mark our passage into wisdom—that time and place when once and for all we will know all there is to know.

When I am 13, I'll be grown up, we say. When I am 16, 18, 21, drive a car, graduate, marry, write a book, own a house, find a job, or retire, *then* I'll be grown up.

When we seek complete transformation, mere insight is disappointing. We find we don't know all there is to know—not at 13 or 35 or 80. We are still growing up.

The baby, the child, the younger person each of us was yesterday is still with us; we continue to love, hate, hurt, grieve, startle, delight, feel.

There is no magic moment of lasting enlightenment, simply a series of fleeting moments lived one at a time each day. They bring us home to who we've always been.

What small thing have I learned today?

*No life is so hard that you can't make it easier by
the way you take it.*

—Ellen Glasgow

Jimmy and Karen were out catching insects for their
science class. Jimmy had caught a gray moth and
Karen a monarch butterfly.

"My moth sure isn't very pretty," Jimmy said as he
looked at the two insects. "Now I'll have to catch
something else."

"Oh, but it is," said Karen. "See what a fat body
your moth has compared to my butterfly, and it's got
fuzzies on its wings."

"You're right," said Jimmy, beginning to smile at his
moth. "I was almost going to let him go."

How many times in the past have we taken just a
quick look at something before rejecting it? Often,
simply because a thing isn't quite what we expected,
we don't give ourselves a chance to discover what it is
that makes that thing beautiful. There is a secret
beauty in everything, even ourselves. When we take
the time to seek it out in other people and things, especially those that have disappointed us, that beauty is
reflected in us, too.

Can I find the beauty in something common today?

The measure of a man's real character is what he would do if he knew he could never be found out.

—Thomas Macaulay

Remember the tale about the poor, tired shoemaker who cut out his last bit of leather and awoke to find a beautiful pair of shoes sewn for him? Night after night two little elves secretly worked from midnight to dawn sewing shoes to help the old craftsman. Helping the shoemaker without his knowing who they were made the elves very happy, and they danced and sang as they worked away. These elves knew their reward was in the doing of the good deed, not in the discovery of their doing it.

What secret gift of kindness can I give today?

People are lonely because they build walls instead of bridges.

—Joseph Fort Newton

Communication is much more than words. Words are merely fingers pointing the direction to understanding—they are not understanding itself. To really communicate with someone, we have to allow ourselves, just for a moment, to become that other person. When we do this, we begin to be able to see beyond the masks that hide what another person is really feeling.

When we take the time to really see others, we may discover they are frightened, timid people longing for understanding. When we get beyond reacting to their outward behavior and move toward viewing their inner selves, it is much easier to extend a hand of friendship, to say we care, and truly mean it.

Who can I see as they really are today?

Growing is like running a twenty-six mile marathon. If we give up on the twenty-fourth mile, we will never know what it feels like to finish the race.

—Anonymous

There will be times in our growth when we will want to give up. Our pain seems to have no end to it. In a sense, we are like the runner of a marathon on her twenty-fourth mile. She may think she cannot finish the race; she may lose her ability to see things as they are.

If she can remember previous successes, she will no doubt make the decision to go on, to at least give the race her best shot. It does not matter how many people come in before or after her. It matters only that she has not given up. When she crosses the finish line, the pain turns quickly into joy.

When we refuse to give up, we give ourselves an accomplishment we can rejoice in, the reward of knowing we have done our best.

What can I finish that I gave up on earlier?

One is forever throwing away substance for shadows.

—Jennie Jerome Churchill

Sometimes we trade possessions with our friends. Maybe we want to add to our collection, or perhaps we just do it to get someone to like us. But if we try to buy friendship, we'll be sad later when we realize we've lost a prized possession and not gained a friend.

Our friendships come when we least expect them, often with people who have something in common with us. They will not be friendships we have to buy, but relationships to treasure and have for years. These friendships will teach us to respect ourselves and our friends.

Am I making good friends, or bad trades?

Down in a green and shady bed
A modest violet grew;
Its stalk was bent, it hung its head,
As if to hide from view.

—*Jane Taylor*

Shyness can be painful. Those of us who are shy do not choose to be this way. There are no quick and easy solutions to shyness, but it isn't the worst thing that could happen to us. And there are some things we can do about it. We can be willing to talk about it with someone we trust. We can exercise to build strength and self-confidence, and we can avoid dwelling on the problem. Most of all, we should not let shyness keep us from doing things. We may be a little uncomfortable, but that doesn't have to stop us from doing the task at hand to the best of our ability.

We can be assured that the ability to succeed is within us, and keep in mind that if we offer love to those around us, their answering love will help us overcome our shyness.

What am I no longer too shy to try today?

One comes in the end to realize that there is no permanent pure relationship and there should not be.

—Anne Morrow Lindbergh

Whether we are teenagers in love for the first time, or parents who have been married for twenty years, relationships can turn into obsessions if we're not careful. We can lose our sense of self and only feel complete when we're with the other person. We can become totally attached and dependent on the primary person in our lives for all our needs.

We need to remember that we can be a good partner in a relationship only if we feel complete within ourselves. Keeping ourselves open to change in our surroundings, our loved ones, and especially ourselves helps us stay whole.

We learn, first, to be ourselves, to make independent choices. We dare to do things on our own, things as simple as going for a walk by ourselves and smelling the scents of nature. Being ourselves means bringing our own world to meet the world of our loved ones, rather than depending on them to make our world.

Am I making my own happiness so I may share it with others?

We all fear what we don't know—it's natural.
—Leo Buscaglia

If we put a blindfold over our eyes and begin to walk around an open field, we would feel unsure with each step. We might be afraid of falling, afraid of walking over some unseen edge and hurting ourselves.

When any of us face something and we don't know what the outcome will be, we often feel blindfolded. We fear we may get hurt. We fear we can't do it. We have a hard time trusting ourselves. A blind person often finds help or guidance from others, or will gain confidence by walking on—slowly at first, finding trust and sureness with each step.

These same things help us when we are afraid. It is also helpful to remember there is no right or wrong way to explore what faces us—only our own way.

What new trust can I place in myself today?

Without solitude, there can be no real people.
—John Euder

We all need some time alone. It's a good idea to set aside a few minutes every day to be alone with ourselves. This is a very special time that is all our own. It's a time to relax and refresh ourselves.

This goes for every member of the family, and it's important that we allow others some time for themselves. It shows them we respect, love, and care about them. Without that solitude, they cannot be truly themselves—and neither can we.

Nature teaches us that each thing, even the earth itself, needs a retreat. Bears hibernate, cats crawl off out of sight, even the plants disappear for the winter. It is this time that refreshes life for the spring to come. If we want to have healthy, fulfilling relationships with each other, we all need time to ourselves every day. Without being "real people"—truly ourselves—how can we be full members of our family?

How can I better spend my time alone today?

We decided that it was no good asking what is the meaning of life, because life isn't an answer, life is the question, and you, yourself, are the answer.

—Ursula K. LeGuin

How many times have we felt like we were drifting aimlessly, constantly searching for meaning in a world that seems so mixed up, seeking direction but getting nowhere? But looked at differently, "nowhere" becomes "now here." When we take things apart, stand back, and examine them from a different angle, we often find we held the answer from the beginning. Sometimes, when we're convinced we are the problem, we discover we were the solution all along.

When we look for true understanding, we can be sure it exists in this moment, and that we can find it within ourselves, with God's help.

What question do I seek an answer to today?

The greater part of our happiness or misery depends on our dispositions and not on our circumstances.

—Martha Washington

We all have friends who seem happy even though they run into lots of bad luck. And we all know other people who seem grumpy all the time. Nothing makes them very happy. It's puzzling, but some people have decided, maybe without even knowing it, that life is fun and should be enjoyed. No bit of bad luck has to make us miserable unless we let it.

A broken bike, a lost math assignment, a rained-out picnic are things that might make us miserable. But we can decide they won't. Feeling happy can be a habit—just like brushing teeth before bedtime.

Will I stop and think today before I let things make me unhappy?

Happiness is not a place to travel to. It's a way of getting there.

—*Anonymous*

Those of us who climb mountains find joy in reaching the top. However, the climb would not make much sense if there were not things to enjoy on the way up. If we groan and complain, it will be hard to feel joy at the summit. However, if we are able to enjoy each day's journey, it makes all the difference in the world. In the midst of each chore, we can notice the sunset or the unique and beautiful surroundings of each day.

Each of our days is different. Happiness is not a goal we are struggling to reach some time in the future. It is a gift we can give ourselves today. If we enjoy some parts of each day of our hike, we will also feel joy at the summit.

What form will my gift of happiness take today?

*I went to sleep with gum in my mouth and now
there's gum in my hair and when I got out of bed
this morning I tripped on the skateboard and by
mistake I dropped my sweater in the sink while
the water was running and I could tell it was
going to be a terrible, horrible, no good, very bad
day.*

—Judith Viorst

Some days, for all our good intentions, seem to go
sour from the start. Maybe we're tired or feeling ill or
preoccupied with a problem that seems insurmountable. Maybe we just got up on the wrong side of the
bed.

Living one day at a time means getting the most we
can out of today. It also means we know today does
not have to doom or dictate tomorrow. If we have a
bad day today, that's all it is—a bad day. It does not
mean we're bad or that the world is against us or that
we might as well give in to our worst attitudes and behaviors since nothing is going right anyway. And it
does not mean tomorrow will be a bad day, too.

When we have a bad day—and everyone does—
there are a few things we can do while we wait it out.
We can slow down. We can be quiet. We can pray.
And we can let go. How else will we be able to recognize a wonderful day?

*Am I living today—good or bad—and not tomorrow or
yesterday?*

All music is what awakes from you when you are
reminded by the instruments.

—*Walt Whitman*

A small group of friends sat in a room around a record player. It was a heavy old thing, with parts that had to be operated by hand and only one speaker— nothing like a modern stereo at all, but more like an antique phonograph. The record—a recording of their favorite music—was old, too, and scratched, its grooves worn smooth as a stone in some places. The tone arm skipped and scratched, and the sound was tinny, hard on the ears.

Most of the friends squirmed in their seats as they listened, and several grumbled that it was impossible to hear the music with such inferior equipment.

But one of the group sat listening, her eyes closed, swaying to the music and humming softly to herself.

"How can you enjoy this?" the others asked.

"Ah," she said with a mysterious smile. "I am listening beyond the recording to the music I know is there!"

Can I find the music that's playing for me today?

Giving up is not giving in, nor is it failing. It is no longer needing to be right.

—*Anonymous*

When someone tells us a riddle, we may give up if we don't know the answer. We give up because we are tired of trying to get it, or because we are eager to find out what it is.

Giving up in other situations may be more difficult. We may need to give up eating something that isn't healthy for us. We may need to give up trying to win an argument. We may need to give up old clothes that we love which no longer fit us. When we don't want to give up, it may be because we have forgotten the knowledge, health, or peace of mind we gain by doing so.

In each case, giving up means growth and going on with our lives. Giving up may mean many different things in different situations, but it does not mean doing nothing. It means doing what seems right for us and giving up the expectation that what happens will be exactly what we want.

What can I gain by giving up something that is harmful today?

The most beautiful thing we can experience is the mysterious. It is the source of all true art and science.

—Albert Einstein

Albert Einstein knew in his heart that the source of all his knowledge was not himself, but a mystery—something or someone outside himself. And it left him in awe and wonder. He knew also that while genius may be 90 percent hard work and only 10 percent inspiration, all the hard work in the world amounts to nothing without that outside, mysterious inspiration.

He was right. We can work hard and play hard. We can paint and draw and write and develop formulas all our lives, but none of it will be new or different unless we are open to inspiration from some power outside ourselves that also, somehow, is deep within us. To be really good at anything, whether it's playing baseball, designing fashion clothing, fixing an engine, or cooking, we must believe in some creative force that helps us excel. When we see that force at work, we stand in awe at the wonderful and mysterious gift we have been given.

How have I been inspired to discover something?

for most this amazing day . . .
. . . for everything
which is natural which is infinite
   which is yes.

—*e. e. cummings*

Let us be thankful today for all simple obvious things: for the sun's rising this morning without our having to awaken it; for another good turn the earth makes today without expecting anything in return; for our ability to know right and wrong by heart. Let us give thanks for all small things that mean the world to us; for bread and cheese and clean running water; for our ability to call our enemies our friends, to forgive even ourselves; for our own bodies, however sagging and worn, which insist on continuing for at least another day.

How much ordinary daily good do I take for granted?

When written in Chinese, the word crisis *is composed of two characters—one represents danger and the other represents opportunity.*
—*John F. Kennedy*

Family crises are unavoidable. At times, things are going to break down. This is no reason to give up and abandon ship. These breakdowns are the things which will strengthen our lives together if we do not lose faith. The Einstein family had a crisis of sorts when their little boy, Albert, did not talk until he was four years old. But what looked like a problem at first did not end up that way in the long run.

We can expect downhill slides once in a while, and we may even start to feel full of self-pity. With faith that these setbacks are meant to help us grow stronger, we won't waste them and end up having to face them again and again until we do recognize their true purpose.

What setback can I use to grow stronger today?

I've never sung anything that I wasn't ready to sing.

— Claudia Schmidt

Most of us are curious about the "olden days" before we were born. We ask our parents what life was like when they were kids, what they did, what they looked like, and what they thought about. But most of us, even those who are parents ourselves, have probably never asked our parents, "Were you ready to go to school, to grow up, to get married, to get a job, to have me?"

So often we are afraid to take even a small new step, afraid of change. We feel so alone in our uncertainty. From our point of view, it often looks as though everybody's ready except us.

Perhaps another way to look at it is that, for most of our lives, readiness really isn't much of an issue. Were we ready to be born? Were we ready to walk, to read, to sing? Maybe we were, maybe not. What's important is what we did, not what we were ready to do. For life is mostly a matter of jumping in feet first, shouting, "Here I come, ready or not!"

What am I going to do today, ready or not?

Go rich in poverty. Go rich in poetry.
                              —*May Sarton*

Poetry lets us put the beauty of nature—the clouds, the flowers, the waterfall—into words. Poetry lets us see that things which appear to be opposites may just be different ways of looking at the same thing. How can we be rich in poverty? Wealth in poverty means finding pleasure in simplicity, finding the core of what's important, and saying it in the fewest possible words.

We are so often caught up in the pursuit of more—more money, more toys, more prestige, that we forget how satisfying the simple things can be. Think of the beauty of a sunset or a walk by the river, the fun of playing in a sandbox or swinging on the swings in the park, or in simply taking time to get something done the right way, without hurry.

What riches lie around me right this moment?

When one is a stranger to oneself, then one is estranged from others, too.
—Anne Morrow Lindbergh

There's a person inside each of us just itching to be known and loved. But if we don't get to know and love that person, how can we expect anyone else to know us?

That's why it's so important to spend time alone getting acquainted with ourselves. And how do we do that? We can sit quietly with ourselves, thinking and listening. Then we can write our thoughts in a journal, or we can draw or paint them. If we play a musical instrument, we can put our thoughts and feelings into music.

When we take the time and make the effort to know ourselves, it encourages others to want to know us, too. Since everything we do and feel begins inside us, we must feel good about ourselves in order to feel good about anything else. What wonders we are, that we have all the power we need to make our world a happy one!

How do I feel about myself today?

I wonder if the snow loves the trees and fields that it kisses them so gently.

—Lewis Carroll

In different times and places, clouds can produce snowflakes, raindrops, or even hailstones. Each one seems to have its own purpose and mood as it falls from the sky. The snowflake is the lightest of these, and so it falls slowly and softly. Rainfall can be soft or hard. It sometimes feels angry, almost cleansing.

No matter how thick the snowfall is, it is still soft. We can rarely hear it land. It covers the world in a peaceful white. If we look closely, we can see that each small snowflake is unique.

Like the snowflakes, each of us has a unique design. Perhaps what we can learn from the snowflakes is how to gently touch the lives and growing things around us. Times of anger and rain are necessary, but a soft snowfall brings peace to all humanity.

How can I show my gentle side today?

They were the first . . . self-created people in the history of the world. And their manners were their own business. And so were their politics. And so, but ten times so, were their souls.
—Archibald MacLeish

There once was a child named Yemaya. Even before she could walk or talk, her mother introduced her to the trees. Yemaya touched them and they accepted her. They told her she was wonderful and she knew it was true.

As she grew up, Yemaya occasionally met people who said unkind things to her. When this happened, she went back to her trees, who continued to tell her she was just fine. She couldn't understand what was wrong with those who were mean to her. Whenever they appeared and insisted on being mean, she pretended what they said was an arrow that sailed right by as she stepped out of the way.

We can do the same. What others say or think is part of them and their lives, not ours. When we are wise enough to let go of things that don't belong to us, we will find our own treasures.

What can I step out of the way of today?

My true god is always with me.
I am learning to trust myself. . . .
—Joan Parsons

Sometimes a book we read at a very young age stays with us our whole lives.

One girl loved *Heidi* more than any other book. She always thought about the grandfather's hut. It was a special place in the world—with the fresh mountain air, the spring flowers, the winter fire on the hearth. But the part she carried with her to adulthood was the part about the grandfather pouring goat's milk into a bowl and telling Heidi to drink it all up so she could grow to be healthy and happy.

Now that girl is a woman. Sometimes, when she wants to feel taken care of, she pours herself a bowl of milk. Then she sits down, picks up the bowl with two hands, and drinks out of it like Heidi. She feels comforted and connected to the universe.

The private rituals we discover in childhood can befriend us all our lives, if we let them.

What do I want when I want comfort?

Believe that life is worth living, and your belief will help create the fact.
— William James

Before Orville and Wilbur Wright ever flew the first airplane at Kitty Hawk, they believed flight was possible. They had a picture of it in their minds. The first step in creating anything is to be able to picture it in our minds. If we can picture it as a possibility, we can work to make it happen.

When we were small, we dreamed a thousand dreams about what could happen in our lives. Anything, even magical things, seemed like they could happen, and our world was full of visions. That part of us that believes wonderful, magical things can happen is still in us. It may have been beaten down for a while, but it is still there waiting to help us seek the wonderful, lovely, and good things in life.

Which of my dreams can I work toward today?

Only people who have joyfully accepted themselves can take all the risks and responsibilities of being themselves.
—*John Powell*

If we have ever gone to school with a black eye, we know how embarrassing it can be. We feel self-conscious and ill at ease. Friends come up to us one after another to ask how we got it. We may want to stay away from people until the eye is better. All of us have things about ourselves we have a hard time accepting. It doesn't have to be as unusual as a black eye. We may think we're too big, too little, too slow, not good readers, not good looking enough, or not popular enough.

We may need to talk about these things with someone else, so these bits of ourselves we don't accept won't limit our freedom to grow. By talking to another, we may find those traits aren't noticed by anyone but ourselves. We may also find that what we once thought of as weak points can be turned to strengths.

What weakness can I turn to a strength today?

If you must love your neighbor as yourself, it is at least as fair to love yourself as your neighbor.
— *Nicholas De Chamfort*

We sometimes find it difficult to accept a compliment. We may feel we don't deserve such attention, and point out reasons why the compliment is untrue. When we act this way, we show a lack of love for ourselves.

God teaches us to love our neighbors as ourselves. Yet, before we can love anyone, we must believe we are worthy of the same love. No creature is undeserving of love, God reminds us of that. We can stop hiding behind feelings of unworthiness. There's nothing stopping us but ourselves. Sometimes it takes courage to say thank you when we get a compliment. Let's exercise that courage, and each time we do, we'll find our self-love growing.

When I thank people today, will I have the courage to smile, too?

Faith is the seamstress
who mends our torn belief
who sews the hem of childhood trust
and clips the threads of grief.
                              —Joan Walsh Anglund

A seamstress takes large pieces of material and cuts them to size. Then, with the help of needle and thread and buttons, she goes to work to create a finished piece. Sometimes, in the beginning, it is hard to imagine a finished product. But the seamstress believes it is possible and goes to work on it.

Faith is like a seamstress. Faith is what can pull all the unfinished pieces of life into some sort of order. Faith is what lets us know we are all right even when life doesn't seem to make sense. We all need the faith to believe our skills and dreams, and even our heartaches can be sewn into a shape that is beautiful and useful.

Our faith is the seamstress who guides the needle, mends the tears, and helps create a shape and meaning to our lives.

How can I show my faith today?

She must learn to speak
starting with I
starting with We
starting as the infant does
with her own true hunger
and pleasure
and rage.

—Marge Piercy

Once there was a writer who was writing a book for children. He decided to ask his son for ideas. "What would you like to tell other children?" he asked. He thought the boy would say something like, "Everybody love everybody." But instead the boy said, "Number one, ignore what your parents say about nutritious food. Number two, don't go to school."

The father laughed and thanked the boy for his ideas, even though they weren't what he expected. He loved his son for being able to feel and express his desires so strongly.

We all have a child within us, no matter how old we are. When we honor that child, we also honor who we have become, and we free ourselves to express our truest feelings.

What does the child within me want to do today?

Feelings are everywhere—gentle.

—J. Masai

Throughout the day we experience many feelings. Losing something makes us angry. Fighting with a friend makes us sad. Perhaps we're lonely because no one is home. Getting an unexpected treat makes us happy. Our feelings come and go just like the hours of our lives.

Letting our feelings be whatever they are is good. They'll go away in time. We may not like all feelings; sadness or anger may be uncomfortable, but being human means we'll have many different feelings each day. If we're quiet with them, they'll help us grow and understand others better, and then they will suddenly be gone, replaced perhaps by a feeling we like more.

Will I be able to accept my feelings today whether I like them or not?

Patience is needed with everyone, but first of all with ourselves.

—*Saint Francis De Sales*

One night Sandra was having trouble putting a puzzle together. Angrily, she pushed all the pieces into a huge pile.

"I can't do this," she said. She got up and walked over to the couch and plopped down.

"Let me tell you a story," said her dad, as he sat down next to her. "There was a daughter who helped her dad take care of her baby sister. Again and again, she helped her baby sister stand and try to walk. One day the daughter tried to put a puzzle together but gave up after only a few tries. She had forgotten how many times she had helped her baby sister."

We are all like Sandra, sometimes. We forget to allow ourselves to fail, even though our growth up to now has been a series of failures that we learned from. With patience, we allow ourselves to take chances we might not otherwise explore, and we widen our world of possibilities. Life has been patient with us so far, now it's our turn.

What have I failed at that I can try again today?

*To heal ourselves is a reclamation of the power
we all have as living beings to live in harmony
with the life energy and to fulfill our potential as
creatures among many on this planet.*
—Chellis Glendinning

We live in a world that tells us healing only comes
from outside ourselves. To some, it may seem odd to
think each of us has the ability to heal ourselves.

How is this possible? Easy—we can do it if we believe we can. Whatever we believe we cannot do will
remain beyond our ability. But believing we can heal
ourselves gives us access to many healing ways. Self-
acceptance is healing. Singing, playing, walking by a
river are healing. Even helping others with their problems can be healing to us. There are as many ways of
self-healing as there are people in the world. Once we
experience what is healing for us, we can go on to discover many more healing acts to share with others.

What healing things do I like to do?

Each day comes bearing its gifts. Untie the ribbons.

—*Ann Ruth Schabacker*

Today will be filled with surprises, big ones and small ones, like the gifts at a birthday party. Maybe we'll see a friend we haven't seen for a while. Or we'll find something we thought was lost. Whatever happens today will be special, and is meant to help us grow in just the right way.

Growing up doesn't always feel easy. We're expected to be more responsible and thoughtful of others. We're expected to be honest about our feelings and needs. If we're angry or scared, we need to tell someone. Sharing our secret about being afraid relieves us of the fear, and we feel lighter, happier, like after opening a special gift.

When I receive today's gifts, will I stop to appreciate them?

Great symphonies begin with just one note.
                                    —*Priscilla Young Pratt*

Sometimes it's really hard to get going. We put off things we don't want to do, or are afraid to try. We occasionally feel overwhelmed by the size of a job to be done, like cleaning out the cellar or reading a long book for a class.

But think a minute. If Beethoven had thought about how complicated it was to write his Ninth Symphony, with all those instruments and voices and notes to blend together, do we really think he would ever have started? But he didn't get overwhelmed. He sat down and wrote just one small note, and then another, and a third. It took him months, but writing one note led to a second, and, one note at a time, he completed it.

We begin the same way with whatever tasks we have ahead of us. Each tiny bit of progress helps us go on to the next part. We begin by reading one page of that book, or taking one box of junk from the cellar. That's all we have to do. The rest will follow almost on its own. The trick is to begin.

What needs to be done today, and how do I start?

Because you're not what I would have you be, I
blind myself to who, in truth, you are.
—Madeleine L'Engle

Sometimes we expect far too much of the people around us, and because no one can ever live up to those expectations, we are almost always disappointed. But wouldn't it be better if we just let go, and let people be who they are? Then we'd be able to see them as they are—with all their beauty and goodness in which we take joy, and with all their faults which we can also see in ourselves.

When we have put someone up on a pedestal, sculpturing them to fit our needs and desires by smoothing out the rough edges and creating new curves here and there, we cannot see the real person underneath our work. All we see is the illusion we have created. That is denying the person's real identity and is disrespectful. It's much better for our friends and for ourselves if we drop our expectations and illusions, and accept them all just the way they are.

_____

What unfair expectations do I have of others?

Volunteers are the only human beings on the face of the earth who reflect this nation's compassion, unselfish caring, patience, and just plain loving one another.

—*Erma Bombeck*

The most precious time we will ever have we give away by doing volunteer chores to help others get more out of life. There is no material wage for this kind of work, but a host of emotional rewards. The height of volunteer giving is doing an act of kindness or love so quietly that none but ourselves will ever know we had a part in it.

What great humility this can bring to us, who live in a world where selfish people often insist on credit for all their deeds—often things they had nothing to do with.

All we need do is think of all we have received without deserving it or asking for it. By taking part in the giving end of life, we find the true wealth of our own generosity.

What secret gift can I give today?

Endurance is nobler than strength, and patience than beauty.

—*John Ruskin*

It's hard to keep from trying to control the lives of others, especially in a family. We can learn from the man whose friend drove twenty miles to and from work on the freeway every day. "How can you do it?" he asked. "I've tried, and I can't go a mile in such traffic without screaming at the crazy drivers who cut in, go too slow, change lanes. Nobody listens. I'd lose my mind if I had to do it your way." His friend replied, "Your trouble is trying to drive every car around you. I relax and drive only one car—my own."

We have only our own lives to live, and this is usually enough to keep us busy. If we pay too much attention to how others live, we will neglect ourselves.

What acts of others can I ignore today?

Open your mind and your heart to be still.
— *Shawn Phillips*

In this time of international conflict and mistrust it is easy to despair. At times we may even feel hopeless as we hear about wars and weapons. But there is hope! Change can grow from within each of us.

The world is like a tree — if the tree is diseased and the leaves brown and brittle, the gardener does not treat the branches, but tends to the roots. Our world is made up of nations, in which there are states containing communities where individual people live. We are the roots of our world tree. As attitudes change; as we accept and love ourselves honestly and learn, in turn, to accept and love others regardless of our differences, slowly, the branches that extend from us and cover the world will grow strong. The peace we can make within ourselves can be reflected everywhere.

Will I find the peace within myself today?

Give to the world all that you have,
And the best will come back to you.
—*Mary Ainge De Vere*

When we share something of our own with a friend, it gives both of us a special feeling. Generosity blesses the giver as much as the receiver. Sometimes we feel selfish, wanting to hoard all our treats or treasures. But when we secretly hide them away, we cheat even ourselves from enjoying them.

Giving love and friendship to others works in just the same way. When we express love and kindness to others, we feel more love toward ourselves. Though we may not understand just how it works, we can be certain it does. The more of anything we give away to others, the greater our own rewards will be.

How can I practice generosity today?

I came to see the damage that was done and the treasures that prevail.

—Adrienne Rich

It takes great courage to face ourselves—to look honestly and fearlessly at our behavior, especially if we have done and said things we are not proud of. We may have caused a lot of sadness in our own and others' lives. It's not easy to look at.

But let's remember, too, that what we do and say is not all of who we are. And let's also look at the treasures in ourselves—those things we have said and done that have brought great comfort, joy, and love into the lives of others.

Beneath the negative parts of ourselves, deep within us, is a kernel of good. Let's look for that as well, and water it so it can grow—so we can grow into the persons we are meant to be.

What is the best part of me, and how can I share it today?

And the seasons, they go round and round
And the painted ponies go up and down
We can't return, we can only look
Behind from where we came
And go round and round and round in the circle
*   game.*

—Joni Mitchell

High in the mountains near Sun Valley, Idaho, is a small cabin. The cabin is always left open for hikers to rest and refresh themselves. There is food in the cabin and wood for a fire. Often, weary backpackers have arrived there, tired and thirsty, to find just the beverage or snack they needed to help them on their way. The cabin operates on a system of trust—if you use something in the cabin, you replace it with something else. Perhaps it is just the thing the next traveler needs to go on. It is a circle game.

We are all part of a big circle. If we give of ourselves or do a favor for someone, eventually—sometimes years later—someone will do something for us that will help us on our way. We do these little deeds without expecting to be rewarded, and we can accept others' little gifts without feeling forever in someone's debt. These unselfish acts, stored in our mountain cabin, stand ready for the next traveler.

What gift can I pass on to another today?

There are no riches above a sound body, and no joy above the joy of the heart.

—*Anonymous*

Holidays are a wonderful and exciting time of year—a time to enjoy snowflakes falling, company coming, and presents. Sometimes we find ourselves concentrating solely on the wrapped presents and forgetting about the presents of the heart. With God's help, we can begin to notice such things as the hug from a brother or sister, the laugh of a grandparent or the hand-drawn card given to us by a friend. All of these wonderful presents and more are ours for the taking; we need only to see beyond the wrapped packages. It is then we will fully experience the joys of the heart.

How many gifts do I see around me right now?

He is Father. Even more, God is Mother, who does not want to harm us.
—Pope John Paul I

God is many things to different people. Some call God "Father," others "Mother," still others "Higher Power," "Inner Light," "Deeper Self," and "Supreme Being."

It doesn't matter what name we use. No one name is ever fully adequate, and each of us has our own private way of trying to understand that which we can't ever understand fully. We give God names which attempt to express what God means to us personally, what God does for us as individuals, and how we see ourselves in relation to God.

Could it also be true that other people can't be labeled and put into one box? Doing so limits them to one particular way of being understood, and it limits the ways we can get to know them. If we are all made in God's image, then we all deserve the freedom to be seen differently by different people.

How does God look to me today?

We have no right to ask, when sorrow comes,
Why did this happen to me? unless we ask the
same question for every joy that comes our way.
—Philip S. Bernstein

All of us have reasons to be grateful. Usually, the word implies we have received something. We often think of gratitude as that warm feeling we get from someone else's generosity. We are particularly grateful when we get unexpected gifts from those who owe us nothing. Within a family, we expect such acts of love because we are close to one another.

But gratitude doesn't always come from being a receiver. Gratitude is warmest when it accompanies the joy of being able to give without expecting anything in return. We find it isn't enough to feel grateful. We have to express our gratitude by showing kindness and service to everyone around us.

Gratitude is the greatest of all heart-openers. When it enters the heart, love pours out. For every kindness we receive, gratitude inspires a hundred acts of giving.

How can I show my gratitude today?

I take it that what all men are really after is some form of, perhaps only some formula of, peace.

—*James Conrad*

When snow drifts quietly down on a winter evening, the hush of nature brings a great sense of peace. Each of us has known times like this. Many of these times did not depend on conditions like snow, or soft music. When we are able to keep a quiet center within ourselves, we are truly in tune with the spirit. Peace of the heart comes from a Power greater than ourselves, and from the faith that all of us, and all that happens to us, are part of a great plan.

Just as the snow falls softly, without fear, without regard for whether it will land on a tree bough or in the street, we, too, can live our lives with peaceful acceptance of whatever comes along, knowing it comes to us naturally and from God.

Am I prepared to accept wherever I will land today?

*In this sad world of ours, sorrow comes to all,
and it often comes with bitter agony. Perfect
relief is not possible except with time.*
                                    —*Abraham Lincoln*

Time may or may not heal all wounds. It depends
on how we use the time. If we deny our sorrow, or
runaway from it, or hope it will just go away by itself,
we will be miserable. But if we turn and face it, and
express our sadness in healthy ways, somehow we are
transformed by the sorrow itself. While the loss is still
there, it begins not to hurt so much.

We can express our sadness in many ways. Crying
is probably the healthiest means of expressing grief.
It's good to cry, even for men, because it releases tension and stress, and we find a little peace afterwards. It
is true that tears are healing.

Getting angry and expressing our anger in appropriate, healthy ways also helps to heal wounds of loss,
strange as it may seem. Yes, in time and with the courage to express our feelings, our wounds are indeed
healed.

What is a healthy way to express my anger at a loss?

I'll walk where my own nature would be leading—It vexes me to choose another guide. . . .
—Emily Brontë

We journey across many intersections in our lives. Some may point in two directions, while others lead off in several. Our choice of direction can be difficult, especially when our friends choose a road we know to be dangerous. When this happens, we can choose to go our own way without them. If they begin to tease and taunt us about our decisions, may we remember that they are as scared as we were about their friends' reaction. We are not, after all, living for someone else. If we would be leaders, we can be assured that true leadership comes from following our own directions with confidence that it's right for us, not from fear of losing others' company.

We can let others live their own lives without us, if their direction is not for us. We can walk away with pride, satisfied in the knowledge that we refused to allow other people's fears change our decisions.

How have I gone my own way recently?

The price of dishonesty is self-destruction.
                    —Rita Mae Brown

There once was a woman who told her husband what she thought he wanted to hear. She told him she was happy when she wasn't. She told him she liked his friends when she didn't. She tried to figure out what he wanted so she could do it for him. She felt hurt when he didn't do the same for her. She felt he should also try to read her mind and do what she wanted without her having to express it. She was scared to tell him how she really felt.

However, her pain and resentment grew so much she couldn't stand it any longer, so she told him her true feelings. He was so used to hearing her lies that he called her a liar when she told the truth. Now she knew how much she had hurt herself by trying to please him at the cost of her own honesty and needs.

Honesty is necessary for a good relationship with anyone. When we lie to ourselves, we cannot tell the truth to others. By being honest, we open our doors to others, we trust them with our true feelings, and they love us for who we really are.

Who can I tell how I really feel today?

Telling the truth is a pretty hard thing.
— *Thomas Wolfe*

Lying can be like sailing in choppy waters. The more we lie, the higher the waves get, and the harder the sailing. When we lie, we feel we've failed ourselves and others. We have to work hard to cover up our lies, and the fear of someone finding out is always with us.

If we ask God for courage to tell the truth, we can be like the sailboat on a clear and calm day. We can enjoy the small waves and the light warm breeze we've given ourselves. Honesty is a good habit, and is easy. With a little faith in our own worth, we can choose the calm waters of honesty and apply our creativity to new, growth-oriented activities instead of covering up old mistakes.

How can I smooth my waters right now?

Finish each day and be done with it.
Tomorrow is a new day; begin it well.
—*Ralph Waldo Emerson*

Two of the most useless phrases in the English language are "what if" and "if only." We waste so much time and energy thinking about what we might have done and wishing we had acted or reacted differently. We imagine how things might have turned out "if only. . . ."

All of us make mistakes. To go back and wonder and wish about our yesterdays prevents us from living fully today. Each day is a fresh chance; a new beginning. We can only squeeze what we can out of the moment and let the drops fall where they may. Some will evaporate and some will form rainbows.

Can I forget about yesterday and start a fresh new day?

INDEX

Hazelden Publishing and Education is a division of the Hazelden Foundation, a not-for-profit organization. Since 1949, Hazelden has been a leader in promoting the dignity and treatment of people afflicted with the disease of chemical dependency.

The mission of the Foundation is to improve the quality of life for individuals, families, and communities by providing a national continuum of information, education, and recovery services that are widely accessible; to advance the field through research and training; and to improve quality and effectiveness through continuous improvement and innovation.

Stemming from that, the mission of the Publishing division is to provide quality information and support to people wherever they may be in their personal journey—from education and early intervention, through treatment and recovery, to personal and spiritual growth.

Although our treatment programs do not necessarily use everything Hazelden publishes, our bibliotherapeutic materials support our mission and the Twelve Step philosophy upon which it is based. We encourage your comments and feedback.

The headquarters of the Hazelden Foundation is in Center City, Minnesota. Additional treatment facilities are located in Chicago, Illinois; New York, New York; Plymouth, Minnesota; St. Paul, Minnesota; and West Palm Beach, Florida. At these sites we provide a continuum of care for men and women of all ages. Our Plymouth facility is designed specifically for youth and families.

For more information on Hazelden, please call **1-800-257-7800**, or access our World Wide Web site or the Internet **[http://www.hazelden.org]**.